The American

BY THE SAME AUTHOR

Robert E. Lee, A Portrait: 1807–1861
Robert E. Lee, The Complete Man: 1861–1870

The AMERICAN

SOUTH YUBA R.

(where wagons were lowered over cliff into Bear Valley)

Nevada City

Dutch Flat

Rough and Ready

You Bet

Grass Valley

Damascu

YUBA R.

N

Marysville

Iowa Hill

Colfax

Yankee Jims

BEAR R.

Forest Hil

FEATHER R.

NO. FK. AMERICAN R.

Auburn

MIDDLE FK. AMERICAN R.

Georgetown

Newcastle

Garden Valley

Pilot Hill

Kelse

Lotus

Coloma

Roseville

FOLSOM LAKE

SACRAMENTO R.

(Old Dry Diggins; later Hangtown)

Placervi

Diamond Springs

FREMONT'S ROUTE

Folsom

Sacramento
Sutter's Fort

AMERICAN R.

EL PASO DE LOS AMERICANOS

COSUMNES R.

0   Miles   15

palacios

BOOKS IN THE
RIVERS OF AMERICA SERIES

RIVERS OF AMERICA   *Edited by Carl Carmer*

As planned and started by Constance Lindsay Skinner

Associate Editor Jean Crawford

THE

AMERICAN

RIVER OF EL DORADO

BY MARGARET SANBORN

Illustrated by Jerry Helmrich

HOLT, RINEHART AND WINSTON

New York   Chicago   San Francisco

For Catherine Sanborn, peerless companion,
who shared the river's exploration;
and for Virginia Borland, in appreciation.

Published simultaneously in Canada by Holt, Rinehart
and Winston of Canada, Limited.

Library of Congress Cataloging in Publication Data

Sanborn, Margaret.
    The American: river of El Dorado.

    (Rivers of America)
    Bibliography: p.
    1. California—History. 2. California—Gold
discoveries. 3. American Rivers. I. Title.
II. Series.
F864.S22   917.94'41   73–15160
ISBN 0–03–012336–4

Designer: Ernst Reichl

Printed in the United States of America: 067

Contents

IV   THE EBBING OF THE TIDE

Preface

THIS STORY of the American River had its beginnings in Colonial Williamsburg one fine October day, when a friend whom we were visiting suggested that I write a book about a river. It was a fresh idea and an appealing one, and upon our return to California I began delving into the history of some of those enchanting Sierran rivers I had known since childhood.

The American was at length decided on because it proved not only California's most important river historically, but one of the important rivers of the world.

Gabriel Moraga and a company of soldiers and padres were the first white men to see the river and name it. Jedediah Smith and his trappers camped on its banks and followed it into the Sierra in search of a pass. John Sutter built his famous fort on a rise overlooking it. Kit Carson and John Frémont followed it out of the mountains. Pioneer settlers from the States let it lead them to Sutter's Fort and the great valley. It played an important role in the American seizure of California. The first transcontinental railroad had its beginnings beside it. Edwin Booth and Lotta Crabtree acted in the towns along it. Indians, empire builders, adventurers, magnates, renowned editors and writers, Argonauts, and noted desperadoes filled out its story.

But it was the discovery of gold in its sands one cold January morning in 1848 that brought the American its greatest fame, and made its name known around the world. Every

country felt the impact of this discovery as thousands of men
from all walks of life set off for the American River, the river
of El Dorado; numbers of them never returned, and their
native lands were often the poorer for their loss. The entire
course of the western history of the United States was changed
by the Gold Rush.

The American's story was, then, California's story, and it
had never been told in full before.

One of the many rewards to be gained from chronicling
such a history is the gathering of material in the field. For
more than two years, the American River, its ghost camps,
former gold towns, and its back country were explored to
track down all sites of historic significance or special interest.
Observations were made throughout the year to record those
subtle or dramatic changes which each month brings to Sierran meadow and forest, to foothill and plain, and to the river
itself. There were walks along its banks and through its glades
to discover wild flowers, to watch and listen for birds, and into
its wilderness to trace tributaries and seek out and follow old
emigrant trails.

Frémont's route along the South Fork was followed as
closely as possible, at the time of the year when he came, to
note what he noted, and to better understand his hardships.

Then there were those invaluable contributions to be had
from lifelong residents of the river country, most of them descendants of pioneer settlers or Argonauts, all possessing funds
of family and river lore, all deeply interested in the American's
past and its future. It was my good fortune to talk many times
with numbers of these well-informed people and, in several
instances, explore parts of the river country with them. All were
helpful and cooperative, but Mr. C. C. Roumage, Professor
Vincent P. Gianella, Mrs. Berenice Pate, Mr. Floyd Locher,
and Miss Annie Yue, of Auburn; Mrs. Mary Bacchi and Mrs.
Virginia Bacchi, Lotus; and Judge Amy Drysdale, Placerville,
were especially generous with their time and knowledge, and

where they had collections of letters, diaries, pictures, and Indian artifacts, they were eager to share them.

Dr. Gianella's scholarly study and careful exploration of Frémont's 1844 passage over the Sierra and down the South Fork has enabled him to establish convincingly the exact route. Readers of this work, profiting by his years of research, will be able to follow Frémont easily through reference to landmarks and contemporary settlements.

It is only through the interest, cooperation, and enthusiasm of many people that such a work becomes possible. I am therefore especially grateful to my editor, Miss Pace Barnes, and to Mr. Carl Carmer and Miss Jean Crawford, editor and associate editor, respectively, of the Rivers of America series; to Miss Virginia Borland, librarian, Civic Center Library, San Rafael, and Miss Jan Fairchild, Mrs. Jacquelyn Mollenkopf, Mrs. Cheryl Hanley, and Miss Regina Jimenez of the staff; to Mr. George W. Taylor, recreation planner, Tahoe National Forest, Nevada City; Mr. W. B. Shackelford, chief civil engineer, and Miss Anne Burnett, librarian, Pacific Gas and Electric Co., San Francisco; Mrs. Elizabeth Anderson, reference librarian, Dominican College, San Rafael; Mrs. Doris Foley, historian and author, Nevada City; Mr. Francis A. Riddell, archaeologist, State of California, Sacramento; Mr. A. R. Buckmann, wildlife-manager biologist, Department of Fish and Game, Sacramento; Dr. and Mrs. Earl E. Rhoads, historians, San Jose; my father, David Warren Ryder, historian and author, Mill Valley; and to my husband, Francis Sanborn, who made exploration of the river possible.

I am further grateful to Mrs. Elsie Heimann and Mrs. Carolyn Barclay, Mill Valley; Miss Lillian Roth and Mr. Lewis Clark, Alameda; Mr. and Mrs. Mardis Gleason and Mr. Rhoads Grimshaw, Auburn.

During the years of research and writing, the interest and faith of Burke Davis, Williamsburg, Virginia, has been a constant source of encouragement.

.I wish to thank Mr. Warren Howell for permission to quote from William Heath Davis, *Seventy-five Years in California*, John Howell-Books, San Francisco: 1967; Harcourt Brace Jovanovich for permission to quote from Constance Rourke, *Troupers of the Gold Coast; or, The Rise of Lotta Crabtree*, New York: 1928; Mrs. Berenice Pate, Auburn, for allowing me to include the late Lizzie Enos' tale, "The Valley Quail".; and Mr. Clyde Arbuckle, San Jose, for permission to use the story of Moses Schallenberger's Christmas dinner.

Unfortunately, space does not allow me to name each one who helped in some way, but they must know that I am grateful to them all.

Chronicling the American River's story has been a joyous experience throughout. Those river-country dwellers who opened wide their doors at my knock and welcomed me to their homes, and all those other total strangers who were so unfailingly kind, resourceful, and perceptive, served to renew my faith in mankind's sterling qualities.

The delights of exploring the American's wilderness were enhanced by the companionship of my daughter, who shared its spell. To wander in sweet, rosiny forests and alpine meadows, tawny in fall and ringed with golden aspen, verdant in spring and flower-filled, or to sit beside the river in its deep canyons and listen to its song, refreshed the mind and body, and gave to the heart, abundant peace.

MARGARET SANBORN

Mill Valley, California
November 1973

1

EDEN

The River Is Introduced

THE AMERICAN is three rivers—three brawling highland rivers each over one hundred miles long. Down the steep slopes of California's mighty Sierra Nevada they rush in spectacularly deep and beautiful canyons of their own making. Foaming, twisting sinuously, tumbling noisily over ledges and dashing against great boulders in their path, the North, South, and Middle forks sweep through a rugged, heavily forested country embracing some two thousand square miles, carving their gorges ever deeper and wider.

There is no time to linger in quiet sunlit pools, for in their first fifty miles they drop six thousand feet, which makes it possible in following one of these rivers eastward—say in April— to experience the amazing transition from spring to winter in an hour's time. The precipitous character of the terrain also makes it possible to pass through four life zones in less than half a day.

After leaving the river's grassy lowlands dotted with great valley oaks, one meets the Upper Sonoran zone in the foothills, heavily treed with Digger pine, maple, blue oak, chinquapin, buckeye, and a thick undergrowth of manzanita, chamiso, ceanothus, toyon and other chaparral. Some fifteen miles higher up, there is the Transition zone with its forests of ponderosa and sugar pine; white and Douglas fir; incense cedar and, along the river, Sierra maple, alder, black cottonwood, ash, willow, and dogwood. Climbing several more thousand feet one comes in quick succession to the Canadian and Hudsonian zones with their stands of red fir, whitebark pine, mountain hemlock, aspen, and, on the bald, windswept domes, the hardy juniper.

Only after the three rivers, by then one, are caught in Folsom Lake, about twenty miles east of the great Sacramento to which the American is tributary, does it lose its impetuosity. Here the wild river is held captive by a dam and is doled out for irrigation, power, municipal and industrial use. After its escape from a second downstream dam and power plant, it races over its rocky course with some of its former spirit, but as it nears its meeting with the Sacramento, it becomes less turbulent—in places even placid. Its waters, mingling with those of five other mountain rivers and countless smaller streams, are carried by the Sacramento into Suisun and San Pablo bays, then into San Francisco Bay where the outbound tides sweep them through the Golden Gate into the Pacific Ocean.

The American's tributary system is a complex maze of alpine springs, lakes, and snow-fed streams of varying size and variety of name: Humbug, Screwauger, Yellow Jacket, Shirttail, Whiskey, Temperance, Hell Hole, and Redskin, to mention some, named by those same carefree Argonauts who called their camps Fleatown, You Bet, Last Chance, Pinchem Tight, Hell's Half Acre, Bogus Thunder, Bottle Hill, and Sweet Revenge.

One branch rivals the American in size. This is the South Fork of the Middle Fork, or more romantically the Rubicon River, named by some now-forgotten classicist who perhaps hesitated before crossing and taking the proverbial irrevocable step.

Another large and important tributary of river size is the Silver Fork American, which rises in alpine Silver Lake, set like a dark blue gem in a granite bowl. In forming its thousand-foot canyon the stream has worn the cliffs into fantastic shapes: ". . . old castles, towers, pillars, pinnacles—all were there," reports an early traveler.

The North Fork American, fed by Mountain Meadow and Needle lakes and Chief Creek, rises south of Donner Lake, scene of the noted Donner Party tragedy. This fork has its own North Fork (and its East Fork, too), the former having its beginnings at Meadow Spring near Emigrant Gap, that point where covered wagons, unable to continue along the spiny ridge above the North Fork, were lowered down the cliff to the opposite valley floor, inched on their way by ropes lashed around trees, and at a later time by iron spikes driven into the solid rock face.

The Middle Fork (also having *its* North Fork) races along through what was once the richest mining region in California. By the fall of 1849 $10 million in gold had already been washed from its bars and banks. This fork also rises deep in the Sierran wilderness, fed by several small springs lying in a basin known as Little American Valley, between Granite Chief and Squaw Peak in Squaw Valley. A shortcut to the goldfields was opened through this valley in 1849. It crossed the western summit at the valley's head, sank into the canyon of the Middle Fork, climbed out to follow a sharp volcanic ridge with a thousand-foot gorge on either hand, dropped again to the river, then rose to another height by a trail so narrow one misstep "would send the horse and rider, or mule and pack, down hundreds of feet, to swift and certain death."

High on Forest Hill Ridge, and clinging to its steep slopes some two thousand feet above the canyons of the Middle Fork and its North Fork, is Michigan Bluff, now a quiet hamlet with its great days behind it. Once its mines shipped out $100,000 in gold each month. Through the gorges below the town the American races to meet the Rubicon, tumbling green and foamy through its own wild canyon from its source in Clyde Lake, lying at an elevation of eight thousand feet, in Rockbound Valley. At that place where the American and the Rubicon meet, the rare bald eagle builds its aerie.

Just outside the foothill town of Auburn, where in the 1850s it was commonplace for a man to take out $1,500 in gold dust and flakes a day, there is a wide, rugged canyon of deep red earth, the slopes thickly grown with pines. At the bottom of the canyon is a rocky promontory forming a Y, where the North and Middle forks round a bend and meet. As the North Fork, they then hurry on to find the South Fork, flowing clear and cold out of a group of Sierran lakes: Echo, Audrain, Medley, Silver, and Twin. But the old tree-lined meeting place of the North and South forks is gone forever, drowned in the depths of man-made Folsom Lake.

The inviting openness of the Sierra woods is one of their most distinguishing characteristics [wrote John Muir]. The trees of all the species stand more or less apart in groves, or in small, irregular groups, enabling one to find a way nearly everywhere, along sunny colonnades and through openings that have a smooth, park-like surface, strewn with brown needles and burs. Now you cross a wild garden, now a meadow, now a ferny, willowy stream; and ever and anon you emerge from all the groves and flowers upon some granite pavement or high, bare ridge commanding superb views above a waving sea of evergreens far and near.

These high- and lowland woods and meadows, wild gardens, streams, and granite steeps support a diverse animal population. Dwellers of the alpine talus are few: chipmunk, golden-mantled ground squirrel, bushy-tailed rat, and pika—and their deadly enemies, the pine marten and weasel. One bird shares the high peaks with them: the rosy finch, which harvests the seeds of sedges and grasses and hunts for insects around the edges of snowbanks.

In the Sierran meadows and around the lakes and streams feeding the river are marmot, beaver, ground squirrel, and jumping mice. In the North and Middle forks area, near swiftly flowing waters, lives the rarely seen water shrew, a tiny creature adapted to a semiaquatic life. It is an expert swimmer, is capable of diving, floating, and walking on the bottom of a stream. Most remarkable, however, is its ability to walk on the surface of the water.

But it is in the coniferous forests and open brushy slopes at various elevations that one finds the largest number of different animals. There, depending on the season, live mountain lions, black bears, bobcats, mule and black-tailed deer, coyotes, spotted skunks, porcupines, badgers, raccoons, ground and tree squirrels, and hare and rabbits of several kinds.

At least two ancient mountain ranges, the geologists say, have in turn occupied the place where the present Sierra Nevada stands, each having been worn down through the ages. As evidence of this, many peaks above thirteen thousand feet have gently sloping or flat summits, indicative of an ancient lowland raised to great heights.

At the beginning of the Cenozoic era (the era of mammals), the Sierra was still a lowland, forming the coastal border of a continent that stretched eastward. Before the end of the Eocene period the area was broadly uplifted and tilted toward the coast. Then, as more time passed, a low, broad mountain barrier arose along the present Sierran-Cascade chain.

Great disturbances of the earth's crust marked the opening of the Pliocene epoch. Yawning fissures gaped along the northern crest of this range, and immense floods of steaming volcanic mud and fiery lava flows poured down the slopes, and heavy ashfalls covered the surface.

Approximately two million years ago, the Sierra Nevada was lifted to its present height: the range did not rise alone; the country to the east of it rose also. Then, after these mountains had passed through their first Ice Age, some three-quarters of a million years ago, great slipping or faulting movements took place. Amid the rush and roar of earthquakes and the thunder of landslides and tumbling boulders, the great Sierran escarpment was formed.

Ten master streams, fed by massive snowpacks and accelerated manyfold, swept down the western slope in torrents, each cutting deeply into the body of the Sierran block to form, over the centuries, the canyons we now know. One of these streams was the American River.

Although the river is no longer fed by such vast snowpacks, or the runoff from glaciers that once covered some two hundred and fifty square miles, during spring thaw it is still awesome, especially when a warm rain hastens the melting of the snow and the river rises hourly. It is then the color of lowering skies, splashed and dappled with the spoils of the forest—leaves, moss, twigs, branches, cones, and glittering scales of mica. Its voice is thunderous, its temper edgy. Listening closely, wrote John Muir, there can be heard, distinct from the "overboom of the main bounding, exulting current, the swash and gurgle of the eddies, the keen dash and clash of heavy waves breaking against rocks, and the smooth downy hush of shallow currents feeling their way through the willow thickets of the margin. And amid all this varied throng of sounds I heard the smothered bumping and rumbling of boulders on the bottom as they were shoving and rolling forward against one another in the wild rush. . . ."

Alder groves are soon waist-deep, "bearing up against the current with nervous trembling gestures, as if afraid of being carried away," as are the mightier firs and pines.

Early summer finds the river's call more dulcet, and its mood, though ever hurried, softer. Its color, too, a clear green, reflects the surrounding verdure. Flowers bloom along the banks, frogs pipe cheerily among the reeds, trout dart into shadowy depths, and water ouzels dive into the white torrents for caddis-fly larvae and fingerlings.

The highlands where the river rises often lie snow-blanketed until mid-June. But when spring comes, it splashes the lush meadows with masses of bright yellow buttercups and deep pink heather. Closer inspection reveals clumps of lavender irises, tiny cream and yellow mimulus, and marsh marigolds. In rocky crevices there are phlox and columbine. In the bogs one may be so fortunate as to encounter the carniverous pitcher plant with its wine-colored flowers almost hidden by long yellow-green sepals. Clustering about their feet, like so many cobras with flicking tongues, are the spotted "hoods" that entrap unwary insects.

On the banks where there are countless newborn streams and waterfalls sprung from the melting snow, grow bleeding hearts and shooting stars, colonies of white, yellow, and purple violets, and, in the water itself, flotillas of aquatic buttercups bobbing in the restless current.

Forest sounds are many along the river at this time. There is the drumming of the acorn woodpecker, the wild cry of the flicker, the call and answer of the quail, the chatter of squirrel and squeak of chipmunk; there is the sonorous drone of bumblebees feeding in streamside gardens and the twitter of gathering swallows skimming the river; and as accompaniment to all other sounds the winds flowing in melody through the treetops.

Too, there is birdsong in every canyon, grove, thicket, and glade—thrush, robin, tanager, junco, grosbeak, bluebird, finch, and vireo; and in the cottonwood groves close to the river, the song- and the golden-crowned sparrow.

There is one songster that is seldom heard, for he never joins in chorus, not even with his own kind, but sings only with the rushing mountain streams. "I have often observed him singing in the midst of beaten spray, his music completely buried beneath the water's roar," noted John Muir.

This is the dipper or water ouzel, as much a part of the river as the water itself, and an expression of its spirit. His clear, ringing song contains the deep notes of the cascades and the trills of the rapids, "the gurgling of the margin eddies, the low whispering of level reaches, and the sweet tinkle of separate drops oozing from the ends of mosses and falling into tranquil pools."

2

The Red Man and the River

DURING THAT ERA of profound earth movement, perhaps two million years ago, when the swift-running rivers were cutting their gorges into the western face of the newly elevated Sierra Nevada, mammals from Asia made their appearance in California. Deer and elk came to browse on the rich grasses of the silty lowlands and to rest in the shade of oaks and sycamores. Bear ambled in the forests of pine, fir, and incense cedar that had spread from the north to replace trees of an earlier humid climate. Dogs, wholly modern in type, snuffed out the trails of rabbits, gophers, ground squirrels, and mice. In the alder-lined streams, beaver built their dams and lodges.

With the end of the Pliocene epoch came the advance of cold climates. When the ice accumulation in Asia was the greatest, population pressures sparked a mighty exodus across the northern straits, into the Alaskan interior that offered an ice-free corridor. Then herds of lumbering mammoth, giant bison, camel, musk-ox, and true horses drifted into California to share the wild pastures with those that had come earlier. Mountain goats and pika invaded the higher, rocky slopes; and saber-toothed cats, dire wolves, and coyotes prowled wood and plain.

Just when man came to California is not known. The earliest physical and cultural remains discovered are only four to five thousand years old; but he may well have come here twice that long ago.

The California Indian's origin, like that of all other native North Americans is shrouded in mystery. There is little doubt that these people came from Asia, following the well-beaten paths of the herds that pressed into Alaska. But our native American cannot be classified as a true Mongoloid; nor, adding to the puzzle, does he comprise a physically uniform population, suggesting strongly that he represents a mixture of several ancestral groups, perhaps both Caucasoid and Mongoloid.

It is believed that these people did not come to California directly from Asia, but that hunters and fishermen already established on the continent wandered in from the southwestern deserts, the northern woods, and the plateaus of Nevada and Utah. They decided to stay. This seems to be the only explanation for the presence in California, which comprises less than one-fiftieth of the area of the continent, of five of the six stocks of superfamilies recognized in native North America (the Eskimo is the only stock not represented), and for the fact that more families of languages were spoken here (104 languages and dialects) than in any other area of equal size.

The Southern Maidu or Nisenan are members of the Penutian superfamily, and their villages were located throughout the entire American River basin. Although they acted largely as a unit and owned certain territory like hunting and fishing grounds in common, they dwelt in separate villages of thirty to thirty-five houses. Their chief was hereditary, and his influence mainly a moral one, for custom and common consent ruled the village. Only after the coming of the white man, particularly the emigrants from the States, did the chief's role grow in importance when his people, confronted by increasingly numerous and complex problems, relied on him to solve them and assume responsibility. Before then his main duties had been to give his people formal public advice (for he was expected to be an orator), welcome visitors, and, when necessary, admonish or counsel. In the larger settlements he lived in the dance or roundhouse; in the small villages his dwelling was used for dances and gatherings.

There were two kinds of shamans among the Maidu: the sucking shaman, with his bag or bowl of charms and herbs, who might be man or woman, and the healing or dreaming shaman who was always a man. It was the latter's primary function to rid the patient of "pain" or "disease objects," his power resting chiefly on his possession of guardian spirits called *kakini*. These could be animals, but were more often the spirits that inhabited lakes, waterfalls, trees, mountains, and rocks.

Sickness was believed due to the presence in the body of some foreign object, and it was the sucking shaman's business to remove that object. The area thought to be the seat of the trouble was first scarified, and the doctor, putting his lips to it, sucked. The "pains" removed were various: pebbles, bits of wood, straws, grains of barley, insects, and worms; these were displayed to the patient and audience and, if the causes of the sickness were alive, they were then buried.

Tobacco smoke from the shaman's ceremonial soapstone or slate pipe was sometimes blown on the patient, and orders given to whatever ailed him to depart. This tobacco was one of three varieties of wild *Nicotiana*, the seeds of which were sometimes sown by villagers. But since it was strong, and tended to produce dizziness and sleep, its use was mainly ceremonial rather than social.

The sweathouse, or *temescal*, was a typical Californian institution, yet it was not universal. Nor was it, as is generally believed, a place of occasional use for the cure of illness, or religious purification through sweating. It was an institution of daily use, and it entered into ceremony indirectly as a means of purification. Since it was the assembly place of the men and their sleeping quarters for about half of the year, it might be more aptly termed a men's club.

A "sweat-house" is an excavation in the earth, to the depth of six or eight feet, arched over with slabs split from logs. These slabs are covered to the depth of several feet with earth [wrote Edwin Bryant who in 1846 camped near a Maidu settlement on the American River]. There is a narrow entrance, with steps leading down and into this subterranean apartment. . . . The door is closed and no air admitted except from a small aperture in the roof, through which escapes the smoke of a fire kindled in the centre of the dungeon. The fire heats the apartment until the perspiration rolls from the naked bodies . . . in streams. I incautiously centered one of these caverns during the operation above described, and was in a few moments so nearly suffocated with the heat, smoke, and impure air, that I found it difficult to make my way out.

The roundhouse had many uses, and one of those on winter nights was storytelling. Narrators were usually men who stood or sat in a circle of listeners. Animal characters were prevalent in Maidu myths, a literary device that spared the teller a description of his characters. The mention of Miss Deer, Mr. Crane, Mrs. Panther, or the favorite Coyote, the hero of countless tales, called up an immediate mental picture, for to each animal was attributed his own as well as human traits. These characters were spoken of as the "first people," and if they had animal names that was only because they had been transformed at some later time into present-day creatures.

A myth that survived the inroads of western ways on native culture was told in these words, a few years back, by Lizzie Enos, a Maidu of the Auburn area. She called it "The Valley Quail."

A long time ago, in the beginning, the people all came from that way [she began, pointing to the north], and as they were tired from their long journey, they stopped and camped. One morning they gathered up their baskets, rabbitskin blankets, and, placing everything in their large burden baskets, they broke camp and continued their journey. One little boy became lost and was left behind. He looked all over the hills and valleys for his people and roamed around calling out, "Wa-Ka-Ka, Wa-Ka-Ka," meaning, "Give me a drink of water, Uncle." He walked and walked, all the time calling, "Wa-Ka-Ka, Wa-Ka-Ka." He was then turned into a quail. That is where the valley quail came from and that is the reason the quail calls, "Wa-Ka-Ka, Wa-Ka-Ka." Even today you can hear him all the time.

There was no concept of religion as we know it, yet Maidu mythology reveals distinct ideas about a creator, genesis, death, and immortality.

Both burial and cremation were practiced by the Southern Maidu. In preparation for the grave or pyre, the body, with strings of shell beads about the neck and feathers in the hair, was laid upon a skin, preferably bear. It was placed in a flexed position, bound tightly with fiber ropes, then wrapped in the skin, and tied again. If the body was to be buried, personal property was broken and burned and placed in the grave beside it, along with acorn bread and meal, pine nuts, and bits of dried meat and fish provided for the journey to the "valley above." In the case of a person of note, his house was burned down.

The soul was spoken of as the "heart" and the phrase "his heart is gone away" meant the person had died. With the rising sun the next morning, the soul, which passed from the body through the mouth, like breath, rose with it. When the meridian was reached, he and the sun would part, the soul traveling alone along the Milky Way, the trail to the spirit world. If the person had led a good life, the path would be well lighted and plainly marked; if not, then he would have to travel in darkness, crawling on hands and knees to painfully feel out the way.

All, whether good or bad, eventually reached the land where the Creator lived, although the latter were restricted to a less desirable part. For the others, there was a comfortable life with plenty to eat, for the Creator had a little basket filled with delicious food, from which they were welcome to take all they wanted; the basket had the property of never being empty.

As a sign of mourning for the loss of a near relative, a man often shortened his hair, but he was not governed by restrictions. However, custom and strict rules dictated the appearance and actions of a widow. Her hair was cropped close, and her head, face, and neck covered with pine pitch mixed with charcoal, a coating that was left on for about a year. She was required to stay in her house during the day, but permitted out for a short time after dark. This restraint was in effect until after the next annual "burning" or "cry," a mourning ceremony held each September or October, and the most important ceremony relating to the dead.

The Southern Maidu or Nisenan had no true garment. At all seasons clothing was scant, although on very cold days in winter a rabbitskin blanket or a deer- or puma-skin might be worn as a loose robe with the fur next to the body. Women's dress consisted of two short aprons of shredded bark (preferably maple), the front panel smaller and tucked between the legs when the wearer sat down. Men, children, and occasionally old women went entirely naked.

Cloth was unknown in aboriginal California, but the Nisenan made the finest feather and rabbitskin blankets, using the nearest approach to a loom that existed here. This consisted of a pair of sticks on which a long cord of rabbit fur or feathered strips of goose or duck skin were wound back and forth and intertwined with a weft of the same material, or with two cords made from the bark or outer fibers of milkweed or dogbane. These plant fibers also furnished material for making dip nets for fishing and nooses for snaring birds and small game, and for heavy two-ply ropes.

Instead of pottery the Nisenan women made baskets by both the twining and coiling methods, an art form in which they have never been excelled. The favorite material was the redbud, which furnished both the white or creamy background that turns a rich buff with age and the reddish brown for designs. Black patterns were less common, although when desired they were obtained by burying pine root fibers in charcoal and mud, or by using the roots of maidenhair and five-finger fern.

Designs were disposed in diagonals, either parallel or zigzag, and in many cases suggest patterns found on Rock Venus clamshells, which could have been obtained by trade. The coarser baskets made for rougher use were always twined and generally without design, while those woven for hats, eating bowls, cooking pots, and ceremonial purposes, were tightly coiled and ornamented with patterns. These people also developed the rare technique of wickerwork, used principally in making seedbeaters. Few primitive people have ever matched them either in making delicately symmetrical chipped arrowheads, knives, and ornaments.

The river was a principal source of food. At certain seasons it abounded with salmon which were speared or caught in deep water with dip nets. Where the river was navigable, fishermen used tule balsas or log rafts. Salmon was eaten fresh, or smoked and dried for winter.

In the foothills and mountains, brown and rainbow trout darted in and out of the deep shadows throughout the year; and there were lamprey eels which the Nisenan relished for their fat, just as the ancient Romans had. Trout and eel were often caught by poison made from crushed buckeye seeds, the juice of wild cucumber, amole, or mullein, and fed into dammed pools, stupefying the fish (but strangely not frogs) and proving harmless to those who ate the flesh.

In the river's rocky pools lived crayfish and freshwater mussels, taken easily by hand. In the reedy shallows of the lowlands were ducks, geese, and swans, trapped by a series of nooses stretched over the water's surface and cleverly held open by a leaf or blade of grass.

Close to shore there were masses of cress, which was eaten raw or slightly cooked. In the trees along the riverbank grew the wild grape with its clusters of small dark-purple bloomy fruit, relished for its sweetness and because it attracted flocks of bandtail pigeons and crows. Crows were sent scurrying from their roosts at night by bands of boys armed with green elderwood clackers and, once on the wing, were driven by shouts and screams into fan-shaped nets.

The grasslands of the plains were home and feeding grounds to large and small game: elk, deer, antelope, rabbit, hare, ground squirrel, and gopher. Here too were wasps' nests which provided larvae that were pounded into a relished pâté; and in summer and fall, myriads of grasshoppers were roasted and eaten like shrimp, or ground into a meal that was rich and spicy and resembled gingerbread. In the damp earth runways of gopher and mole, there were earthworms, a favorite ingredient for soup.

The meadows and dells were rich in sweet grass, clover, filaree, dandelion, mustard, and Indian lettuce. These were all cooked slightly or eaten raw, sometimes consumed right where they were harvested, which gave rise to the curious belief among whites that the Nisenan pastured like cattle. Bulbs, roots, and tubers—mariposa lily, brodiaea, camas, arrowhead, cattail, and tule potato—were boiled or baked. Mushrooms were highly prized and eaten raw or cooked.

The seeds of sunflowers, peppergrass, chia, tarweed, and lacepod were gathered in pitch-lined conical baskets, to be parched with hot coals, eaten fresh, or ground into a fine flour and baked in thin cakes in the hot ash. The small gray-brown seeds of the chia were often stirred into water to make a lightly flavored and refreshing drink; these seeds, very glutinous, have a high food value: the equivalent of one teaspoonful was said to be enough to sustain a hunter on a day's march.

The flour made from peppergrass was also used for poultices and as a remedy for diarrhea.

In the ravines there were blackberry thickets, elderberries, and gooseberries, and strawberry patches on the dry banks. Thimbleberries were abundant in the deep woods. On drier slopes grew coppices of manzanita, with its little apples which could be eaten fresh but most often were dried and stirred into water to make a pleasant drink. Digger and other large-seeded pines provided nuts which were an excellent source of nourishment. The fresh pitch or resin from the sugar pine was used as a mild laxative and, when dried and ground, as a cure for sores and ulcers.

But the staple of their diet was the acorn. A chronicler with Juan Cabrillo's expedition of 1542 makes the first mention of the acorn as food for the California Indian. Failure of the acorn crop meant hardship, although there was never actual starvation, since buckeye seeds and starchy bulbs were ground and used instead, but these substitutes were neither as plentiful nor as satisfying.

Acorns were harvested from the many varieties of oak growing along the ridges and in the canyons of the American River. When dry they were shelled and pounded into a flour that was then leached in a sand basin hollowed out on the riverbank, to remove the bitterness. In oak groves along the river today are found flat boulders or low, tablelike outcroppings, pocked with numerous smooth, deep or shallow holes, made long years ago by patient hands rotating the stone muller. Where natural slabs did not exist, a portable, flat metate was used. The globular mortars usually associated with Indian grinding were thought by the Nisenan to possess magical properties; supposedly they had once been people. Called "spirit baskets," they were used only by shamans as receptacles for charms and sacred meal.

Acorn meal was made into a solid bread, baked in the ashes or in a pit oven, or boiled to make a soup or mush called *atole*.

This atole was cooked in watertight baskets, the heat produced by red-hot stones dropped into the mixture and stirred constantly to spread the heat and keep the basket from being burned. As soon as the stones cooled, they were replaced by others, two forked or looped sticks being used to pick them out of the fire.

Atole was flavored either by the stick selected for stirring—usually incense cedar—or by dropping in a few sprigs of cedar and cooking them three or four minutes. Today "acorn" is relished as a gourmet food among the Nisenan, and it would be unthinkable to hold such important ceremonies as the Bear Dance without it. Since worked spoons were virtually unknown, the four fingers of the right hand were used to scoop up the soup or gruel, which was sucked off.

Plants, seeds, nuts, roots, bulbs, insects, mollusks, birds, and small game furnished the greater part of the Nisenan's diet, for elk and deer were hard to kill. These were usually hunted by companies of men who drove them over a cliff or past archers hidden in the chaparral near runways. Individual hunters stalked with deerhead masks, or ran the animal down.

In the valley the Nisenan built substantial round, earth-covered lodges from twenty to forty feet in diameter. In the foothills they constructed conical huts, ten to fifteen feet across, supported by poles tied together over a shallow excavation. The outside might be thatched with cedar bark or with bundles of gray willow twigs, tied together with grapevine, the leaves all hanging in one direction to shed water, and each row overlapping the next in the manner of shingles. Bedding, according to locality, was hides or tule mats, while deerskins and fur or feather blankets served as covering.

The bounty of this river land was not taken for granted; there was humility in the Nisenan's attitude toward nature's gifts. In the fall, after the first rain, an Acorn Dance of great solemnity was held to thank the spirits of the mountains for rain at the proper time, and to propitiate the spirits of the oak trees for an abundance of acorns next season. There were days of fasting prior to this dance to ensure the right conditions to thank the spirits properly. In April and May the old men gathered in the dance house to pray again for a bountiful crop of acorns and other food.

When the salmon began to run, the shaman caught the first one and, with prayer and rite, roasted it on the riverbank and divided the flesh among all the villagers. This opened fishing for the year.

Deer and elk drives were always undertaken with rite and prayer, while the hunters' families were governed by strict taboos. Bear hunts were opened ceremonially just before the end of hibernation.

When the wild clover was ripe, the young girls were sent out to pick it; and they came home at the day's end with flowers in their hair and their sweet-smelling harvest in their arms, singing an ancient song taught to the first clover pickers by the sandhill cranes.

3

Hunting the Land of Gold and Griffins

GOLD WAS their passion. Visions of limitless wealth haunted them. After Cortés' conquest of Mexico, accounts of the fabulous treasure-houses of the Aztecs fired Spanish explorers and conquistadores with a new zeal to find in North America kingdoms even richer than Montezuma's.

Their minds were dazzled as they listened to the tales the Indians of the New World told of strange treasure-laden islands; of the incredibly rich kingdom of La Gran Quivira where even the lowly kitchen utensils were made of pure gold; of El Dorado, the Gilded One, that high priest of the mountains whose body was anointed each morning with oil and painted with gold dust, and washed off every night in a lake whose waters had become thick with the precious metal.

Men still believed in the fabulous. Myth was closely interwoven with fact. They accepted the existence of dragons, griffins, mermaids, and Amazons as easily as they did their own barnyard animals and human neighbors.

The most popular books of the day were those romances of chivalry that were an outgrowth of the crusades of the eleventh century. One of the earliest and best was *Amadís de Gaula,* attributed to the Portuguese author Vasco de Lobeira. It was immediately popular, and Lobeira had scores of imitators who wrote continuations of the tale. In Spain, the people's craving for these romances reached such a point that there was talk of banning their publication.

Around 1510, García de Montalvo, who had translated *Amadís* into Spanish, wrote a sequel, called *Las Sergas de Esplanadián*, recounting the adventures of the son of Amadís, a doughty knight named Esplanadián, who had been suckled by a lioness and grew up to perform heroic deeds. Although considered inferior to its forerunner, it was extremely popular, especially with the explorers.

In the end it was ridicule, in the hands of such masters as Cervantes, that dealt the deathblow to Spain's passion for these romances. There is a scene in *Don Quixote* where the curate, housekeeper, and barber decide to burn those works that have affected the old knight's brain. *Amadís*, as the best of them, escaped, but *Esplanadián* was not so fortunate. "The goodness of the father shall avail the son nothing," decrees the old priest. "Take him, Mistress Housekeeper; open the casement, and throw him into the yard, and let him make a beginning to the pile for the intended bonfire."

Interest in this work was revived in 1862 when Edward Everett Hale brought it to the world's attention that the book contained the name "California," applied to a fabulous island. With this discovery Hale ended a long controversy over the origin of the word.

"Know then," wrote Montalvo, "that on the right hand of the Indies there is an island named California, very close to the Terrestrial Paradise, and it was inhabited by black women without any man amongst them for they lived in the manner of Amazons. . . . Their weapons were all made of gold. The island everywhere abounds in gold and precious stones. . . . In this island . . . there are many griffins. In no other part of the world can they be found."

In 1535 Cortés wrote his king about just such an island which he had been told lay "ten days' journey from Colima." It was peopled by "Amazons or women only" and abounded in "pearls and gold." It was the search for this island that sent the explorer sailing north along the Pacific Coast.

So the long narrow peninsula that he discovered and mistook for an island was called California because it seemed to him to lie "on the right hand of the Indies." What Cortés had found was that barren sandy waste now known as Baja California.

The search for the long-sought Strait of Anian led to the discovery of Alta California. Romance again played its part since it was said that cities of gold lined the ice banks of this northern passage.

In 1542, Juan Cabrillo, looking for this shorter route to the Spice Islands, sailed up the California coast in spite of continuous storms, going as far north as Cape Mendocino, where the winds shifted and drove him south. On his way back he discovered the bay that would later be named for Sir Francis Drake. Buffeting his way in, he took possession in the name of the Spanish king, in forty-five fathoms of water, not daring to land because of high seas.

Thirty-seven years later Drake made his memorable visit to California and, sailing into this same bay, claimed the land for his queen. News of this act prodded the Spaniards to renewed exploration of the coast and search for the Strait of Anian.

If it had not been for rumors of gold and silver deposits near the China coast, Spain might have settled California early in the seventeenth century. But reports of the existence of two islands, Rica de Oro and Rica de Plata, diverted them, and for nearly two hundred years California was all but forgotten.

Word of a Russian settlement at Sitka finally worked its way down to New Spain, and in its wake came disquieting rumors that these fur hunters might extend their operations southward. England already held eastern Canada and was steadily moving west. Spain, forced to act, resurrected its old plans for colonization. In January 1769, the first expedition sailed from La Paz.

Seventeen sixty-nine was a notable year. On the other side of the world were born two men whose paths were destined to cross strangely—Napoleon Bonaparte and Arthur Wellesley, the future Duke of Wellington. In our own land the frontier had been pushed as far west as the Alleghenies, and Daniel Boone with a party of hunters had tramped through the Cumberland Gap to explore the enchanting wilderness of Kentucky and prepare the way for settlement. In civilized New Hampshire, Dartmouth College was founded under a charter granted by George III, and in Boston, Samuel Adams, his rage at white heat, was fanning the revolutionary embers and setting the stage for American independence, with polemical writings aimed at this same king.

This time the Spaniards were not starting out in search of chimeras; political rivalry was the impetus and populating the land the goal. José de Gálvez, the no-nonsense visitador general of New Spain, took personal charge of the expedition, dividing it into four parts: two to go overland and two by sea, setting out at intervals, and all to meet on the shores of San Diego Bay. The last land division was headed by Gaspar de Portolá; his companion was the missionary Junípero Serra, who, as *padre presidente*, had with him five other Franciscans, for it was the Spanish way to march sword and cross together.

After many hardships, about eighty soldiers and friars were united at San Diego where the first mission in the chain that was to extend northward through California was founded on July 16, 1769.

Progress was rapid: the following year a second mission was established at Monterey, then another at San Francisco, so that by 1787, when members of the Federal Constitutional Convention were meeting in metropolitan Philadelphia, there were already nine California missions. Their chief significance lies in that they marked the beginning of California's settlement.

The old tales of gold were forgotten as men struggled to shape the wilderness. The missionaries learned after a time that gold existed along the rivers and streams of the Sierran foothills because Indian neophytes, returning from visits to home villages in those regions, often brought them a few flakes or a quill full of gold dust. But the priests, fully aware of the effect of gold on men's minds and souls, warned them not to talk about it, and they kept the secret well.

Spain was attempting the impossible in trying to hold California with a handful of soldiers and settlers. Once, when rumors reached Monterey that pirates were about to ravage the coast, the governor directed the *commandantes* of the several presidios established in the territory to collect bows and arrows, since muskets were at a premium. Forty was the total force to guard Monterey, whose principal defense lay in the eight cannons of its presidio, all but two of them in poor condition.

To make up for lack of strength, Spain passed stringent laws aimed at the foreign encroachment she so dreaded. Californians were not allowed to trade with other countries, whose vessels were forbidden entry into the bays and harbors. They were even discouraged from trading with Spanish vessels other than the two scheduled supply ships that came once a year from La Paz. Forts were built on the hills overlooking the harbors, and though their little guns barked at the arrival of strange craft, a few still came in from time to time, to take on water and wood.

On the morning of April 5, 1806, a Russian ship, the *Juno*, sailed into San Francisco Bay to dispose of her cargo and buy or trade provisions for the starving and scurvy-ridden settlement at Sitka. On board was the czar's chamberlain and colonial administrator, Count Nikolai Rezánov, who had come to Alaska on official business and discovered the colony's plight. He knew the law of California but hoped to work around it and negotiate a trade agreement; if he could not, the Russian colony was doomed.

Although the governor, José de Arrillaga, admitted the convenience of trade for his people, he was incorruptible. The only concession he finally agreed to, after hearing Rezánov's arguments and pleas, was the purchase of grain for cash. But this was not enough, and according to Rezánov's report, desperation forced him to adopt an age-old tactic.

From the time of his arrival he had been visiting the home of the commandante, José Argüello, where he had admired the beautiful daughter of the house, fifteen-year-old Maria de la Concepción Marcela. Beyond support of Sitka, Rezánov had ambitions for Russia's colonial expansion and plans to establish a post in northern California. He saw marriage into this prominent family as a stride toward promoting these political objects, and he set about wooing Concepción.

She was said to have been the most beautiful girl among many beauties in California, and intelligent as well. Before the Russian was done with this exercise in diplomacy, he may have found himself in love. Whatever his feelings were, the aging but still handsome widower won her heart, and they became engaged. "From this time, I managed the port of his Catholic Majesty as my interests required," he wrote.

The *Juno's* cargo was soon exchanged for a load of food-stuff, and on May 21 she sailed with Rezánov on board. After reaching Sitka he planned to return to St. Petersburg, where he would propose to the czar that he be sent to Madrid to negotiate a trade treaty with Spain. After that he would return to Yerba Buena, as San Francisco was then called, and marry Concepción.

But Nikolai Rezánov never returned. While crossing Sibera on his way to the capital, he died a miserable death from the combined effects of a fever and a fall from his horse.

Concepción waited resignedly if not always patiently for him to come back. Word of his death did not reach her for several years, and thirty-six were to pass before she learned the details. She chose to remain faithful to his memory and refused all other offers of marriage. Eventually she joined the Third Order of St. Francis and devoted the rest of her life to caring for the sick and teaching the children of the poor. Her story, and her youth and beauty, made her even in her own day one of the most famous and appealing figures in the romance of colonial California.

On his return to Sitka, Rezánov took careful observations

along the California coast, and reported favorably on its possibilities for settlement. Although later explorations of the area confirmed his report, no permanent settlement was made in California until June 1812, when a party of Russians and Aleuts began work on a stockaded fort set on a bluff overlooking a small harbor thirty miles north of Bodega Bay.

From the beginning this Colony Ross, or Fort Ross as it came to be called (Ross thought to be derived from *Rus*), was a source of anxiety to the Spanish who feared an advance down the coast. But when New Spain and South America began to have troubles, and the annual supply ships for California fell prey to privateers, Governor Arrillaga was thankful for his Russian neighbors with whom he could trade for necessary articles.

It was not long until the Boston traders got wind of California's plight and instituted a flourishing contraband: hides, tallow, and soap being exchanged for manufactured goods. The officials, who were no better off than the rest, made only token attempts to stop the smuggling. One Yankee sea captain justified his illegal operations by writing that he had served "to clothe the naked soldiers of the king of Spain, when for lack of raiment they could not attend Mass, and when the most Reverend Fathers had neither vestments nor vessels fit for the church, nor implements wherewith to till the soil."

The situation was changed when New Spain declared her independence and emerged as the republic of Mexico. The mission fathers remained loyal to the king while the military and rancheros sided with the new government. The result of this divided allegiance was the eventual secularization of the missions.

A commission was sent from Mexico in 1822 to see that the new order was properly established and to elect a governor. But after this initial show of interest, the colony was left to run its own affairs.

Foreign trade became legal, and the era of Boston ships and

great cattle ranches opened. Boston came to be spoken of as though it were the only city in the United States; Americans were known as "Boston men," and their cargoes as "Boston goods." For the first time those vast acreages granted by Spain as an inducement to settlers were made to pay, and a new class of gentry grew up as a result of the prosperous commerce in hides and tallow. Yankee ships flocked into California ports with tempting consignments of mahogany and rosewood furniture, dishes and glass, linens and carpets, silks and laces, and, from the Orient, jade and jewelry, fans, and embroidered Chinese shawls. Life for the Californians became something more than mere existence.

For nearly forty years Spanish occupation of California was limited to a narrow strip along the coast, stretching from Yerba Buena to San Diego; the vast interior was regarded as a *tierra incognita*, and spoken of as such officially. Then, in 1808, a desire to expand the mission system prompted exploration of that interior, and expeditions were sent up through the great valleys and along the rivers, penetrating the Sierran foothills.

On September 25 of that year, Gabriel Moraga, an energetic officer, described as "brave, gentlemanly, and the best Californian soldier of the time," set out with his chaplain and a party of soldiers from Mission San José to explore the northern end of the great valley. They headed eastward across the parched plains. The hot wind, blowing constantly, gave no relief from the scorching sun. It rippled the tall bleached grasses on the distant slopes so that they seemed to have unending flocks of golden sheep running down their rounded sides.

On reaching the San Joaquin River with its occasional groves of fragrant willow, which brought welcome shade, they turned north to follow the stream. On October 7 they camped near the junction of the American and Sacramento rivers. With a small party Moraga followed the American upstream for about twelve miles, passing eleven Indian villages, but finding no suitable mission sites, he reported.

From a high clearing he looked across the wooded ridges and saw the snowcapped Sierra Nevada towering in the distance. Below him, in the bottom of a rocky gorge, he watched the river fighting its tortuous way. Its struggles reminded him of Christ's passion, and he named it *Las Llagas*.

4

Jedediah Smith Defies the Land Barriers

CALIFORNIA's days of isolation were over. The Boston ships had opened wide the sea gates and now the land barriers would be broken down. The vast deserts and rugged mountains so long believed impassable were to be conquered by a young man named Jedediah Strong Smith, who would be the first white man to reach the Pacific Coast overland from the United States. Following the trails that he opened, thousands of his countrymen—trappers, explorers, settlers, and gold seekers—were to follow and change the whole course of history.

If Smith had not read a book about the travels of Lewis and Clark, he might have stayed in his native Jericho, New York, and become a clergyman, for he had a deeply religious strain and a liking for study. But his imagination and love of adventure, perhaps stronger characteristics, were stirred by the descriptions of strange sights and natural wonders, and he became eager to explore that mysterious land west of the Rocky Mountains. More practically, he had learned that the Far West promised a fortune in the fur trade. Times were hard, and there was a flock of younger brothers to get started in life. In the spring of 1822, Smith packed his Bible, a book of Wesleyan hymns, a copy of Rollins' *Histoire Ancien*, and the work on Lewis and Clark, and, taking his musket and a few provisions, set off for St. Louis.

He could not have arrived there at a better time. General William Ashley, an emigrated Virginian who had prospered in the fur trade, was advertising for hunters and trappers. "A very intelligent and confidential young man" was his comment after he had hired Smith as a hunter. Two years later Smith had become Ashley's partner, and at age twenty-seven he bought Ashley out and became senior partner in the largest company engaged in the mountain fur trade: Smith, Jackson, and Sublette. He was then, in the vernacular of the mountain men, the "booshway" (a corruption of bourgeois) of three hundred hunters and trappers.

Jedediah Smith has been described as "a mild man and a Christian." But underneath the quiet unassuming exterior of this lean, muscular man, who stood six feet two inches tall in his moccasins, were all the requisites of the frontiersman and explorer: untiring energy, total indifference to privation, courage, a desire to investigate his surroundings and chronicle his findings, and a positive genius for leadership. There was never any doubt who was in command. "Old Jed" some of his men might call him behind his back, but to his face he was Mr. Smith or Captain.

In his brief life he saw more of the West than Lewis and Clark, and he knew as much or more about it than did Kit Carson after a much longer career. If Smith had not been murdered by the Comanches when he was thirty-three, knowledge of the Far West would have been advanced at least fifteen years.

Besides making the first overland journey into California, he opened the South Pass in the Rocky Mountains, made the first crossing of the central overland route west of Salt Lake, was the first white man to traverse the present state of Nevada, the first to cross the Sierra west to east, and the first to blaze a trail from California to the Northwest.

On the afternoon of November 27, 1826, an Indian vaquero from Mission San Gabriel, in present Los Angeles County, stared in amazement at a troop of ragged men and bony horses straggling along the trail to the mission. At their head rode a commanding figure dressed in a shirt of fringed buckskin and trousers of scarlet wool. His long brown hair was tied back with a blue bandanna.

The Indian hurried off to report that a party of white strangers had appeared from nowhere, having penetrated the impenetrable. In a short while they were called on by the mission guard. The captain, noticing the men's starved looks, thoughtfully ordered a beef butchered and sent to the granary for cornmeal, before asking Smith to return with him.

The head priest, Father José Sánchez, described as a "very jovial, friendly gentleman," received Smith cordially and gave him food and drink. It was his duty, he explained apologetically, to take his arms and hold him until he could get orders from the governor. In the morning he reported the party's illegal entry and asked for instructions. Smith also wrote the governor to explain how he and his men, "worn out with fatigue and hardships and emaciated from hunger," had entered the province hoping to get supplies and fresh horses. They then intended to travel on to San Francisco Bay, follow the largest river that emptied into it, and cross the range to the east to keep a rendezvous with Smith's partners in Cache Valley, near Salt Lake.

Twelve days later a messenger arrived with orders for Smith to report to San Diego for a meeting with the governor. He set off by horse the next morning with Captain William Cunningham, a Boston shipmaster who had been at the mission on business, but whose vessel lay at San Diego.

Smith's interviews with Governor José de Encheandía were protracted and unsatisfactory. He questioned and cross-questioned the American, and examined and reexamined his papers, license, and journal. It was impossible for him to imagine men taking such risks merely for the sake of furs. The stranger's firm bearing smacked of the military; trapping, the governor presumed, was merely a front. This tall American was in reality a captain of soldiers come to spy. He hinted at detention for three months until an answer could be had from Mexico.

The meeting with Captain Cunningham had been fortunate. In the end it was through his efforts and those of several other Boston seafarers in port, that Smith was finally released. On December 20 they drew up and signed a document attesting to the authenticity of his license and papers.

Once the responsibility was shifted from his shoulders, the governor willingly granted Smith a passport and permission to buy horses and supplies. But there was one stipulation: he must leave the province by the route over which he had come.

By January 10 Smith was back at the mission, fitting out the party, and a week later they were ready to start, their pack animals laden with parting gifts from Father Sánchez.

Smith and his men reached the desert on February 1, and feeling that he had complied sufficiently with the governor's order, he turned back and began traveling northwest, careful to keep a good two hundred miles between himself and the coastal settlements.

They took their time, hunting and trapping along the way, so it was already the end of April when the party reached the American's South Fork and camped near what is now Folsom.

No white man knew anything firsthand about the land that lay between the Sierra and the Rocky Mountains. Indians told of a great river flowing westward on the other side of the divide, and navigators familiar with San Francisco Bay were aware of some large river emptying into it. Maps of the day, based on hearsay and imagination, showed the Buenaventura River flowing from the Rockies to California and the ocean.

Jedediah Smith was eager to explore that great unknown territory. By following the river on which they were now camped east to its source, he might find a pass through the range. Once on the other side he could leave most of his men to trap on whatever streams were there, while he went on to his summer rendezvous.

The first week in May found Smith and his men caught in a storm in the high Sierra, floundering through drifts of fresh snow, and making but a mile or two a day. Nights were so cold men and animals huddled together to keep from freezing. "I then thought of the vanity of riches & of all those objects that lead men in the perilous paths of adventure. It seems that in times like those man returns to reason & makes the true estimate of things," Smith was to write.

Five horses were caught in the deep snow and, unable to get out, starved to death. Provisions began to run low, and spirits sank. Reluctantly Smith gave up his attempt to force a crossing at this point, and turned back to the valley. The voice of the river and the thunder of its cascades were harsh and menacing, he would remember.

After resting, the party made another vain effort to penetrate the Sierra, farther south. Smith decided this time that the only way to make a successful crossing was alone, and by May 20 he was ready to try again. Silas Gobel, a blacksmith, and Robert Evans, a hunter, volunteered to go with him. The rest of the men were left in a base camp set up on what Smith called the Appelamminy River, thought to be the present Stanislaus, in charge of Harrison Rogers, the company clerk and second in command, or "little booshway." Here they would hunt elk and trap beaver until Smith's return, which he expected would be within four months.

Details of this memorable first west-east crossing of the Sierra (which Smith called Mount Joseph in honor of Father Sánchez) are meager. All that is known firsthand is from Smith's letter to General William Clark, which is sparing with words. They took seven horses and two pack mules to carry the hay and provisions, he wrote. The ascent and crossing took eight days, with the loss of only two horses and mules. The snow on the summit was from four to eight feet deep, but packed so hard it bore the weight of men and animals. "After traveling twenty days from the West side of *Mount Joseph* I struck the S. W. corner of the great Salt Lake. . . . My arrival caused considerable bustle in camp, for myself and party had been given up as lost. A small cannon brought up from St. Louis was loaded and fired for a salute. . . ."

There is no agreement among historians as to which river he followed into the Sierra or where he crossed, since his map and that part of his journal that described the passage are missing. The most widely accepted theory takes him up the Stanislaus and over the Sierra near today's Ebbetts Pass.

In ten days he had finished his business in Cache Valley and was recruiting men and packing supplies for the return to California, by the southern route. His main purpose was to relieve the party on the Stanislaus and trap more beaver, but he admitted that he was also anxious to explore the coast and all land lying between the Sierra and the sea.

The trip was uneventful until they reached the Colorado River. On the previous trip Smith had made friends with the Mojave Indians living there, and now they seemed as well disposed as ever, trading corn, melons, and dried pumpkins, and even supplying a reed raft to ferry the baggage.

But just as the horses were coming out of the river on the west bank, and the raft was being sent back for another load, a war party made a sudden attack. It was brief and one-sided, for most of Smith's men were unarmed, and in a matter of minutes ten of them lay dead; among these was the faithful Silas Gobel. Jedediah and eight companions managed to escape unharmed and to survive a second attack. Later, when he had had time to reflect, Smith concluded that the Mojaves had been ordered by Mexican officials to keep all Americans out of the province and to kill them if necessary.

After dark the survivors started off with little hope of getting across the desert. All their horses had been taken, and of their food supplies only fifteen pounds of dried meat had been salvaged; further, they had no containers in which to carry water.

After a journey of almost incredible hardship, when they traveled at night to avoid the blistering sun and lay during the day in the shadow of boulders and at springs which Smith had found on his first trip, they eventually reached base camp. But instead of the expected supplies and horses, they brought only a tale of disaster and death.

Smith was forced to turn to the missions again for help, but this time there was no cordial reception; the head priest at San José clapped him in the *calabozo*.

The pattern of ensuing events was identical with what had happened before: a summons to appear before the governor—this time at Monterey, by then the capital; prolonged and indecisive meetings with him; even a shipmaster coming to the rescue. This time it was Captain John Rogers Cooper, although an English trader, William E. P. Hartnell, acting as the governor's interpreter, thought up the plan. Hartnell recalled that in cases of emergency involving British subjects in a foreign port, their law allowed four English sea captains to appoint one of their number consul. He surmised Americans must have a similar law, so Captain Cooper was appointed agent for the United States government in the port of Monterey. On November 20, Cooper and three other seafaring men went Smith's bond, and the governor issued a passport. But again there was that stipulation that he go back over the trail by which he had come.

Returning at once to the mission, he made hasty preparations to get on his way and out of the reach of Mexican authorities. This time there were no parting gifts. For two days he traveled innocently enough to the south, but on the third he turned eastward and crossed the San Joaquin River. On its farther shore he breathed freely once more. He had, he wrote, seen enough of the "folly of men in power," and "returned again to the woods, the river, the prairie, the camp and the game with a feeling somewhat like that of a prisoner escaped from his dungeon and chains."

On February 20 he and his company reached the American's South Fork. It was raining steadily, and the river was a torrent. He wrote that seeing it again in this mood stirred unpleasant recollections of his first vain attempt to fight his way up its rugged, snow-packed canyon.

Two days later they crossed the flooding river in elkhide canoes, and made camp on its north bank. Here they stayed for ten days, to hunt and trap, while Jedediah looked for a practicable route to the Northwest.

One day as he and a small party were riding along the river, they came to a Maidu village. The Indians were so frightened they all fled, some in their terror plunging into the river, others stumbling and falling down the banks, while still others took to a raft and hastened downstream. Spurring his horse, Smith galloped after a group of women running along the shore and, overtaking one, convinced her of his goodwill by giving her presents. He then rode on to where he had seen another fall. She was lying perfectly still, a girl of eleven or twelve, he judged. Dismounting, he found to his amazement that she was dead.

"Could it be possible," he mused, "that we who called ourselves Christians were such frightful objects as to scare poor savages to death?"

He covered her gently with a blanket and left some gifts beside her. Because of the "singular wildness" of these Indians, he called the river the Wild.

And now it had two names.

5

The River Is Settled and Named Again

ENGLISH-BORN John Rogers Cooper, the sea captain who had befriended Jedediah Smith, was the first person to take up a grant in the Sacramento Valley. This was 1833. By then Cooper was a Mexican citizen, known as Juan Bautista Rogers Cooper, and the land he selected lay along the American's South Fork, near what is now Folsom. On the map accompanying his petition, Cooper called the river Rio Ojotska, thought to be a phonetic spelling of the Russian word *okhatskaia,* meaning hunter, for men from Fort Ross had begun setting their traps in the thickets along the river each winter and spring.

So now the river had been named three times. But after Jedediah Smith, that amazing *Americano,* had camped on its banks in direct defiance of Mexican orders and had followed it up into the Sierra, Californians began calling it Rio de los Americanos, and the ford across it, which Smith and other trappers used, El Paso de los Americanos. Then as settlers from the States began following its forks down from the Sierra, the name Rio de los Americanos became firmly fixed.

Cooper did not develop the land and later renounced the grant. The first white settlement of the valley and the American River was to be made by an affable and visionary Swiss, John A. Sutter, who had fled his country in 1834 to avoid arrest after he had failed in the dry-goods business, and bankruptcy charges were filed against him. At that time there was no better place in the world to recoup one's fortunes than the United States.

Toward the end of May, Sutter sailed for New York, leaving behind a wife and five children to be sent for when his fortune was made. After his arrival he spent several unprofitable years in the Santa Fe trade, then opened a small store in Westport, Missouri. It was at this time that he began signing his name "J. A. Sutter, Capt." To those who asked, he told of his service in the Royal Swiss Guards at the court of Charles X. This fiction was to open many doors during his career.

But Sutter had no head for business; he was too trusting and openhanded, and what little he made was spent on fine clothes and books. It was inevitable that he should fail. When this happened, he talked of suicide to a close friend; but reconsidering, he made plans to emigrate to California. On a misty morning in the spring of 1838, he started off on an Indian pony, with a little band of emigrants, all of whom later joined a caravan going by way of the Oregon Trail.

It was October when the party reached Fort Vancouver, the Pacific headquarters of the Hudson's Bay Company, and too late in the season to go on by land to California. But Sutter, who had during his cross-country trek been making plans to found a colony in California, had no intention of idling away his time until spring. Seeing his impatience, James Douglas, commander of the post, gave him free passage to Honolulu on a company ship. With luck, he would be able to find a vessel there ready to sail for California. Douglas, who was greatly impressed with the captain of the Royal Guard, gave him a sheaf of introductory letters to persons of importance in the Islands.

But Sutter just missed the last ship going to California. Five months passed, and it seemed as though he were going to be stranded in Honolulu. Then a merchant to whom he had an introduction came to his aid by offering him free passage as supercargo on a vessel bound for Sitka: he would have the privilege of taking the ship on to California.

On April 20, 1839, Sutter sailed aboard the *Clementine*, taking with him more introductory letters and, as a nucleus for his colony, eight Kanaka men and two women, three Caucasians, two of them German carpenters—and a large bulldog. He also had a stock of carpenter and blacksmith tools, farm implements, and three brass cannons to tame the wilderness.

On July 3 the *Clementine* anchored at Monterey, and Sutter was shortly presenting his credentials to the governor, Juan Alvarado. "He had never seen so many letters of recommendation," Sutter was to write. The Swiss asked permission to settle along the Sacramento River, which he had heard was a region of great "beauty and fertility."

Alvarado was receptive to the suggestion of an outpost in the heart of the *tierra incognita,* seeing it as a possible solution to some of his most vexing problems. As a representative of the Mexican government this military officer could banish the Russian and British trappers from the rivers, keep in line the troublesome "Horse-thief Indians" who made regular raids on the rancho herds, and discourage emigrants from the United States. He gave Sutter a passport and permission to select whatever land he liked. Come back in a year and he would be granted his citizenship and land.

At Yerba Buena, Sutter bought a four-oared pinnace (on credit) and chartered the schooners *Isabel* and *Nicholas,* commanded by William Heath Davis; then, loading them with provisions, seeds, and the equipment brought from Honolulu, he started up the Sacramento River on August 9. His party now included several mechanics and runaway sailors picked up in the pueblo.

It took eight days to sail up the river. During this time Sutter talked enthusiastically to Davis about his plans. As soon as he found the right site, he said, he would build a fort, not only as protection against the Indians, but also against the Mexican government, for he intended to pursue his own policy toward the natives (using their labor to build up his settlement), to establish independent trading ventures, and to monopolize the fur trade. He had the vision to foresee that his post could become a rendezvous for emigrants from the United States whom he intended to encourage to settle the valley, for it was of such men he planned to build his colony into a sovereign state. He also spoke of his desire to induce a large number of his own countrymen to emigrate there.

Every day they would stop, and Sutter would take off in the pinnace to explore the country for the ideal spot. On the afternoon of August 17, the two schooners nosed their way into the South Fork American, sailing up as far as deep-draft vessels could go in summer. A landing was made on the south bank, just north of what is now B Street in the city of Sacramento. Equipment and provisions were unloaded, tents were pitched, and the brass cannons mounted.

In the morning the two vessels headed back for Yerba Buena. Davis was to write:

> As we moved away, Captain Sutter gave us a parting salute of nine guns . . . which produced a most remarkable effect. As the heavy report . . . and the echoes died away, the camp of the little party was surrounded by hundreds of Indians, who were excited and astonished at the unusual sound. A large number of deer, elk, and other animals on the plains were startled, running to and fro, stopping to listen, their heads raised, full of curiosity and wonder, seemingly attracted and fascinated to the spot, while from the interior of the adjacent woods the howls of wolves and coyotes filled the air, and immense flocks of water fowl flew wildly about over the camp. . . .
>
> This salute was the first echo of civilization in the primitive wilderness so soon to become populated. . . . We returned the salute with nine cheers. . . . The cheers were heartily responded to by the little garrison, and thus we parted company.

Sutter selected a knoll about a mile upriver from the landing place as a site for his fort. By the time the first rains came the tule thatch was finished on a one-story adobe structure that was forty feet long and contained a blacksmith shop, a kitchen, and quarters for Sutter. This was the first permanent white habitation on the American River, and the first in the Sacramento Valley. "When I first came into the valley, my closest neighbors lived more than a hundred miles distant," he wrote. He named his settlement New Helvetia.

The Indians from nearby villages watched the stranger furtively, refusing to venture near his camp. To gain their confidence he left bags of Hawaiian sugar, strings of glass beads, and brightly colored handkerchiefs near their settlements. Soon they were coming to ask for more gifts. By giving them presents to run errands and perform small tasks, he gained their confidence, and it was not long until he had them helping him clear the land. Then he taught them how to plow and plant, to use the whipsaw and plane, and later, after he began to build up herds and flocks, to tend horses, cattle, and sheep. It was upon their friendliness and cooperation that he had to depend if he was to succeed in his plans, and by a policy of kindness tempered with firmness, he retained their goodwill. Many of them came to hold responsible positions, and he had among them many faithful friends.

In August 1840, Sutter went to Monterey to receive his naturalization papers, and as Don Juan Agosto Sutter, he took the oath as a Mexican citizen. With his new position went those trappings in which he delighted: the dazzling uniform of a Mexican army officer, which satisfied at last the yearning for martial pomp and lent authenticity to his claims to military fame.

One of his first acts as representative of the government was a proclamation that excluded all "foreign" trappers from his domain. But proclamations without the means of enforcing them are worthless, and the Hudson's Bay men flocked in just the same. Sutter had expected to reap his largest profit from the fur trade during those years when he was getting started. Later, after he had built a distillery, he retaliated by secretly trading his brandy for the greater part of the Hudson's Bay fur harvest, and managed to make more than if he had kept a large hunting establishment of his own.

The following June he returned to Monterey to receive his grant of eleven square leagues (48,818 acres). While in the capital he hired a number of workers, mainly mechanics. One of them was a Negro cooper, who was to be the first black to settle in the valley.

On his return, Sutter began building the adobe fortress he had been planning for so long. Fir and pine timber for beams and planking were felled upriver and rafted down, and thousands of adobe bricks were made by his Kanaka and Indian workers; until the protective walls were up, Sutter worked with them at this task.

When the fort was finished four years later, it covered five acres and contained a two-story residence for Sutter and his clerks; offices, kitchen, bakery, gristmill, and storerooms; shops for the cooper, blacksmith, carpenter, and shoemaker; barracks for the garrison; quarters for the vaqueros, farmers, gardeners, sawyers, and hunters; a corral, guardroom, and jail. By 1847 it would include spinning and weaving rooms, a hat and blanket factory, a gunsmith shop, a brewery, and a distillery where the wild grapes that grew so plentifully along the river were made into brandy. Near the landing was a tannery.

Around these structures was a spacious courtyard, and enclosing the whole a formidable adobe brick wall eighteen feet high and two and a half feet thick. Cannons bristled from projecting bastions at the corners and commanded the main gate through embrasures.

The fort was run by strict military rule. A sentry was on duty at the gate night and day, and the guard, composed of fifteen young Indians dressed neatly in uniforms of blue drill trousers and white shirts with red bandannas on their heads, made the rounds all night, marking each half-hour with a stroke on the bell and an "All's well!" Dr. G. M. W. Sandels, the eminent

Swedish scholar who visited Sutter, reported that "the discordant notes of a Mexican drum" assembled the men for work. Winter and summer all hands rose at daybreak. Except for a siesta during the hottest part of summer days, work was continued until sundown. Sutter set an example by beginning his day at four each morning, and going back to his desk for several hours after supper.

The garrison also consisted of Indians—a hundred foot-soldiers and fifty cavalry—officered by two Germans, an Indian chief, and a former mission neophyte. Every evening after work the infantry was drilled, marching to the music of fife and drum.

On August 23, 1841, Sutter ran up his flag and fired his cannons in honor of the first official visitors from the United States. Lieutenant Cadwalader Ringgold of the naval vessel *Porpoise* came up the river with a company of seven officers and fifty men, who were amazed to find a flourishing settlement in the wilderness. They were part of Lieutenant Charles Wilkes' scientific expedition, the first of its kind to be authorized by Congress, and after three years of travel which included discovery of the Antarctic continent, they had reached the California coast. Ringgold and his men were detached to explore and survey the Sacramento River.

Sutter's Indian fishermen, who acted as scouts, brought notice of their approach, and a clerk was sent to the landing to identify them. As soon as Sutter learned who they were, he sent them horses, put on his uniform, and ordered up a banquet. In the morning they went on, but on their return from the Upper Sacramento, they stopped by again, camping along the American not far from the fort.

Shortly before their return, Sutter had another unexpected caller. The Russian schooner *Constantine* landed Count Alexander Rotchev, author and translator for the Russian theater, who was governor-general of the North American colonies. He had come to offer Sutter a chance to buy the holdings at Fort Ross and Bodega. The fur trade was no longer profitable, for their own zealous hunters had nearly exterminated the seal and sea otter; the climate had proved too cold for the wheat and peach orchards set out in the valleys along Salmon Creek and the Slavianka (Russian) River, where fingers of sea fog are driven by prevailing winds. Even their efforts at shipbuilding and manufacturing had not been successful. Rotchev was anxious for Sutter to return with him to Fort Ross and discuss details with Peter Kostromitinov, the sales agent from Sitka. Seeing how this acquisition could materially strengthen his position, Sutter readily agreed to go.

One night after supper Kostromitinov made the formal offer of sale: $30,000 with a down payment of $2,000 in cash, and Sutter's holdings, fixed and movable, as security. For the first three years the payments would be made in produce: wheat, peas, beans, soap, suet, and tallow. The fourth and final one of $10,000 was to be paid in coin. Each September a ship from Sitka would call for the produce; in case of failure to deliver, Sutter was liable for the expense of sending the vessel.

So Sutter, who had a mania for undertaking more than he could handle, agreed to the conditions of sale, and the deal was celebrated with a banquet aboard the Russian schooner *Helena*, anchored in Bodega Bay. Present, surely, was Rotchev's bride, Princess Helena de Gagarin, a niece of the czar; an adventurous young woman, she had that summer led an expedition to explore the interior of California. At the party "champagne flowed freely; we drank the health of the Russian Emperor, and I was toasted as the new owner of Ross and Bodega."

Toward the end of September he began transferring the Russian herds and flocks to his wild pastures along the American —some 1,700 cattle, 940 horses, and 900 sheep. With the down payment of cash, he received the twenty-ton *Constantine*, which he renamed *Sacramento*, and four smaller boats; farming and woodworking tools; carts, halters, harness; household furniture; bells from the Orthodox chapel, which he hung at the fort and used to call his men to and from work; "forty-odd pieces of old rusty cannon and one or two smaller brass pieces, with a quantity of old French flintlock muskets," said to have been abandoned by Napoleon's army on its retreat from Moscow; ammunition, and a large supply of blue and green uniforms piped with scarlet, in which the Indian garrison was soon clothed.

Buildings were taken down just for their lumber. It took two years of constant ferrying and overland hauling to transfer all the stock and material to the American River.

When Sutter returned from Fort Ross he found that in his absence the largest party of emigrants yet to come overland had arrived. This was the Bidwell-Bartleson Party, numbering thirty-three men, one of whom, Benjamin Kelsey, had brought his wife and child. Twenty-two-year-old John Bidwell, a teacher, and co-captain of the party, wrote that Sutter received them with "open arms and in a princely fashion," and that he proceeded to hire all who wanted to stay and work for him. Bidwell was among these, and he shortly became Sutter's chief clerk, trusted assistant, and confidant.

"He employed men—not because he always needed and could profitably employ them," Bidwell recalled, "but because in the kindness of his heart it simply became a habit to employ everybody who wanted employment. As long as he had anything, he trusted anyone with anything he wanted, responsible or otherwise, acquaintance and strangers alike."

Word of this refuge in the wilderness worked its way back to the States, and nearly all who came to California made it a point to go to New Helvetia, where they knew a warm welcome awaited one man or a hundred. Sutter made no charge for room and board, and men could stay as long as it suited them. When they were ready to go on, he furnished them with passports that were recognized throughout the province. Often the fort was so crowded with "wet, poor, and hungry immigrants," he himself had trouble finding a place to sleep. He helped many get started by giving them land from his own grant, and horses and cattle from his herds. "These men were allies and buffers to my empire," he explained.

Edwin Bryant, a young Kentuckian of education, who led a company of emigrants from Missouri in 1846 and crossed the plains partway with the ill-fated Donner Party, has left an interesting account of Sutter's hospitality under trying conditions. At the time of Bryant's arrival that September, California was in the throes of being taken over by the United States, and Sutter was no longer master of his domain. After crossing the American River at the ford, the party followed a well-beaten path to the fort. Riding up to the front gate, Bryant saw two Indian sentinels pacing back and forth, and several Americans dressed in buckskin trousers and blue sailor shirts, sitting in the gateway. He asked one of them if Captain Sutter was there.

A very small man, with a peculiarly sharp red face and a most voluble tongue, gave the response [Bryant wrote]. He said, in substance, that perhaps I was not aware of the great changes which had recently taken place in California; that the fort belonged to the United States and that Captain Sutter, although he was in the fort, had no control over it. He was going into a minute history of the complicated circumstances and events which had produced this result, when I reminded him that we were too much fatigued to listen to a long discourse, but if Captain Sutter . . . could conveniently step to the gate a moment, I would be glad to see him.

Sutter soon came out and greeted them "with much gentlemanly courtesy and friendly cordiality"; he regretted that he did not feel authorized to ask the party to stay inside the fort. Bryant assured him that this did not matter, but if he could supply them with a little meat, salt, and a few vegetables, they would be content.

Bryant continues: "A servant was immediately dispatched with orders to furnish us with a supply of beef, salt, melons, onions, and tomatoes, for which no compensation would be received." Taking the provisions, they camped in an oak grove west of the fort.

John A. Sutter

A few days later Bryant and two or three of his party were invited to have dinner with Sutter. "He is a gentleman between forty-five and fifty years of age, and in manners, dress, and general deportment, he approaches so near what we call the 'old school gentleman,' as to present a gulfy contrast from the rude society by which he is surrounded," Bryant noted.

Neither the dining room nor "table furniture" presented a very luxurious appearance. The room is unfurnished, with the exception of a common deal table standing in the centre, and some benches, which are substitutes for chairs. The table, when spread, presented a correspondingly primitive simplicity of aspect and viands. The first course consisted of good soup, served to each guest in a china bowl, with silver spoons. The bowls, after they had been used for this purpose, were taken away and cleaned by the Indian servants, and were afterwards used as tumblers or goblets, from which we drank our water. The next course consisted of two dishes of meat, one roasted and one fried, and both highly seasoned with onions. Bread, cheese, butter, and melons constituted the dessert.

The parlor, he saw, was furnished with simple heavy pieces that had been made from native laurel trees by the Russians at Fort Ross.

Until 1842 Sutter had no immediate neighbors. That year John Sinclair, a jovial Scotsman, described as "a talented man and capital company where grog and cards were stirring," and "of great enterprise in business," took up land for two wealthy Honolulu merchants, Eliab and Hiram Grimes. Since the ford, El Paso de los Americanos, was on the property, he named the holding Rancho del Paso. On a piece of rising ground two miles east of the fort, he built what was a distinct novelty for California—a wooden house, modeled after those in the States. For years it was the first "civilized" dwelling reached by emigrants journeying down the western face of the Sierra. Bryant spoke for many when he wrote that the house and outbuildings presented "a most comfortable and neat appearance. It was a pleasant scene, after having traveled many months in the wilderness, to survey this abode . . . resembling so nearly those we had left in the far-off country behind us."

Like Sutter, Sinclair also welcomed all newcomers to the territory, treated them to his hospitality, and gave help to those in need. Later he became a figure of considerable importance when he was appointed *alcalde* of the Sacramento District.

John Bidwell has written that because of Sutter's generosity and his ever-expanding enterprises, many of them impractical, he found himself "immensely—almost hopelessly—in debt." He seemed "to owe everybody" and, in his struggles to save himself, sank still deeper in the morass. The year after he took over Fort Ross was a dry one, crops were short, and there was no wheat for the Russians. He got his most necessary supplies that season by bartering elk and deer tallow and wild grape brandy. He paid off his most pressing debts with beaver pelts; the rest of his obligations, including those to the Russians, were simply put off.

At this time he began diverting the American River into irrigation ditches and sowing more and more bottomland to wheat, peas, and beans. But agricultural tools were few in California, and farming methods primitive and wasteful. Wheat was harvested by his Indians, some armed with sickles and butcher knives, some with pieces of iron hoop, and others with dry willow sticks, having only their hands with which to gather the brittle grain. Piling the harvest in the middle of a strong, round corral, three or four hundred wild horses were then turned in to thresh it, the Indians keeping them on the run by yelling at them, and reversing their course occasionally by dashing in front of the band suddenly.

Within an hour the grain was thoroughly threshed and the dry straw broken into chaff. Next came the winnowing, which could only be done in the wind, when shovelfuls of grain and chaff were thrown high in the air, the lighter material being blown aside, while the grain fell in its own pile.

With such archaic methods the yield was always short. Beyond this there were those years of unseasonable rain, late or early frost, drought, heavy winters with deep snowpacks in the Sierra followed by thaws, when the American overflowed its banks and turned the valley into a vast muddy sea, washing out newly planted crops, and drowning horses, cattle, and sheep.

Each passing year found Sutter more deeply in debt. At times he could feel the foundations of his cherished empire shaking, and in these moments of doubt he considered leaving the river and settling at Fort Ross.

6

The River Trail Is Opened

ON THE AFTERNOON of February 20, 1844, Lieutenant John C.
Frémont and twenty-five members of his exploration party
camped on the summit of a gap through the Sierra, about half
a mile south of the present Kit Carson Pass. It had been pointed
out by an Indian, from the eastern side of the range.

Frémont called it Snowy Mountain Pass, a name that was
kept well into the 1850s. Later it was renamed in honor of his
guide, Kit Carson, remembered as a small, laconic, "stoop-
shouldered man, with reddish hair, freckled face, soft blue
eyes," and nothing in his manner to "indicate extraordinary
courage or daring."

It was a cheerless camp in the windswept gap. The men, exhausted by physical exertion and hunger, were low-spirited.
For sixteen days they had been struggling to get the camp
gear, scientific instruments, and starving animals up the steep
slope. Snowstorms and gales had buffeted them constantly, and
many nights were so cold sleep was impossible.

One after another horses and mules had sunk to their ears
in the deep drifts and, being too weak to pull themselves out,
gave up and froze to death. Of the one hundred and four animals that started up the mountain, only fifty-three came through.
Precious hours were lost in making sleds to carry the loads animals were too weak to tote, and in fashioning snowshoes for
those men who had become the burden bearers.

It was not as though there had been no warning. On the night of February 4, two Indians had joined the men as they huddled around the campfire on the eastern slope. With darkness a strong wind had sprung up, and the temperature dropped to ten degrees. All at once one of the Indians stood up and began to speak. He was an old man, but his voice was strong and clear. Repetition of certain phrases gave music and power to his speech.

"Rock upon rock—rock upon rock—snow upon snow—snow upon snow," he had said. "Even if you get over the snow, you will not be able to get down from the mountains," and he made the sign of precipices, and showed how their horses would slip and be thrown off the narrow ledges. "Turn back—turn back—and I will show you a better way," he urged.

A Chinook with the party, who understood the old man's words better than anyone else, covered his head with a blanket and gave way to tears. The situation seemed hopeless, but Frémont refused to turn back.

Provisions had been low when he made his decision to cross into California, but the ascent had taken so much longer than expected, supplies were nearly gone. Only a few handfuls of flour were left, and these would be used to give body to the horsemeat and pea soup that was now their mainstay. There had been no game on the wintry mountainsides, and the weaker horses and mules were shot for food. Once, when the advance party was cut off from its ration of horsemeat, they were forced to eat their pet dog, to keep from starving. Then salt ran out, everything was unpalatable, and men began developing strange symptoms.

For seven days the advance party had camped three miles from the summit, waiting for the animals to be brought up. During this time they lived like wild creatures in two large snow-free holes made by setting fire to two old fir trunks; these burning downward, had melted the eight-foot drifts. One pit was used for sleeping, the other as a kitchen.

On one of these days, February 14, Frémont and Charles

Preuss, the expedition's cartographer and artist, climbed the highest mountain to their right, the present Red Lake Peak, to view the country and give Preuss a chance to map and sketch it. From the summit they saw a large lake of the deepest blue, nestled in a great basin rimmed by rugged, snow-blanketed peaks. This was Lake Tahoe, and they were the first white men to see it.

But the next day something of more importance to the whole camp occurred: rock salt was bartered from some Indians they met, and the endless peas and horsemeat became bearable again.

With the entire party finally gathered at the summit of the pass on that pale winter afternoon of February 20, Frémont felt elated: the Sierra had been conquered. He stood with his back to the fire and tried to give heart to his men, many of them giddy from fatigue and hunger. The worst was behind them, he said. There was only the descent now, which would be rapid, and he reminded them of what was said about the Sacramento Valley, the land of no winter, its plains teeming with fat deer and elk, and its rivers with salmon. There would be many days of rest there, with plenty to eat, while the party refitted for the homeward journey at "the house of Mr. Sutter."

This was Frémont's second expedition. It had set out the previous May with the blessing of the federal government, to explore those regions lying south of the Columbia River and between the Rocky Mountains and the Pacific Ocean. It was intended to tie in with his expedition of the year before and give a connected survey of the western half of the continent. This was the acknowledged purpose—but there was something more. In Washington there was a powerful group of senators—Frémont's father-in-law, Thomas Hart Benton, their leader—who was advocating and working for United States expansion to the Pacific. Frémont had his instructions from them to observe closely the strength of British and Mexican settlements, and to determine the feasibility of taking over California whenever that opportunity offered.

There was reason, then, to go into California, but there was no call for haste or necessity for a crossing of the Sierra in midwinter. The party could have settled into camp comfortably along the Truckee River, east of the range, where fish and game and grass were plentiful. With the spring they could have made their ascent of the mountains without hardship.

On the morning of February 21 the party was stirring before dawn in order to cross the vast snowfields that stretched down the western slope, before the sun melted their icy crust. It was soon seen that the descent was not going to be as easy or rapid as supposed, for beyond the snow, and between them and the valley, stood barriers of wild and rugged mountains through which a passage had to be found.

Once safely over the first snowfields that morning, the men turned northwest to follow that high ridge between the headwaters of the Upper Truckee River and the Silver Fork American. Six miles were covered that day, and camp was made in a grove of pines where there was a little grass for the animals, and where Frémont found a few delicate blossoms of blue flax.

"We had hard and doubtful labor yet before us, as the snow appeared heavier where the timber began farther down, with few open spots," he noted in his journal, after a climb to the heights to trace out a line for the next day's march.

After dark they noticed fires lighting up as if in answer to their own, twinkling like distant red stars among the pines of the nearby ridges, and the sight was comforting. Later they would learn that these fires were along the shores of San Francisco Bay, where the Indians were burning tules.

Breakfast was over that next morning long before sunrise to enable passage of frozen snowfields that were often fifteen feet deep. There were but two meals a day now, of peas and horse or mule meat, a diet many felt gave little strength.

In places the trail had to be stamped and beaten to get the animals across, and only three miles were made before it was time to camp again.

"But what an atmosphere!" exclaimed Charles Preuss, in spite of the rigors of the day's march. He noted that the sky was blue as forget-me-nots, and the air held a hint of spring. His spirits rose still more after he consulted a pocket atlas and found they were in the latitude of Smyrna and Palermo.

The following day, February 23, proved the worst yet. "Terrible march," Preuss commented grimly. Deep drifts among the trees drove them off the ridge onto rocky slopes that were "steep and slippery with snow and ice . . . the tough evergreens . . . impeded our way, tore our skins, and exhausted our patience. Some of us had the misfortune to wear moccasins with parflèche [smooth rawhide] soles so slippery that we could not keep our feet, and generally crawled across the snow-beds," observed Frémont, who was wearing moccasins.

In going ahead to reconnoiter that afternoon, he and Carson came on the American's South Fork and had an unwelcome baptism in its freezing waters. In crossing, Carson made a leap clear over, but when Frémont came to jump, his moccasins glanced off an icy rock and shot him into the river. "It was some seconds before I could recover myself in the current and Carson, thinking me hurt, jumped in after me, and we both had an icy bath. We tried to search awhile for my gun, which had been lost in the fall, but the cold drove us out." Later the gun was found lodged under the ice shelf that lined the river's edge.

At the end of this day's nine-hour march, which again took them only three miles, Frémont saw how poorly his men looked. Most of them were mere skeletons—gaunt, and hung with rags —and each mile took its toll in strength. By the time his tepee was pitched and camp set up in a dry, open spot at the present Strawberry Valley, many were ready to give out.

Still, the party was astir at three the next morning to make astronomical observations. After eating, the line of march was taken up along the south face of the canyon wall where, during the morning, they struck an Indian trail. The footing was no longer sharp and rocky, but sandy, and covered with pine needles and a thatch of last year's leaves. Frémont saw that the river was now "a raging torrent," and was pleased to note how rapidly it raced downhill.

As they neared the present Kyburz, they found patches of new grass and an occasional bank covered lightly with it. Countless cascades fed by melting snow on the ridgetops tumbled down the canyon walls into the river; and they filled the gorge with the roar of muffled thunder. Full-throated streams rushing along the valley floor poured into the river; their shallows were rank with succulent reeds, and on their banks grew a legion of horsetail. The weaker animals were left in the care of a mess, to feed on this luxuriance.

Oak trees hung with balls of mistletoe now appeared among the conifers; a warm wind stirred the fallen leaves, and there was birdsong in the thickets. The men found these certain signs of spring "intoxicating," and hurried on "to escape entirely from the horrid region of inhospitable snow," Frémont wrote. By evening they had gone as far as today's Riverton.

On the morning of February 25 the company parted. Frémont, who was sure the worst was over, decided to press on as fast as possible with the sturdiest men and the best of their "miserable beasts" to Sutter's Fort to obtain food and fresh animals and return to relieve the others. He took with him Carson and Preuss, Jean Baptiste Derosier, Charles Towns, Raphael Proue, and Jacob Dodson, an eighteen-year-old free Negro from Washington, whose ambition it had long been to accompany Frémont on an expedition.

The advance party made a good twenty miles that day by keeping close to the river "which pursued a very direct westerly course through a very slight and narrow bottom," covered with pine, fir, oak, and lush vines.

The next day the face of the river country changed abruptly; the canyon sides suddenly rose high and steep, and locked the river between such narrow walls the party had trouble getting their animals through. A sudden rain in the afternoon caused

the river to rise with such turbulence that within twenty minutes they were driven to the heights to escape being swept
away. By sunset the storm had passed, and they went back to
the river to camp. Most of the animals went to sleep without
any food for the terrain was rocky, and grass sparse.

The following day the rugged nature of the river gorge again
forced them to the heights. At three that afternoon they stopped
to rest. The valley was still far off. Charles Preuss, stretched out
on the crest of the ridge, wrote in his diary: "I'll be damned if
I don't see at least fifty miles ahead of me nothing but forest.
That's a nice prospect." If no grass were found this day, there
would be no chance of saving the animals.

Toward the close of the afternoon, as they were plodding
wearily on, Charles Towns suddenly darted off and plunged
into the heart of the forest.

"Towns! Towns!" they shouted after him. "What are you
about?" He did not answer, but they could hear him crashing
on through the thickets.

"Go after him, Jacob!" Frémont ordered. He wondered how
many more minds would give way before help was reached.

Around dusk they straggled down the side of a ravine, to
make camp along a stream at the bottom. Jacob had brought
in Charles Towns, but morale was low. Then all at once there
came a shout from ahead. It was Kit Carson.

"Life yet! Life yet!" he called. "I've found a little hillside
sprinkled with green grass enough for tonight!" Frémont brightened. The animals were saved—but what about his men?

They spent all of the next day, the twenty-ninth, in the narrow, grassy ravine to let the animals eat their fill. Charles
Preuss spread his buffalo robe in a sunny spot and, stretching
out on it, lighted his pipe, listened happily to the music of the
river and the wind in the pines, and thought about the effect of
weather on men's spirits.

But poor Charles Towns, still delirious, wandered off to the
river and plunged in for a swim, "just as if it were summer and

the stream placid, when it was a cold mountain-torrent foaming among rocks," Frémont wrote. Someone was sent in to drag him ashore.

Jean Derosier volunteered that day to go back on their trail to look for Towns' horse, Proveau, which had been unable to climb the last ridge. There was a general fondness for this animal that had shared the adventures of the first expedition.

By dark Derosier had not come back, and when in the morning he was still not in, it was feared he had lost his way in the jumble of mountains. Still, it was impossible to wait; they must press on to find more feed for the horses.

After traveling about six miles along the river a halt was called near a grassy hillside. Here there were swarms of large black butterflies with wings edged in lemon yellow. Ceanothus and manzanita filled the air with honey-sweet fragrance, and shooting stars dotted the banks.

That night Derosier came back to camp and, seating himself by the fire, began to talk wildly about all the things he had done during the many days he had been gone. Times were indeed hard, Frémont noted, when "stout men lost their minds from extremity of suffering," when horses and mules dropped dead from hunger, and men ate their stringy meat to keep from starving.

The next morning (March 1), Charles Preuss, who had been anxious to explore the river and map its course, went ahead alone, planning to join the others in camp that night. Toward sundown he climbed out of the river canyon to look for his companions and, when he could not find them, went back on his trail to hunt for them. But darkness overtook him before he had gone far, and he gave up the search. Tired and hungry, he returned to the river to build a fire of driftwood and go to bed supperless, for he carried no food. "A fine mess!" he jotted in his diary. What he could not know was that for the animals' sake Frémont had set up camp at a little meadow, after traveling only a few miles.

Concern was expressed over his absence that night, but in the morning they felt better when they picked up his trail and followed it to his camping place. He was not there so they shouted and fired guns. They got no answer, but presumed he was merely out of hearing downstream, and that they would soon overtake him.

Coming shortly to a slope that was, in Frémont's words, "covered with an exuberant sward of grass," they stopped to let the animals graze. Here they shouted for Preuss again, and their hopes were raised by answering calls from the river. Then, just as they expected to see him emerge from the brush, an Indian stepped out, stopping short to stare at them in amazement. He soon backed off and disappeared among the trees. They then grew uneasy, for Preuss was unarmed, and the character of these Indians was not known.

That noon, after fording the present Rock Creek (a name Frémont gave to this stream that dashed "with great velocity . . . among large boulders"), and climbing "about three thousand feet up the opposite hill," and down again, they stopped to make a serious effort to find Preuss. One man volunteered to go back upriver, and another to follow a spur leading to the river, in the hope of crossing his trail. "To the successful man was promised a pair of pistols, not as a reward, but as a token of gratitude for a service that would free us of much anxiety." That night both scouts came back without having seen a trace of their man.

By this time Preuss was beginning to consider his situation serious, after another fruitless search for his companions at sundown. He decided they must have taken another route and that now his only salvation lay in following the river into the valley. Meanwhile he hoped to find some Indians from whom he could beg food, for since the first morning he had had nothing to eat beyond a few wild onions and part of a red ants' nest, which he had learned from the Columbia River Indians was edible. It had, he found, "an agreeable acid taste."

In their travels this day Frémont's party came to a small Indian settlement from which all the inhabitants fled at their approach. Near the dwellings they noticed structures resembling large hogsheads set up on poles but made with interlacing sticks, brush, and grass. On investigating, Frémont found these were acorn caches, and that they were full. He tasted a few, and finding them "sweet and agreeably flavored," resembling the Italian chestnut, took half a bushel, leaving a shirt, handkerchief, and a few trinkets in exchange.

Around three that afternoon, Charles Preuss, finding himself very weak, began his daily search for dry moss, fallen branches, and driftwood. He had still found nothing to eat. But now in looking for firewood he came on a number of small frogs in the reedy shallows and managed to catch several with his hands. He was so ravenous he did not wait to build his fire and cook them, but cut off their legs with his pocketknife and ate them right there.

Toward noon the next day Frémont and his men came on three Maidu women filling their conical harvest baskets with the filaree that carpeted the ground, its dark pink flowers spreading a rosy haze over the plains. They offered him some and made him understand that it was good to eat, fresh or cooked; but the men preferred their own fare and, building a small fire, broiled some bits of horsemeat.

That morning, March 5, Preuss started slowly on down the river valley, aware that his strength was failing fast. In about two hours he came on mule tracks which he knew must belong to their animals, and began following them, although with small hope of catching up. They led shortly to the little Maidu village with the acorn granaries. Seeing several Indians sitting in front of a house, he walked up boldly, sat down among them, and made them understand that he was hungry.

An Indian brought him a handful of acorns which he started to eat, then remembering that he must provide for the miles ahead, he put the rest in his pocket. Seeing this, they then

brought enough acorns to fill "both my pockets to capacity."
He expressed his gratitude and went on his way happily, certain this ration would carry him through to Sutter's Fort.

At two o'clock he came to a smoldering fire, and seeing more
mule tracks, knew his party must not be far off. "I collected
my last ounce of strength" and pushed on. Before sunset he
saw the familiar tepee ahead of him. He had caught up with
them in the beautiful valley of Coloma.

In going along the river this day the party passed that place
where four years later James Wilson Marshall was to discover
gold and so change the course of history.

Their animals were now strong enough to carry them again,
so the party made better time, traveling at the rate of over four
miles an hour. This day they came to the confluence of the
American's forks: "together they formed a beautiful stream,
sixty to one hundred yards wide," which Frémont mistook for
the Sacramento.

They pushed on eagerly now. Coming to a place where the
river swept in a large bend to the right, they suddenly found
the valley spreading out before them. It was "gay with flowers,"
Frémont wrote, and some fields were "absolutely golden with
the California poppy." Mixed with them were short dark blue
lupine, pink owl's clover, creamcups, tall blue brodiaea, and
rosy hollyhocks.

Rounding a corner they came suddenly on a large Maidu
settlement. The villagers "immediately crowded around us,"
and "a well-dressed Indian came up, and made his salutations
in very well-spoken Spanish. In answer to our inquiries he
informed us that we were upon the *Rio de los Americanos* . . .
and that it joined the Sacramento about ten miles below.
Never did a name sound more sweetly!"

"I am a *vaquero* in the service of Captain Sutter, and the
people of this *rancheria* work for him," the Indian explained.
When Frémont asked for directions to Sutter's house, he said
that if they would wait, he would get his horse and show them
the way.

They soon came in sight of the fort and, crossing the river at El Paso de los Americanos, made camp on its banks.

Toward sunset as Sutter was walking outside his gates, two gaunt and nearly naked men came riding up.

"You are Captain Sutter?" the younger man asked. Sutter said that he was and, noticing their Scotch caps, asked if they were Hudson's Bay Company men. Frémont laughed and introduced himself and his companion, who was Kit Carson.

He briefly explained his plight—by then a familiar story to Sutter, and asked for provisions and horses to take back to the main party still in the mountains. Sutter invited the two men to have dinner with him and spend the night. He led the way into the courtyard, calling to servants to take their horses, and sending orders to the cook to prepare for company. But Carson spoke up, explaining that he could not stay, for the others in this advance party camped just up the river would be expecting some supplies. If the captain were able to spare a little beef and bread, he would take it back to them. Sutter then turned to Frémont. Would the lieutenant be able to stay? He said that he would.

In the morning, Frémont and Carson, furnished with horses, mules, and still more provisions, started back on their trail to find the main party. They met on the second day near where the American's forks join.

"A more forlorn and pitiable sight than they presented cannot well be imagined," Frémont reported. "They were all on foot—each man, weak and emaciated, leading a horse or mule as weak and as emaciated as themselves." Several of the men were sick from having eaten "strange and unwholesome food which the preservation of life compelled them to." There had been great difficulty in coming down the slopes, slippery from rain and melting snow, and a number of horses fell over the cliffs and were killed. One of these was carrying all the botanical specimens collected over a two-thousand-mile trail.

Camp was made as soon as they met, and "a repast of good beef, excellent bread, and delicious salmon, which I had brought

. . . were their first relief from the sufferings of the Sierra." The next day, which was March 8, they joined the others in their camp near Sutter's Fort.

The party stayed for eighteen days, living all the while in "luxury," according to Charles Preuss: "Drinks, fish, bread, butter, milk, beef, pork, potatoes, and wonderful salmon."

Since they were in need of everything, the fort was soon bustling to supply them with horseshoes, bridles, reins, packsaddles, ropes, and blankets. Vaqueros were sent out to collect horses, mules, and cattle; and the gristmill worked night and day grinding wheat and corn. There were boots and moccasins to be made, and buckskin and cloth to be turned into trousers and shirts. Preuss found the price of drill so high he decided to save the additional cost of tailoring by making his own trousers, a decision he came to regret after he found that he had sewed both legs together for one, and all the tedious stitching had to be done over.

"I gave Frémont everything he wanted, and what I did not have was fetched from Yerba Buena by my schooner," Sutter writes. By March 22 the party was completely fitted out, and made a preparatory move a few miles up the river to a place near Sinclair's rancho. At this camp, Jean Derosier, his mind still affected by his hardships, disappeared and was never seen again.

Two days later Frémont broke camp and started on the homeward journey which he would make by a southern route, crossing the Sierra through a pass in the Tehachapi Mountains. During his stay on the American he had learned much about the Mexican regime and its tenuous hold on California, and the French and British threats, from his talks with Sutter and other well-informed men at the fort.

He was starting out with a large stock of provisions, 130 horses and mules, 30 oxen, 2 milch cows with calves, and an Indian vaquero to manage them since they were "nearly as wild as buffalo." Sutter rode with the party for several miles to see them well on their way.

Some other man might have profited by supplying the thousand needs of this destitute band. But Sutter's heart was touched and, ignoring his own mounting debts, he furnished them everything at cost or below. In payment he accepted drafts on the United States Topographical Bureau. But when he came to cash them, he found they could be redeemed at only one-fifth of their face value.

"In the goodness of my heart I thought I would do the American Government a favor by not taking advantage of Frémont's distress, but I only cheated myself thereby."

7

Wagons over the Sierra

A WELL-ORGANIZED company of emigrants, the Stevens-Town-send-Murphy Party, made camp during the afternoon of November 14, 1844, in a grassy bottom along a tributary to the river they had been following and had named "Truckee" in honor of their faithful Paiute guide. This was not his real name, writes his granddaughter, Sarah Winnemucca, but is a Paiute word meaning "all right" or "very well." It was his friend Frémont who first called him "Captain Truckee," she says. The old chief's frequent use of the expression doubtless prompted the explorer to give him this name.

The Stevens Party had suffered no extreme hardships or any deaths in crossing the plains and deserts; their number had even been increased by one with the birth of a girl along the way. Nor had there been any of those strident quarrels to which emigrant parties were subject.

Elisha Stevens, a Georgia blacksmith, trapper, and miner who had come west "with the express purpose of finding gold," possessed the necessary qualifications for leadership of such an enterprise. The others, more than half of whom comprised a close-knit family unit, were intelligent, courageous, and congenial.

There were twenty-six men, eight women, and seventeen children; one of these was the four-month-old baby born to Mrs. James Miller on Independence Day at Independence Rock, and named commemoratively Ellen Independence.

The year was fast waning, and provisions were low. One of
their women, Mrs. Martin Murphy, Jr., was nearly nine months
pregnant. Twelve inches of snow buried the grass from their
hungry animals, and two feet lay on the Sierran peaks. Hanging
over them like a menacing cloud was the threat of winter
descending in earnest and trapping them in the mountains. An
immediate decision had to be made as to the best route from
this point on.

Scouts reported that the creek at which they had stopped
flowed through a flat bottom due west toward the range, and its
cut looked more promising for wagons than the rough and
rocky canyon of the Truckee River, which bore south.

A council was held, and it was decided to divide the company as a precautionary measure. A party of six, all young and
well mounted, would follow the Truckee and strike west across
some practicable pass. Traveling light and fast they could get
over the Sierra before the snow grew deep, press on to New
Helvetia, alert Captain Sutter to the coming of the main party,
and be ready to rescue them in case of need. This horseback
group included two women, Ellen Murphy, who was single, and
Elizabeth Townsend, wife of the company's physician, Dr.
John Townsend.

A few miles of travel the next day brought the wagon division to a deep blue lake lying in a narrow valley whose steep
granite sides were darkly wooded with pine, fir, and cedar.
Ever grateful for the Paiute chief's help, they called the lake
Truckee. Later the name was changed to Donner to commemorate the tragedy that took place near it during the winter of 1846,
when more than half of that ill-fated party, so riven by dis-
sension, was trapped by early snows, and starved to death.

Now only one towering mountain wall lay between the
Stevens Party and their goal, but its formidable face, topped
with what looked to many like a menacing fort with bastions
and turrets, appeared impassable. While their scouts hunted
for a passage, the party waited in camp in the same grove of

pines that was to offer scant shelter to the Donner Party.

Another council was held to discuss the advisability of scaling the mountain with wagons. Opinion was divided, five members being for it, and six against. Dr. Townsend and his wife's seventeen-year-old brother, Moses Schallenberger, had brought with them an assortment of "broadcloth satins and silks," to sell at a profit in California. The doctor was one who decided to leave his wagon, and young Moses volunteered to stay and guard it until the party could send back fresh animals from Sutter's Fort. Two young men, Joseph Foster and Allen Montgomery, offered to keep him company and look after the other wagons.

When the scouts came back with news that they had found a gap between the towering crags (south of the present Donner Pass), the party moved on around the northeastern shore of Truckee Lake where they saw thickets of wild raspberry canes that in another season were laden with delicious fruit. The going was slow, for in many places the steep slopes were so boggy their animals "sunk to their bellies in the mire."

It was found on closer inspection that the mountain face held several abrupt pitches on the line of ascent; between these lay a few fairly level shelves where teams might stand and draw up an empty wagon. So the wagons were unloaded and their contents packed to the summit; then oxteams were doubled, and the ascent begun.

In the words of one emigrant who came after, the climb proved "one continued jumping from one rocky cliff to another. We would have to roll over this big rock, then over that." Some gaps could be spanned with logs, but in most cases wagons had to be lifted "by main force up to the top of a ledge of rocks that it was impossible for us to reduce, bridge or roll our wagons over." At times the granite was so rough it defied passage; at others so glasslike the animals slipped and fell to their knees, their blood staining the trail with deep purple patches.

Halfway up they were faced with a solid perpendicular wall, ten feet high, and it then seemed as though the wagons would have to be abandoned after all. But these were determined men, and they set off to find some way of either scaling or bypassing it. After a careful search a breach was found just wide enough to let one ox at a time pass through.

Teams were unyoked and led through to the summit. Next, chains were fastened to the wagon tongues, carried up to the gap, and attached to the oxen that were yoked again. Then, while men and boys pushed and hoisted from below, those on the summit urged the animals to pull on the chains, swearing at them mightily, it is recalled. One by one the wagons were drawn up the sheer rock face. Later parties were to devise windlasses, construct rollers, or take their wagons apart and pack them piecemeal to the top.

As nearly as can be reckoned, for the journal kept by Dr. Townsend and Moses Schallenberger was lost, and there seem to have been no other diarists with the Stevens Party, this day was November 25, 1844, a memorable one that marked the opening of the Truckee Pass or California Trail. In their wake thousands would follow, those on foot or horseback traveling to the valley along the crest of the narrow divide that rises steep and high above the North Fork American, while those with wagons were forced to abandon the ridge at a gap some twenty-five miles west of the summit, and travel on through Bear Valley.

After resting at the pass from which the view was "inexpressibly comprehensive, grand, and picturesque," they moved on to make camp at a small lake surrounded with grass. In the morning they started on in good spirits, expecting a short, easy downhill run; they were soon to discover that the descent led uphill as well as down, "over the Damdist mountains I ever see or hird tell of for a wagon to be drove over," one emigrant was to write. The whole day was spent in dragging the wagons over rocky ledges and hoisting and lowering them over the "jump-offs." The downgrades were so steep wheels had to be locked, or trees felled and tied on behind.

"Bad road," one diarist noted at the end of his first day west of the summit. "Bad Bad Road," he wrote on the second day. On the next, "distressing Road"; and on the fourth, "if possable worse Road."

After several days' travel, the Stevens Party came to what was to be called Devil's Hill, at Hampshire Rocks, and made camp near the present Big Bend. A bitter wind had been gathering thick clouds all day, and in the morning it began to snow. It may have been during this first night in camp that Mrs. Murphy gave birth to a girl. Like her cousin Ellen Independence, she was given a commemorative middle name after her mother learned that they had camped on the Yuba River. The baby was called Elizabeth Yuba.

Here another council was held and the decision made to leave the women and children (and the wagons) in care of two older men, James Miller and Patrick Martin, Sr., while the others hurried on to Sutter's Fort for supplies and fresh animals. Before setting off they put up a log shelter (some sources say several), and butchered enough beef to last until their return; they took the rest of the cattle with them.

These wagons were the first to come across the plains and over the Sierra. Until then the Mexican *carreta* was the only wheeled vehicle known in California, and it was used for business and pleasure. On workdays this clumsy cart with its rimless wheels of solid oak toted incredible loads of hides; on gala days it was swept out and a roof and curtains of gay calico were fixed over a top of arched hoops. Transformed into the family carriage, it then transported bevies of women and children and pretty girls on rounds of visits, or to church and fiestas.

When young Moses Schallenberger and his two companions offered to guard the wagons at Truckee Lake, they expected the experience to be something of a lark. Game was plentiful, they were all good hunters, and they looked forward to several weeks of fine sport. It did not occur to any of the party that more than two feet of snow would fall there, or that it would not melt between storms, as it did in the part of the country they knew. But with the foresight that had characterized all their acts, the leaders insisted that the young men keep two cows.

The morning after the others went on, the three started to put up a cabin for, as Moses was to write, they wanted to be "as comfortable as possible, even if it was for a short time." They built it of pine logs notched close, twelve by fourteen feet, with a lean-to roof covered with rawhide and pine brush, and they made a good-sized fireplace of mud-plastered logs and large stones. They did not bother with windows. "A hole was cut for a door, which was never closed. We left it open in the day-time to give us light, and as we had plenty of good beds and bedding that had been left with the wagons, and were not afraid of burglars, we left it open at night also."

This little cabin became historic after it gave shelter to the Breen family, who were members of the Donner Party, and a lean-to was built against one wall by Louis Keseberg, the most controversial figure in that heterogeneous group of emigrants who set out for California in the spring of 1846. Later, Keseberg was to be accused falsely of many crimes, the most serious, the murder of Mrs. Tamsen Donner.

At Fort Bridger, the company that included the Donners divided, the greater part following the proven trail by way of Fort Hall and reaching California in safety. But eighty-seven persons, including the Donner brothers, George and Jacob, and their families, took the untried Hastings Cut-off, a supposedly shorter route. Much of the country proved impassable for wagons, and a road had to be hacked out of the most rugged wilderness. Blaming each other for their plight, the men began to quarrel bitterly.

By the time the party reached the Sierra, an early winter had set in, the pass was closed, and they were forced to make camp in these same woods where Moses Schallenberger and his friends had put up their cabin.

Twenty-two feet of snow fell that winter and trapped the Donner Party. Several unsuccessful attempts were made to get to Sutter's Fort for help. In December a party of fifteen made a final effort. After incredible hardships, five women and two men got through to Johnson's Rancho (on the site of today's Wheatland). From there word of the plight of those left in the mountains was taken on to Sutter, but it was not until February that the first relief party got through to the lake. The last of the forty-seven survivors were rescued in April.

"On the evening of the day we finished our little house it began to snow," Moses Schallenberger recalled, and by morning three feet covered the ground. The hunt he and his friends had planned for that day was postponed for the next. But when they wakened in the morning it was still snowing, and it kept on for a week, and they had to kill the cows to keep the animals from starving to death. Not even at the week's end did the snow stop falling, and it was not long until the little house was nearly covered.

They found the surface of the snow so "light and frosty" it would not bear them up, and Moses admits, "we began to fear we should all perish." Their only hope was to devise some means of getting about to hunt.

None of them had ever seen snowshoes, but Foster and Montgomery had a general idea about their construction and set to work making each one a pair from the hickory bows that held up the wagon covers; they bent them into oblongs, and filled them in with a network of rawhide. When they were finished, the three set out hopefully on their long-delayed hunt, but as they trudged through the snowy wilderness they were appalled to find there was no game.

"We now began to feel very blue," Schallenberger recalls,

"for there seemed no possible hope for us. We had already eaten about half our meat. . . . Death, the fearful, agonizing death by starvation, literally stared us in the face." After talking it over they decided to start out for the Sacramento Valley.

Each man carried ten pounds of smoke-dried beef, a pair of blankets, a rifle, and ammunition, but being ignorant of the proper way to fasten snowshoes, they were soon adding at least ten pounds of weight apiece to their feet; they had tied the shoes at both heel and toe, and at every step these would sink and collect large amounts of snow.

Moses was still growing, he says, and had "weak muscles and a huge appetite, both of which were being used in exactly the reverse order by nature." In the middle of the afternoon he was seized with cramps: "I fell down with them several times. . . . After each attack I would summon all my will power and press on, trying to keep up with the others. Towards evening, however, the attacks became more frequent and painful, and I could not walk more than fifty yards without stopping to rest." By the time they reached the summit he could barely drag his feet. Here they stopped for the night.

In the morning as they ate their beef they talked over the prospects, which were far from bright for Moses. He was so stiff and sore he could hardly move, and his companions knew he could not travel far; circumstances might be such that when he broke down they would have to leave him behind.

It was then that he announced his decision to go back to the cabin. He could live for a while on the quarter of frozen beef that was there and the ten pounds he was carrying; when that was gone, perhaps the weather would be better and he could start again for the valley. The others were reluctant to have him stay there alone, but he finally convinced them that there was no other solution.

"We did not say much at parting. Our hearts were too full for that," he remembered. "There was simply a warm clasp of the hand accompanied by the familiar word 'Good-by'. . . . The feeling of loneliness that came over me as the two men turned away . . . will never be forgotten, while the 'Good-by Mose,' so sadly and reluctantly spoken, rings in my ears to-day."

His companions were not gone long before he got hold of himself and, strapping on his load, began retracing his steps to the cabin.

The next morning he put on his snowshoes and, taking his rifle, scoured the wood for some signs of game. He saw many fox tracks but no foxes, and came back to the hut "discouraged and sick at heart." But as he was standing his gun in the corner, he saw something he had not noticed before: some steel traps that belonged to Elisha Stevens. Here was hope, and his spirits rose. He hurried to bait them with some scraps of beef and set them in a likely spot.

He was almost afraid to look the next morning in case the traps were empty, but when he did go out, he found he had caught an old coyote. He soon had him skinned and his flesh roasting in a Dutch oven. His mouth watered in anticipation of the treat, he says, but when he came to eat it, he found the taste "revolting." Thinking that boiling might improve it, he put the meat into a pot, but the result was just as disappointing.

On the third day he caught two foxes, one of which he roasted. The flesh was lean but delicious. "I was so hungry I could easily have eaten a fox at two meals, but I made one last me two days." After that he devoted his whole attention to trapping, and caught, on an average, a fox every two days, with a few coyotes in between, which he hung outside the cabin to freeze and be used only as a last resort. His hope was that the supply of foxes would last, for he was determined to save the beef.

His existence was miserable, he recalled. "The daily struggle for life and the uncertainty . . . were very wearing. I was always worried and anxious, not about myself alone, but in regard to the fate of those who had gone forward." What he wanted most was enough to eat, "and the next thing I tried hardest to do was kill time." Something that made the long hours pass more quickly was the large stock of books his brother-in-law, Dr. Townsend, had brought with him.

"I used to read aloud, for I longed for some sound to break the oppressive stillness. . . . At night I built a large fire and read by the light of pine knots as late as possible, in order that I might sleep late the next morning and thus cause the days to seem shorter." His favorite reading was Byron, and Lord Chesterfield's letters to his son.

On Christmas Day Moses roasted a fox, and brewed the last cup of coffee, which he had been saving for this time. But as he prepared to eat, he began thinking gloomily of home and far happier Christmas Days, and his appetite left him. To raise his spirits he decided to conjure up a festive gathering and people his bleak little cabin with imaginary friends and family members. He put another log on the fire, and stirred it up so that its warm glow brightened the room. By the time he was ready to carve the fox, which his mind's eye had turned into a plump young turkey bursting with sage and onion stuffing, the table was lined with cheerful faces. Taking up a knife, he addressed an imaginary guest: "And what will you have? Light meat or dark? Dark meat? Very well," and he began slicing from the fox's thigh. He then asked another guest the same question, and since the answer this time was light meat, he cut from the fox's breast. And so he went on down the table, asking each one his or her preference, and laying the pieces carefully on his own plate until he had served himself his ration for that day.

When he came to eat the monotonous fare he found himself relishing it as he had not done in months. It seemed to taste far better than usual. Although he could not be sure, he thought he could even detect a trace of sage and onion in the meat.

One day in late February 1845, as he was standing outside his cabin a little before sunset, looking at the mountain that shut him off from all knowledge of family and friends, he saw a man approaching. At first he thought it was an Indian, but as he drew near he saw that it was Dennis Martin, a member of the party. "My feelings can be better imagined than described," he says.

One of his first questions was about his sister, Elizabeth Townsend. She and the other members of the mounted party had reached Sutter's Fort safely, Dennis told him. He had seen her just a few days ago, when, learning that he was packing in some food to the party at Big Bend, she had begged him to go on over the summit and find out what had happened to her brother.

After leaving the wagons, the horseback party had ridden down the Truckee River Valley to Lake Tahoe, the first white people to reach its shores. Fording the river there, they traveled south along the lake for about seven miles and then turned west, probably to follow the course of McKinney Creek at whose head they crossed the summit. Continuing along the present Miller Creek they would have come to the South Fork of the Middle Fork American, known today as the Rubicon River. This they crossed and, taking perhaps a westerly course, passed above Mud Lakes to Gerle Creek; then, striking up Deer Creek, met the Rubicon again, swimming their horses over, possibly at today's Hale's Crossing. They then kept to the narrow, twisting gorge of the swift-running Rubicon which falls 6,500 feet, on an average of 130 feet to the mile, in its race to meet the Middle Fork American.

It was rough country, and they were compelled to cross the river's many windings, but its rapid descent soon had them out of the snow and into the foothills. Striking the American, they probably kept close to it, either along the river itself or on higher ground, letting it lead them to Sinclair's Rancho del Paso, where they were received "with warm hospitality" on December 6. They had been twenty-one days on the way. On the tenth they rode on to Sutter's Fort which was bustling with preparations for war: California was on the eve of an insurrection.

That fall, while Sutter and John Bidwell were on their way to Monterey they learned of a plot to overthrow the Mexican-born governor, Manuel Micheltorena, exile him, and select a new governor from among the Californians. His enemies, led by General José Castro and former Governor Juan Alvarado, accused him among other offenses of being too friendly toward Americans and of granting them too much land.

Sutter and Bidwell hastened on to warn the governor, and Sutter, alarmed at the prospect of a revolt directed in part against foreign settlers, returned at once to New Helvetia, leaving Bidwell to follow.

A few days later the first blow was struck when the insurgents seized all the government horses at Monterey, completely crippling the governor by converting his crack cavalry into foot soldiers.

Bidwell, setting out on horseback for Sutter's Fort, met the governor and his men returning from a vain pursuit of the horse thieves, and they stopped to talk. Micheltorena asked him to "beg the Americans to be loyal to Mexico; to assure them that he was their friend, and in due time would give them all the lands to which they were entitled. He sent particularly friendly words to Sutter," Bidwell recalls.

Riding on, he came next to the headquarters of Castro and Alvarado, who treated him "like a prince . . . protested their friendship for the Americans, and sent a request to Sutter to support them."

On his return to the fort, Bidwell and Sutter discussed the situation and decided to support Micheltorena. "He had been our friend," Bidwell writes, "he had granted us land; he promised, and we felt that we could rely upon, his continued friendship. . . ." A dispatch was sent him saying that Sutter was organizing troops and preparing to join him.

Those twenty men from the wagon division of the Stevens

Party arrived at New Helvetia just in time to be recruited. Their joining Sutter's forces seems like a rank desertion of their women and children, but Sutter probably convinced them their families would be better off in the mountains, safe from the hazards of a revolution. Too, there was the promise of land that the governor held out to his supporters, an inducement difficult for prospective settlers to resist.

On June 1, the men from the Stevens Party rode off to the south, "with music and flying colors," as part of Captain John Gantt's mounted rifles. With them went a detachment of artillery and some hundred Indians armed with bows, arrows, and muskets.

The opéra bouffe revolt was over by February 20 when Governor Micheltorena flew the white flag and graciously conceded the insurgents' victory. While it lasted, the revolt had included many heartwarming scenes of intimacy between sides. Once when one of Sutter's officers, Isaac Graham, was captured he cried out, "Don't kill me!", and his captor, Joaquin de la Torre, jumping from his horse, embraced him and said: "Captain, how could I kill you? You are my friend!"

And there was one memorable occasion when a woman, said to have been Alvarado's mistress, came into Sutter's camp with her little boy who was carrying a present for Captain Gantt. On opening the white napkin in which it was wrapped, he found a stack of fresh tortillas and, slipped between them, a friendly note from the insurgent leaders inviting the foreign settlers in Gantt's command to visit their camp and make friends.

And, once again, when Sutter came upon a company of riflemen who were talking instead of advancing as they had been ordered, he asked Gantt what was going on. "Oh, we are voting to see who is for one side and who is for the other," the captain told him.

Long before the surrender, many Americans in Sutter's ranks had tired of the farce and slipped off. Sutter must have given the Stevens Party men permission to go to the relief of their families, and sent instructions for Pierson B. Reading, left in charge at the fort, to furnish them with provisions and horses.

Among the first to return was Dennis Martin, whose father was with the camp near Big Bend. He prepared to leave at once with emergency supplies and, at Elizabeth Townsend's request, go on over the pass.

He found all well at the mountain camp, although food had run short and one family had been forced to live on rawhide for two weeks. He divided the rations, cheered them with the news that relief was on the way, and, remembering his promise to Mrs. Townsend, strapped on his snowshoes (he was a Canadian, and an expert snowshoer), and pushed on toward the summit, but with little hope of finding Moses alive.

That night as Dennis sat by the fire in the little cabin, giving an account of the happenings over the last three months, he was at work improving Moses' snowshoes. In the morning, after showing him how to fasten them properly, they started off.

The boy's limited diet and lack of exercise had not fitted him for the climb, but by resting often, he says, he got over the summit and on to the party's camp, without breaking down. Sutter's supplies and horses had arrived by this time, and he was able to ride on to the fort.

He stayed there as Sutter's guest until June. Then, completely recovered from his ordeal, he began worrying about the wagons and decided he must go back to Truckee Lake; Dennis's brother, Patrick, offered to go with him.

Patches of snow still lay in the deep shade, but it had melted from around the little house. The wagons were there, but everything had been taken from them and the cabin, except the guns and ammunition.

The following month men from the party drove in oxen, hauled out the wagons from beside the lake, and picked up those left near Big Bend. But they could keep to the narrow ridge above the American's North Fork only as far as the present Emigrant Gap, to become known as the "jumping-off place." Here they had to lower the wagons down a rock face that was "almost perpendicular," into the valley of the Bear River.

"By taking out the leaders of our teams & back locking & every other kind of locking, & attaching a rope behind & holding it around a tree, our wagons & all, with a great deal of work, trouble, & fatigue, were moored safely in the valley," reports a later traveler.

Until the opening of the Carson Emigrant Road in 1848, this trail that the Stevens Party forged through the unexplored wilderness was the main route into California. The summit came to be known as the "great bugaboo," and anticipation of its terrors brought "disturbed dreams" and "many a sleepless night" to countless emigrants.

Some parties seeking an easier route followed the Truckee River south, then, turning west at Squaw Creek, crossed the crest at the present Watson Monument, southeast of Granite Chief. They came to the headwaters of the American's Middle Fork and traveled along it to the Forest Hill Divide, the ridge that separates this fork from its North Fork. There were also variations of the Stevens horseback route, with parties continuing along the shore of Lake Tahoe to Sugar Pine Point, and turning west there to follow McKinney Creek, the Rubicon, and the American's other forks.

During those years the river kept its secret well. Of the hundreds who rode and tramped along its banks, not one seems to have recognized those yellow flakes in the sand as gold. Or if any did, the discovery was dismissed lightly. Who but the wildest dreamer could ever have conjured up visions of the vast treasure the river was guarding?

8

"Manifest Destiny"

THE AMERICAN'S SOUTH FORK was destined to play an important part in the coming struggle for California.

On December 10, 1845, John C. Frémont, by then brevet captain, appeared unexpectedly at Sutter's Fort; with him was his inseparable companion, Kit Carson. Sutter was away, and John Bidwell was in charge. He recalls that "Frémont at once made known to me his wants, namely, sixteen mules, six pack-saddles, some flour and other provisions, and the use of the blacksmith shop. . . . I told him precisely what could and could not be furnished. . . . He became reticent, and, saying something in a low tone to Kit Carson, rose and left without saying good-day. . . . As they mounted to leave, Frémont was heard to say that I was unwilling to accommodate him. . . ."

Bidwell admits that the accusation hurt him, for "we were always glad of the arrival of Americans, and especially one in authority. Besides I knew that Captain Sutter would do anything in his power for Frémont."

He hurried over to Frémont's camp to explain how circumstances had changed since his last visit, when Sutter was able to furnish him with everything. Frémont replied "in a very formal manner," saying that since he and Sutter each represented different governments, and there were now difficulties between those governments, he could understand the reluctance to supply him.

In the morning Bidwell sent out a vaquero to round up mules, and fourteen were delivered to Frémont's camp. Two days

81

later the explorer left for Yerba Buena to get his supplies, while his men marched south to meet the main party.

This was Frémont's third expedition, organized late in the year, ostensibly for scientific purposes to tie in with the last survey but keeping in mind the inevitability of war with Mexico.

"As affairs resolved themselves," he wrote, "California stood out as the chief subject of the impending war; and with Mr. Benton and other governing men at Washington it became a firm resolve to hold it for the United States. . . . This was talked over fully during the time of preparation for the . . . expedition, and the contingencies anticipated and weighed. . . . For me no distinct course or definite instructions could be laid down, but the probabilities were made known to me . . ."; and to this end, a party of sixty well-armed men and two hundred horses was recruited.

On the eastern side of the Sierra, Frémont sent his main party, under Joseph Walker, to explore the Humboldt Valley and cross into California by way of the present Walker Pass. Meanwhile he, with a select company of fifteen, among them several Delaware Indians, made his second winter crossing of the Sierra.

This time it was rapid and unattended by hardship. On December 5, he passed over the summit, following the trail Elisha Stevens had opened, but keeping to the ridge above the North Fork American all the way to the foothills. Near where Auburn now stands, he turned off to find the South Fork and follow its familiar windings to Sinclair's Rancho, which he reached on December 9.

Now, failing to find his main party at the rendezvous, and supposing them still east of the Sierra, he returned to his old camp on the American. On his arrival Sutter invited him to a "sumptuous dinner" and, when he came, fired a seven-gun salute in his honor.

But Frémont's behavior puzzled Sutter: "He acted strangely

toward me, as if he were guilty of some crime." Five days later he was off again, this time to Monterey, to ask permission to winter in the San Joaquin Valley, for "refreshment and repose." Mexican officials were not at all anxious to grant permission, and it was only after he had convinced them of the wholly scientific nature of his expedition, and promised to keep away from the settlements, that it was given.

Riding on, he soon met up with his main party which had been waiting all this time and, growing tired of the delay, had set out to look for him. They had missed each other before through a misunderstanding about the place of rendezvous. With his forces united, he now proceeded to travel through the most populous parts of California and to set up a permanent camp within twenty miles of the capital.

The governor, Pio Pico, and his general, José Castro, suspecting that the American officer's interest in the countryside was not strictly topographical, ordered him to move, since his actions were illegal.

"I peremptorily refused compliance to an order insulting to my government and myself," he wrote, and promptly moved his men to the top of Gavilan Peak where he built "a rough but strong fort of solid logs." Then, setting up a trimmed sapling as a flagstaff, he ran up the Stars and Stripes and waited quietly to see the results of his defiance.

On the second day a small body of Mexican cavalry reconnoitered the area, but, unwilling to attack such a formidable position guarded by riflemen of noted marksmanship, they withdrew.

On the third day the flagpole fell down, and Frémont, interpreting this as an omen, slipped away in the predawn darkness, leaving his campfires blazing. To his wife he wrote of his flight: "My sense of duty did not permit me to fight them, but we retired slowly and growlingly. . . ."

By March 22 he was back at his favorite encampment on the South Fork, and two days later he was off again, seemingly in great haste. He followed the river east for about ten miles, then turned north and headed toward Oregon.

"Frémont's conduct was extremely mysterious," Sutter observed. "Flitting about the country with an armed body of men, he was regarded with suspicion by everybody."

On the evening of April 28, a little after sunset, a small boat came up the river and landed another inscrutable American at the fort. He introduced himself as Archibald H. Gillespie, a merchant, traveling for his health. He had with him a packet of family letters for Captain Frémont, whom he hoped to find encamped on the river. Sutter explained that Frémont had left for Oregon several weeks before. "I want to overhaul him," Gillespie said anxiously.

In the morning he asked for the loan of a horse and a guide. Sutter let him take his favorite mule ("he returned it windbroken," he remembered) and an Indian to lead him through the wilderness.

Sutter was certain Gillespie was not an ailing merchant, and Gillespie's anxiety to find Frémont made Sutter suspect he had something of more importance for him than personal letters. There was a military air about the man; he was a special courier, Sutter decided, an army officer perhaps, carrying messages from his government.

Gillespie was, indeed, a lieutenant of marines, and had left Washington under orders from the President. He had been entrusted with oral instructions from George Bancroft, the naval secretary, for Commodore John Sloat with the Pacific Squadron at Mazatlán, and with a secret dispatch from Secretary of State James Buchanan for Thomas Oliver Larkin, the American consul at Monterey, appointing Larkin a confidential agent of his government. Just before leaving Washington, he had been given the packet of personal letters for Frémont and been instructed by Buchanan not only to show Frémont a copy of the message to Larkin but to familiarize him with his own instructions.

Gillespie was sent across Mexico, from Vera Cruz to Mazatlán, the most direct although not the safest route to California, for it was beset with highwaymen. But taking no chances he memorized the secret message during the twenty-five-day voyage to Vera Cruz and, before landing, destroyed the original, having it fixed in his mind. On reaching Monterey he wrote out the message from memory.

As special agent, Larkin was instructed to use conciliatory approaches to win the confidence of the Californians and encourage friendly feelings to counteract the work of British and French agents. "If the people should desire to unite their destiny with ours, they should be received as brethren," Buchanan wrote. Gillespie had orders to cooperate with Larkin in carrying out these objectives.

It was a practical policy, for most thoughtful Californians were anxious to have a strong government, and men with foresight, like General Mariano Vallejo, favored United States annexation.

Mounted on Sutter's mule, Gillespie and his guide set off through the wintry wilderness, on Frémont's trail. At Lassen's Rancho he recruited a party to accompany him into hostile Indian country. "Daring and gallant" Sam Neal, who had been one of Frémont's blacksmiths on the last expedition and had since settled in California, agreed to guide them.

"How fate pursues a man!" Frémont mused as he stood by his campfire on the north shore of Klamath Lake. His reverie was suddenly interrupted by the sound of hoofbeats, and Fate, in the guise of Sam Neal and a companion, rode into the circle of firelight to announce Gillespie's coming.

At early dawn the whole party went back over the snowy trail to find him. Near sunset they met him as he and his companions rode out of the forest. There in a glade ringed with large cedars three campfires were built, for the night was bitter cold. While his men smoked and talked around two of them, Frémont, beside the third, listened eagerly to Gillespie's messages and by the flickering firelight read a copy of the secret dispatch to Larkin.

Frémont has written of this meeting with Gillespie: "Now it was officially made known to me that my country was at war." This was historically impossible since the interview took place on the night of May 9, and war was not declared until May 13.

Ignoring Larkin's appointment as secret agent (he later claimed never to have heard of it, although Gillespie under oath testified before a federal committee that he had shown "the duplicate copy of the dispatch to Mr. Larkin"), Frémont, without authority, appointed himself to take California—not by the peaceful means Buchanan had stipulated, but by force. He now decided to return to the Sacramento Valley, "in order to bring to bear all the influences I could command."

On May 29, Gillespie left the party north of New Helvetia and hurried on to Yerba Buena for supplies. He applied to Captain John B. Montgomery of the sloop-of-war *Portsmouth*, at anchor in the bay, for provisions and clothing, and, more significantly, for eight thousand percussion caps, a keg of powder, and three hundred pounds of rifle lead.

Frémont's sudden return to the valley excited great curiosity, and people from all over flocked to his camp. He took this opportunity to recruit a citizens' army, made up of what he termed "picked men," selected from the vagabond population of trappers, runaway sailors, and professional horse thieves. He welcomed to his ranks such men as "Hellroaring" Thompson, Jim Savage, "Growling" Smith, and "Stuttering" Merritt—all with nothing to lose and everything to gain.

Ezekial Merritt, a tall, rawboned, hard-drinking trapper and squawman, who could neither read nor write, was singled out for special honors. His reputation for bravery was based, so John Bidwell remembers, on his "continual boasting of his prowess in killing Indians. The handle of the tomahawk he carried had nearly a hundred notches to record the number of

Indian scalps." Frémont made Merritt his "Field-lieutenant." This army was encouraged to make aggressive moves throughout the province and provoke General Castro to strike the first blow.

On the night of June 8, 1846, Lieutenant Francisco Arce and eight soldiers arrived at Sutter's Fort with a band of two hundred horses that were being sent by General Vallejo at Sonoma to General Castro. The lieutenant stayed overnight with Sutter and, in the morning when he left to ferry his animals across the river, remarked with a laugh to his host: "California is like a pretty girl—everyone wants her!"

Within forty-eight hours he and his soldiers had been captured, and the horses driven off to Frémont's camp by a party of twelve armed citizens led by Merritt, under orders from Frémont. This constituted the first hostile act in the conquest of California.

Believing that this action called for "prompt precautionary measures," Frémont sent Merritt on to Sonoma, with orders to surprise the garrison and arrest General Vallejo.

In the early morning hours of June 14, a motley band of thirty-three horsemen was advancing on the pueblo of Sonoma. If there were any among them attuned to nature, they would have marked the peculiar sweetness of the warm air, laden with the fragrance of short blue lupine which in late spring carpets meadow and hillside in that valley, and heard the fluty morning song of meadowlarks, and the piping of plover from streamside and marsh. But they were, in the main, reckless adventurers bent on plunder: "thick-bearded, fierce-looking fellows, who wore ornamented hunting shirts of buckskin, gartered leggins" and heads "turbaned with colored handkerchiefs."

In the lead rode Merritt with "Rachael," his faithful rifle, across the saddlebow; a visionary named William B. Ide, whom the philosopher Josiah Royce likens to the Bellman in *The Hunting of the Snark*; and Dr. Robert Semple of Kentucky, "six feet eight inches in his stockings" and "fifteen inches in diameter." Semple was a man of education and ability, but affected the frontiersman's manner, and his dress of fringed buckskin and fox fur hat. As "the tallest man in the country," he cut a ridiculous figure in a leather suit that was too short in the sleeves and trouser legs; his spurs bristled midway from bare shanks, since there was no horse in the province tall enough to accommodate him.

The leaders, so Ide recalls, did not know exactly what they were to do after demanding the garrison's surrender and arresting General Vallejo. They had orders to commit depredations that would provoke Castro further, but at the same time they were to avoid "unnecessary violence."

To their surprise they found the barracks empty. General Vallejo, having grown tired of maintaining troops at his own expense, had disbanded them eight months before. Making the best of this major disappointment, they marched on up the street to surround the general's house on the plaza.

He came to the door "and asked what they wanted, to which no one answered, for the good reason, I believe, that none of them knew what reply to give," admits a member of the party. "He then asked if they had taken the place, to which they answered in the affirmative. He then returned to his room, but soon reappeared with his sword girded on, which he offered to surrender to them. But as none of the party manifested any disposition to receive it, he returned to his room again and replaced the sword."

He held some parley with Semple and Merritt at the door, then invited them in to explain their object and draw up articles of surrender. A servant was sent across the square to ask Vallejo's brother-in-law, Jacob P. Leese, an American, to come over and act as interpreter. Leese admitted later that he was "astonished to see such a rough-looking set of men. I supposed to find them regular troops ordered by the United States government."

The general next produced something to drink, "the high

commissioners tarried long," and to those waiting outside, the meeting seemed interminable. Their patience drawn thin, they selected one Grigsby to go into the house and find out what was causing the delay. He was "likewise long lost to view," whereupon William Ide was sent in. "He found all the high contracting parties moderately drunk, and still poring over the written articles of capitulation." He "indignantly seized them and rushed forth to read them to the company outside."

Merritt, aroused to a befuddled sense of duty, began arresting everyone in the room: the general's secretary, Victor Prudon; his brother, Captain Salvador Vallejo; and Jacob Leese. He then committed the crowning indignity and unpardonable affront by tying General Vallejo to his chair. This was not easily forgotten: "And they tied me to a chair! Me! Vallejo!" he recalled angrily.

The general had expected by agreeing not to engage in hostilities, to secure the personal liberty of himself and the other prisoners. He was therefore shocked to hear "the long captain in leather" say that they were all to be delivered to Frémont on the American River.

Among those left behind to hold Sonoma was William L. Todd, a nephew of Mrs. Abraham Lincoln. Looking up at the naked flagstaff in the plaza one day, it occurred to him that he ought to make a flag to represent the independent republic his party had just declared, and fly it there. Rounding up two assistants, Peter Storm and Nennigan Taylor, he set out in search of cloth for the field. Mrs. John Sears, who had recently come across the plains, donated two yards of coarse, unbleached cotton from a bolt she had brought with her.

By this time the project had become a kind of community one, and an ex-sailor and express rider, known as "Dirty" Mathews, who was standing by offered to furnish the red for the border Todd thought would look well along the lower edge. Mathews raced home and took from the clothesline a red flannel petticoat belonging to his Mexican wife. After the border was stitched on by Ben Dewell, a saddler, the field was ready for its emblem.

There were many ideas, but a grizzly bear, suggested by another onlooker, Henry L. Ford, seemed to strike everyone as best. Then up spoke a sailor to say there should be a star lying just beyond the bear's snout.

Someone next produced a container of old red-brown paint and a brush, and Todd went to work with most of the pueblo watching. A sudden gust of wind lifted a corner of the cloth and nearly smeared the paint. Looking up, Todd called to a little black-haired, dark-eyed boy who was standing near, "Here, sonny, just put your foot on it." The child obeyed at once. He was Platon Vallejo, the general's five-year-old son.

When the paint was dry, the flag was sent rattling to the top of the pole, but as the breeze caught and spread it, it was realized that in Todd's inept hands the grizzly had turned into some zoological freak. Native Californians staring up at it were heard to exclaim: "*Coche!*" meaning pig.

When the party with their prisoners reached Frémont's camp, General Vallejo stepped forward: "Captain Frémont, I am your prisoner," he said.

"No," Frémont replied, waving his hand toward the escorts, "you are the prisoner of these people."

According to Jacob Leese, he then launched into a drawn-out "rigmarole" enumerating all of Castro's supposed offenses, and then ordered them to Sutter's Fort, to be held "indefinitely."

Frémont rode with them, and he and Sutter met for the first time since the return from Oregon. Sutter was shocked when he saw who the prisoners were and told Frémont bluntly that the arrest was "wrong and unnecessary," that General Vallejo was the best friend the United States had in California. John Bidwell was in the room and, although not close enough to over-hear their words, he sensed the stormy nature of the interview.

"In a few minutes," he wrote, "Sutter came to me greatly agitated, with tears in his eyes, and said that Frémont had told him he was a Mexican and that if he did not like what he (Frémont) was doing he would set him across the San Joaquin River and he could go and join the Mexicans."

Sutter was hurt, for in opening his gates to the Americans, he had, as he says, renounced all allegiance to the Mexican government and frankly declared for the United States.

Frémont preferred his camp on the riverbank to quarters in the fort, but he left about ten of his men there and put it under the command of Edward Kern, the exploring party's young topographer and artist.

"I assure you," Sutter wrote his friend William Leidesdorff, vice-consul of the United States, "it is not pleasant to be second in command in one's own house and establishment!"

John Bidwell was given charge of the prisoners who were kept in Sutter's parlor. He saw to it that they were made as comfortable as possible, that their meals were regular, and served properly. Sutter, who regarded them as his guests, stopped by daily to see that they lacked nothing and usually stayed for a short visit.

One day Dr. Townsend, who was now the fort's physician, and had apparently heard some rumor, warned Sutter not to be too friendly with the prisoners, or he might find himself incarcerated in his own house. His advice was timely, for a day or two later Frémont sent word that if Sutter visited the prisoners once more, he would hang him on the oak growing in the courtyard.

On July 2, Commodore Sloat sailed into Monterey Bay with orders to take possession of California, only to find that it had already been declared an independent republic. Unnerved by this discovery and uncertain what to do next, he waited five days before carrying out his order. On July 7, 1846, he raised the American flag over California.

Two nights later a courier, William Scott, arrived at Sutter's Fort with an American flag and orders to fly it at sunrise. Sutter had the whole establishment roused long before dawn the next day and his guns ready. Then as the Stars and Stripes were hauled up, the cannons broke out with their salutes and kept them up, at his orders, until, as he writes, "nearly all the glass in the Fort was broken."

On the twelfth, Frémont received an express from Sloat asking him to come to Monterey, and a few days later he left his camp on the American for the last time. Wearing "a sailor's blue flannel shirt, with a star in each corner of the broad collar," buckskin leggins, moccasins, and a broad-rimmed Mexican hat, he rode his gray horse, Sacramento, at the head of that "wildest wild party." Following right behind him were his five Delaware Indian bodyguards, and after them, riding two by two, came the others, lean, tough, weather-beaten, most of them darker than the Indians.

Officers and men favored the Mexican hat, most having trimmed it with a narrow band of bright red flannel. For shirts they too wore sailor blouses, or buckskin, with buckskin trousers and moccasins, their clothing "all generally much the worse for wear, and smeared with mud and dust," wrote Edwin Bryant, who rode with them.

"A leathern girdle surrounds the waist, from which are suspended a bowie and hunter's knife, and sometimes a brace of pistols," he continued. "These, with rifle and holster-pistols, are the arms carried by officers and privates. A single bugle (and a sorry one it is) composes the band." But in the expert hands of William D. Miller this bugle roused the camp at daybreak with such unmilitary selections as "The Merry Swiss Boy," and "Behold How Brightly Breaks the Morn," which was a perpetual satire on the weather, since it rained nearly every day.

Kern was left in charge at Sutter's Fort, with instructions not to release the prisoners except on a direct order. Not until August 1 did this order come, and then it was for the parole of General Vallejo only; his companions had to wait seven days more for their release.

With the signing of the surrender on January 13, 1847, at a

ranch house near Cahuenga Pass, the Mexican War in California—which had consisted of several skirmishes—came to an end. Frémont, who had received the surrender, hurried off to Los Angeles, arriving just in time to take part in a bitter controversy between Commodore Robert F. Stockton, Sloat's successor, and General Stephen W. Kearny, over who was in command. Kearny, the last officer to arrive on the scene, fresh from his conquest of New Mexico, brought orders from the War Department to establish temporary civil government there; Stockton refused to recognize his authority since he had been instructed by the Navy Department to occupy and administer the ports of California which he interpreted to include the settlements around them.

Frémont immediately jumped into the quarrel on Stockton's side, and when Kearney, who was his superior officer, sent him orders concerning his troops, he refused to obey them. Stockton's next move was to appoint Frémont civil governor, an office he accepted with pleasure and held for fifty days.

Lieutenant William T. Sherman recalls that there was much speculation among the younger officers, as to what the general would do to Frémont, not a few believing that he would be tried and shot. All agreed, Sherman says, that "if anyone else than Frémont had put on such airs, and had acted as he had done, Kearny would have shown him no mercy."

In February, Kearny received orders from Washington investing him with direction of land operations and civil government. He sent Frémont a copy of his orders and the proclamation whereby he assumed the governorship, and asked him to surrender all papers and documents pertaining to the local government. Frémont refused to obey this order, too, claiming later that he had known nothing about the proclamation and had presumed Kearny was simply trying to depose him.

Later, when the two met (Frémont appeared for his interview in the dress of a native Californian, even to the "high broad-brimmed hat with fancy cord"), tempers flared and Frémont accused the general of having set one of his officers, Colonel Richard B. Mason, to spy on him.

At a subsequent meeting with Mason, a remark of Frémont's caused the colonel to explode: "None of your insolence, or I will put you in irons!" At this Frémont immediately challenged him to a duel. Mason accepted, and the general had to step in to prevent it.

Kearny now decided to take this young hotspur with him to Fort Leavenworth and charge him with insubordination. On June 13, 1847, the general with his staff and escort stopped at Sutter's Fort on their way east. Sutter, who was now master of his domain again, put on his uniform (he was a lieutenant of United States Dragoons), fired a salute, lined up his Indian garrison on parade, and gave a banquet in Kearny's honor.

Three days later the party took up the line of march, to follow the American's North Fork and cross the Sierra through the pass opened by Elisha Stevens. In the retinue rode John Charles Frémont, "more or less a prisoner," as Sutter was to note.

9

In Pursuit of Happiness

"THERE ARE no people that I have ever been among who enjoy life so thoroughly as the Californians," wrote a widely traveled New Englander in 1846. "Their habits are simple; their wants few. . . . They attach no value to money. . . . Their happiness flows from a fount that has very little connection with their outward circumstances. . . . Their hospitality knows no bounds; they are always glad to see you, come when you may; take pleasure in entertaining you while you remain; and only regret that your business calls you away."

"*No se apure*" ("Don't be in a hurry"), the host says to his guest. "Let us ride out this beautiful April morning. See how fresh and green the hills are! It is the finest time of the year." And so they ride out together, the business of the day momentarily forgotten.

There were no inns in California then, and a man riding a long distance would pull up toward dusk at a rancho where, whether large or small, he could count on a welcome. Here he shared the hearty supper of "good beef broiled on an iron rod, or steaks with onions . . . mutton, chicken, eggs," tortillas, beans, corn, and tamales; most dishes well spiced with red peppers, "their favorite seasoning." Then after an evening of music, for every family contained at least one musician, and probably dancing, he was shown to a room where the elegance of the bed contrasted sharply with the other pieces that were often plain and crude. "The women were exceedingly clean and neat in their houses and persons," and took great pride in "the excellence . . . of their beds and beddings, which were often . . . highly and tastefully ornamented, the coverlids and pillow cases being sometimes satin and trimmed with beautiful and costly lace," wrote an early Californian. If his host were a man of means, there would be a buckskin bag of coin on the table, to which the guest might help himself without thought of repayment. In the morning there would be an ample breakfast, usually beef, beans, and eggs, and a fresh horse at the door.

Men of all classes lived in the saddle, and were trained to the horse and the use of the *riata* from early childhood. It was said that a small boy's first act as soon as he could stand alone was to throw his toy lasso around the neck of a kitten, and that he learned to sit a horse about the time he learned to walk. Women were equally at home on horseback; they often accompanied the men on bear hunts into the mountains and on other expeditions that called for mettle and hard riding.

"The dance and the dashing horse are the two objects which overpower all others in interest with the Californians," it was noted. "It appears as natural for Californians to dance as to breathe or eat. Often I have seen little girls, scarce six years of age, flying through a *cotillon*, or circling in the giddy waltz, or dancing with great skill their favorite *jotah* or *jarabe*. The girls are all elegant waltzers, and will exhaust the strength of an ordinary American gentlemen," an "ordinary American gentleman" reports from experience.

The *valecito casaro*, or little home party, was a favorite way to entertain guests, for an impromptu ball could be gotten up "in five minutes by calling in a guitar or harp player." The *fandango* was another informal dancing party, popular with the rancheros who invited neighbors in for an evening of fun. The *baile* or ball, however, was exclusive and formal and restricted to the gentry who usually held them in their town houses. The highlight of every *baile* was the *jarabe*, an ancient dance performed by a single couple who faced one another and at a certain point stopped to recite original verses "complimentary of the personal beauties and graces of those they admire, or expressive of their love or devotion."

During carnival one of the chief amusements at a fandango or *baile* was the breaking of *cascarones* (eggs blown and filled with cologne or bits of gold and silver paper), over the heads of the opposite sex. "Much manoeuvering and various ingenious devices were resorted to by the ladies to catch the gentlemen off guard," recalls an early Californian. "The gentlemen, at the same time, exercised all their tact and skill to get a similar advantage." One of the challenges was to slip up behind a dancer and crack the egg over his or her head without interfering with the steps of the figure.

A less well-known custom at carnival was for revelers to try to smear each other's faces with colored dyes, carried in little vials. Guests often arrived at a ball resembling Indians in war paint, for "it was the great sport to ride against each other, each endeavoring to stain his opponent's face, while himself escaping," recalls Brigida Cañes Briones. "As we neared Monterey the carnival spirit grew wilder, and the ladies' dresses and faces suffered, but we all took it in good part.

"On our arrival . . . we found every one already dancing. The assembled guests, rushing to us, lifted us from our horses and led us in, smearing our faces with more paint and breaking cascarones on our heads with much laughter. . . ." In the evening everyone washed, put on dancing slippers, sat down to a banquet, and afterward danced the night away. The spirit of "wild revel" was replaced by "the most courtly behavior."

Around midnight a supper of cold chicken, roast beef, salad, pudding, and cake was served, and washed down "with generous libations of champagne and crusty old port of native manufacture."

Picnics, musicals, and amateur theatricals were other popular home pastimes, with horse racing, bullfights (usually held on

Saints' days), bear hunts, cockfights, and bull-and-bear baiting, the favorite public amusements.

In those areas where the wild strawberry grew abundantly, harvesting them called for a camping excursion, lasting about a week, and taken part in by a hundred or more men, women, and children. These expeditions harked back to the first days of the country's settlement when the Indians pointed out to the Spaniards those places where the strawberry was plentiful.

The cavalcade of carretas, laden with hampers of food and wine, tents, bedding, and clothing, and old women and babies, started ahead to the strawberry grounds, the rest of the party following on horses that were gaily decked with red and green ribbons. In their hats the men stuck sprigs of evergreen, while the women and girls wreathed theirs in wild flowers.

Each midafternoon the women would spread large snowy tablecloths over the grass and pile on them "every kind of meat and game—from the ox down to the hummingbird—and all sorts of cakes and sweetmeats." There were jugs of lemonade and coffee and bottles of light California wine, "a gallon of which would not intoxicate."

Evening called out the guitar, harp, and violin, and the green in front of the tents was soon filled with dancers; or there might be songs, or games, and storytelling. On the last day one of the wealthier rancheros would hold a *merienda* to which the whole encampment was invited. Then several bullocks were roasted on spits over coals (*carne asada*), wine flowed like water, and music and dancing were kept up until the rising of the morning star. To wind up a strawberry festival in proper style, a dance would be given at the house of one of the rancheros, on the way home.

The outcome of the Mexican War made no change in this happy, gracious way of life. The New England traveler, meeting a Californian one day who was "reeling off a merry strain" on his guitar, asked how he could be so lighthearted when his country's flag was passing into the hands of a stranger. "Oh," he answered with a smile, "give us the guitar and the fandango, and the devil take the flag!"

Even the discovery of gold in the early 1840s made only a slight ruffle in the normal calm of daily life. The old Spaniards had been obsessed by gold, but for their children's children this was no longer true.

In 1841, Jean Baptiste Ruelle, a French-Canadian trapper who had worked in the placer mines of New Mexico, found gold in the mountains of present Los Angeles County. But the yield was small and the discovery made only a slight stir. The next spring a much larger deposit was found by Francisco Lopez, majordomo of Rancho San Fernando, who was rounding up stray horses and cattle. While resting in the shade of an oak in Placerita Canyon, he dug up a clump of wild onions to eat with his dried beef, and in the earth clinging to them found some glistening particles he took to be gold; probing about in the ground with his knife he uncovered more.

At the pueblo of Los Angeles he was assured that what he had found was gold, and news of his discovery sparked California's first gold rush in which several hundred local residents took part. They were able to use only the crudest methods to extract the gold, for there was not even water nearby to wash the earth. Later that year when some experienced miners from Sonora, Mexico, came in to try their luck they introduced the method known as "dry washing," which is simply the old agricultural principal of winnowing in the wind.

Although it was claimed that $80,000 to $100,000 in gold were taken out in the first two years, Lopez's discovery had no far-reaching or lasting effects.

One day in 1843, Ruelle, who was by then working for Sutter, showed him and John Bidwell a buzzard quill (in which New Mexican miners invariably carried their gold) filled with flakes he said he had found along the American River's South Fork. He wanted to follow the river into the mountains and asked Sutter to outfit him with a quantity of provisions, tools, two mules, and two Indian workers for a prospecting trip. But Sutter suspected that he had it in mind to go on to Oregon rather than hunt for gold and refused to supply him. After gold was discovered on the river in 1848 by James Marshall, Ruelle protested that he should be given credit as the real discoverer.

"After the war things went on prosperously for me, and my empire seemed assured under the new flag," Sutter wrote. "I planned night and day to advance it and render it a permanent place in the California sun."

Some twenty houses had been built within that area of which the fort was nucleus, and Sutter and his neighbors were operating six water-powered mills and a tannery. Demand for leather, saddles, boots, bridles, spurs, hats, and blankets increased steadily as more settlers came into the valley and the San Francisco Bay area, and Sutter was soon employing six hundred men. Good mechanics were more plentiful, for with the disbandment of the Mormon Battalion, many of whom were skilled workers, a large number came to the fort asking for employment, and Sutter hired them. "The best people which I has ever employed," he said.

"I could raise 40,000 bushels of wheat without trouble," he recalled of these years. He had eight hundred beaver traps set along the river, his salmon fisheries were paying well, and his herds and flocks were counted by the thousands. Two miles below the fort he had laid out what promised to be a thriving city, Sutterville.

"Now I needed mills—a grist-mill and a saw-mill for lumber." In May 1847 he set his Mormon mechanics to work building a large gristmill at Natoma, four miles east of the fort, on the west bank of the American. In a letter to Leidesdorff, he predicted that within a year of the mill's operation, all his debts would be paid.

For some time he had been sending parties into the mountains to look for a suitable site for the sawmill. Now that his own enterprises were calling for more lumber, and foreseeing a

market with the continued settlement of the valley, he made
another effort to find a good location.

That July he selected from among his workmen James Wilson
Marshall, an eccentric man of thirty-eight who had worked in
his native New Jersey as a coach- and wagon-maker and carpenter. He was an ingenious person who could turn his hand
to almost any trade and had been making plows, spinning
wheels, looms, and shuttles for Sutter. Marshall's peculiarities
were so evident that "almost everyone pronounced him half
crazy or hare-brained," John Bidwell recalled.

On his return from this excursion up the South Fork, Marshall
reported that he had found the ideal place, well timbered and
accessible, right on the river, about forty-five miles northeast
of the fort. It was in a little valley which the Maidu called *Cullumah,* meaning, it was said, "beautiful vale."

With characteristic enthusiasm, Sutter entered at once into
a partnership with Marshall and called in John Bidwell to write
up the contract. Sutter would furnish the means; Marshall was
to build and operate the mill, taking a share of the lumber as
his compensation.

The contract was signed on August 27, and the next day
Marshall was off for the mountains to select a place to set up
the mill, taking with him young John Wimmer. The boy's parents, Peter L. Wimmer and Jennie (who was to be the party's
cook), several younger brothers, and a Mormon named Gin-
gery came up on the twenty-ninth with two wagonloads of provisions. Two days later Sutter sent up an additional force of
five Mormons and five Indians, and "a Wagon with 3 Yoke of
Oxen and 20 Sheep."

As there would be a crew there all winter, the first task was
to fell pine timber for "a nice doble log cabin," as one worker
described it; it was built beside a spring on a hillside about a
quarter of a mile from the millsite. "This was done in less than
no time, for my men were great with the axe," Marshall tells.

It was "wild and lonesome" country, one of the Mormons has

written, and "infested with wolves Grizly bears and indians."
These Indians came to the camp, and Marshall immediately
made friends with them and hired forty to help him build the
dam.

Daily entries in the fort's logbook show that construction of
the two mills absorbed much of Sutter's time and thought, and
took precedence over other enterprises: eight grinding stones
for the gristmill were being cut from the quarry at Stoney
Creek; Oliver Larkin (who was also a merchant) was shipping
iron for the sawmill; the Indian workers were cutting a wagon
road through the woods to Cullumah; Sutter was riding his
mule upriver to inspect the raising of the gristmill frame; Marshall was making models for the mill irons, and Levi Fifield,
the blacksmith, was getting ready to forge them; John Bidwell
was surveying "a straight road to the Mill at Natoma"; and
wagonloads of food and supplies were being sent each day to
both mills.

But the entry for December 4, 1847, notes something different: "Afternoon the little Steamboat arrived here from San
Francisco . . ." (as Yerba Buena was now called officially). This
was the *Sitka,* the first steamboat to navigate the American
River. It had been built as a pleasure craft for the governor of
the Russian colony in Alaska, and William Leidesdorff had recently bought it. After a trial run around San Francisco Bay
and an excursion to Sonoma, Leidesdorff headed the thirty-
seven-foot vessel with its "pocket engine" up the Sacramento
River to pay Sutter a call. He took with him a party of nine,
including one dauntless woman, Mrs. Gregson, wife of a work-
man at the fort, and her baby.

The little boat was so touchy, a passenger recalls, that the
weight of one man would set her on beam ends, and whenever
the order came to trim boat, they would "pass Mrs. Gregson's
baby over starboard or larboard."

It took the *Sitka* six days and seven hours to cover the hundred miles to New Helvetia. One passenger, who had urgent

business at the fort, grew so impatient he asked to be set ashore seven miles below it, so that he could walk the rest of the way: he beat the steamer by seven hours.

Although the *Sitka* set no records for speed, it did achieve a landmark in the maritime history of California by introducing steam navigation to her inland waters.

California's last decade before the Gold Rush is considered the happiest period through which any country ever passed. Certainly it saw life lived easily and graciously. Although more and more foreign settlers were drifting in each year, there were not enough to make any change in this way of life.

Eighteen forty-seven had been a memorable year in California's history, and it was fast drawing to a close. On Christmas Eve native Californians, as was their custom, lighted bonfires on hill and plain and set off skyrockets and Roman candles. Young men dressed as shepherds, their tall staffs wound with streamers of colored silk and bright paper flowers, filed through the streets of the pueblos. Leading them was the Angel Gabriel with sheeny purple wings and gossamer robes. At the procession's tail stalked the Devil, dressed all in black, with eyes, lips, and tongue stained a fiery red. Into the churches they all marched to enact their sacred drama before the high altar.

During the Christmas season these players, accompanied by musicians, wandered through the streets, stopping before this house and that to sing and to receive cakes and wine.

December 25 was marked at Sutter's Fort by the arrival of several wagonloads of timber for the sawmill; more in keeping with the season was the coming of a canoe laden with pumpkins and fowl. A Christmas dinner, given by the tanners and shoemakers, was held at the hatter's house.

At the sawmill no work was done that day. Henry Bigler, one of the crew, who was a Mormon preacher, led a party of his brethren to the top of Mount Murphy on the north side of the river. There they joined in prayer and hymn singing, and Bigler preached a Christmas sermon.

The year 1848 promised much for settlers along the river. More and more of its rich earth would come to know the mastery of the plow and yield good crops; more and more horses and cattle would grow sleek in feeding on the rank wild grasses and herbage of its slopes and plains. Sutter was looking toward a time, not too far off, when all his debts would be paid and his wealth and position would make him one of California's most important men. The ranchero in the coastal valleys foresaw only good in the year to come, and looked forward to devoting much of it to the continued pursuit of happiness.

But James Wilson Marshall, the simple wheelwright, had been singled out to play a major role in the destiny of the West.

The end of Eden was much closer than anyone knew.

II
THE END OF
EDEN

James W. Marshall

10

Gold!

JANUARY 1, 1848, dawned clear and bright, an auspicious opening for the new year. Robins sang in the sycamores along the
river, and brown towhees scratched in last year's fallen leaves.
At Cullumah the alders were in catkin, and manzanita blossoms
filled the air with the tangy fragrance of wild honey. It might
be May rather than midwinter, a New England diarist reflected.

But a week later skies were leaden, rain was drenching the
land, snows were melting, and the river was a foaming torrent.
On the eleventh it rose eight feet in a few hours, and Marshall
and his crew had to work night and day to save the sawmill
and the brush dam. Two nights later, swollen still more, it
swept over its banks and flooded the pond behind Sutter's, turning it into a moated fortress.

John Bidwell writes that in spite of storms and floodwaters,
and the difficulties of location and terrain, James Marshall suc-
ceeded in building a substantial mill that incorporated many
innovations that were improvements. But on its trial run it was
found that "the old-fashioned flutter wheel that propelled the
upright saw" had been placed too low, and could not turn;
"the gravelly bar below the mill backed the water up, and sub-
merged and stopped the wheel. The remedy was to dig a channel or tail-race through the bar . . . to conduct away the water."

The digging was hard and took several weeks, but as soon
as water began to run through the tailrace, "the wheel was
blocked, the gate raised, and the water permitted to gush

through all night." It was Marshall's practice to examine this channel every morning while the water was running through so as to be able to tell his Indian workers where to deepen it.

He went down as usual, around seven thirty, one morning in late January—"it was a clear, cold morning: I shall never forget that morning," he says—and, shutting off the water, stepped into the race, near the lower end. There, about six inches below the surface of the crystal-clear water

> my eye was caught with the glimpse of something shining in the bottom of the ditch. . . . I reached my hand down and picked it up; it made my heart thump, for I was certain it was gold. The piece was about half the size and of the shape of a pea. Then I saw another piece in the water. After taking it out I sat down and began to think right hard. I thought it was gold, and yet it did not seem to be of the right color . . . this looked more like brass. . . . Suddenly the idea flashed across my mind that it might be iron pyrites. I trembled to think of it! The question could soon be determined. Putting one of the pieces on a hard river stone, I took another and commenced hammering it. It was soft, and didn't break; it therefore must be gold. . . .

He put the pieces in the knocked-in crown of his old white hat and, carrying it cradled in his hands, went back to the cabin for breakfast. On the way he saw William Scott, a carpenter, already at work, and going up to him said: "I have found it."

"What is *it*?" Scott asked.

"Gold," Marshall told him.

"Oh, no, that can't be," Scott said doubtfully.

"I know it to be nothing else," Marshall replied, and showed him what lay in the hat. "Mr. Scott was the second person who saw the gold," Marshall states.

At the millyard he stopped again to call out: "Boys, by God, I believe I have found a gold mine!" and he set his hat down on the workbench. The hands crowded around. None had ever seen free gold before, and one of them, Azariah Smith, a young Mormon, drew out a five-dollar gold piece from his purse, to compare it. There was a difference in color, but they accounted for this by the presence of alloy in the coin. Still, there were doubts, so one of the pieces was heated in the fire. It came out untarnished, but to test it further, it was dropped into the kettle in which Mrs. Wimmer was making soap. It was boiled all day and night, and when fished out the next morning, seemed to be all the brighter for its experience.

Marshall was now certain that he had found gold. Although most of the men were inclined to make fun of his optimism, they still kept a sharp lookout for shining flakes and within several days collectively picked up about three ounces. Then the rains came again, the river raced through the channel, and gold hunting came to an end.

On the stormy afternoon of January 28, James Marshall rode into the fort and hurried over to Sutter's office next to the guardhouse. His felt hat was dripping, and his serape and buckskins soaked and mud-splashed. He seemed greatly excited, and asked Sutter if they could talk in his private office where there would be no chance of anyone's overhearing. Sutter, smiling to himself at this whim of Marshall's, led the way to his bed-sitting-room.

"Are we alone?" Marshall asked anxiously, and Sutter assured him that they were.

"Is the door locked?" It was not, so Sutter turned the key.

"I want two bowls of water," Marshall said next. A servant was called, and the water brought.

"Now I want a stick of redwood and some twine and sheets of copper."

"But, Marshall, what do you want with all these things?"

"I want to make some scales."

"But I have scales enough in the apothecary's shop," Sutter reminded him and went out to get them. On his return he forgot to lock the door and Marshall, not noticing the oversight, reached into his pocket and pulled out a dirty rag. Just as he was unfolding it, the door opened and one of Sutter's clerks walked in to see him on business. Marshall stuffed the rag back in his pocket and glowered.

As soon as the clerk left, he burst out, "Lock the door! Didn't I tell you we might have listeners?"

Sutter obeyed, but assured him he need not suspect the clerk, for this was a usual procedure. Pacified, Marshall pulled out the rag again and, unfolding it, showed the contents to Sutter.

"I believe that this is gold," he said, admitting though that many at the mill still doubted it.

Sutter carefully examined the collection of flakes and grains and agreed that it did look like gold. Then going to his bookshelf he took down a volume of the *Encyclopedia Americana* and turned to the article on gold. After reading it he put the metal to several suggested tests.

It was not affected by aqua fortis, he found, and when placed on the scales with an equal amount of silver and then dipped in water, the yellow metal sank, outweighing the silver. Sutter then told Marshall that he, too, was convinced that this was gold, and of the finest quality.

Marshall wanted to return to the mill at once, although it was by then suppertime and still storming, and he insisted that Sutter go with him. But Sutter had business that would keep him at the fort for several days, so he persuaded Marshall to stay over until morning.

This discovery did not come as a surprise to Sutter. In 1841, James Dana, a mineralogist with the Wilkes expedition, had told him of finding proof that gold existed in this area; and in 1843 Dr. Sandels, the Swedish scholar, had made the same discovery. Then there had been Jean Ruelle with his buzzard quill of gold that came from the American River, and Pablo Gutiérrez, another of his workmen, who had shown him and Bidwell gold he had found along the river's upper reaches.

Still, Marshall's certainty that this deposit was extensive and very rich made Sutter wakeful that night, for there was more than one side to the picture. This could prove the final solution to the nagging problems of finance—complete freedom from debt was an exciting thought. But then there was the disquieting realization that if his workmen got wind of the gold mine they would all desert and leave his two mills unfinished and worthless. These represented a large investment of capital so far: $25,000 for the gristmill, and $10,000 for the sawmill. He decided that he must convince the crew in the mountains to keep the discovery a secret until both projects were completed.

Then he began to wonder how many people at the fort had become suspicious of his prolonged closeting with Marshall behind locked doors, and his bustling back and forth with telltale articles. As he was to learn, there was considerable guessing, some of it coming near the truth. Before Marshall left in the morning, he was cornered and asked if he had found a quicksilver mine like the one recently discovered near Monterey that was making its owners rich. But he had refused to answer.

By the time he reached the sawmill he was bursting with the news. "Oh, boys! By God, it is the pure stuff!" he shouted to the hands. As they crowded around he talked with unusual volubility about how he and the "old Cap" had locked themselves in a room and were "half a day trying it"; and how the "Regulars" at the fort had begun to wonder "what the devil was up" and, putting their heads together, hit on the quicksilver notion. "But we let them sweat," he added.

On the following Tuesday afternoon, Sutter, riding his favorite mule, Katy, set off for the sawmill; he had with him Olympio, his faithful vaquero, and his usual bodyguard of Maidu, who were armed with lances. The riverbank was clothed in fresh green, and the skies clearing; a good omen, perhaps—the future might well be as bright.

Marshall's spirits were still high, and as soon as Sutter came he hurried down to the hands' cabin to tell them the "old Cap" had arrived; playfully he suggested that they pool their gold and salt the tailrace before Sutter inspected it. Seeing all that gold, the Old Man would get so excited he would pull out the pocket flask he always carried and treat them to brandy. The idea was approved, and after the water was shut off the next morning, Henry Bigler, whom Marshall had appointed to do the job, sprinkled the community gold "prity plentifully" on the base rock.

Just as the crewmen were finishing breakfast they saw Sutter walking down the hill with Marshall and Peter Wimmer. As they hurried out to meet them, Bigler noticed that Sutter was as usual "very well dressed," was wearing a broad white hat, and was "stubbing along" with a gold-headed cane. He greeted them with "politeness and cordiality" and, as they had hoped, asked them to join him.

But a minute later Marshall's little joke backfired when one of Peter Wimmer's young sons came running up from the tail-race. Holding out his hand, he said breathlessly, "See all the gold I've found, Father!"

Examining the little pile in the boy's hand, Sutter excitedly "jabed his cane into the ground" and cried out: "By Jo, it *is* rich!"

Although there was no sharing of the flask then, before he left for the fort he gave the crew presents of pocketknives— and a bottle of brandy: "So we got our drink after all," Azariah Smith reported.

Sutter now asked his workers to keep the discovery a secret for six weeks, when both mills would be finished. These represented security for the future, he said. It was still not certain that this was gold they were finding, and even if after further tests it proved to be, no one could tell how extensive or rich the deposit was. But the mills, he stressed, would go on grinding wheat and corn and sawing lumber for years to come; they were guarantors of future prosperity for all. The request was reasonable enough, and the men readily agreed.

The chiefs from the neighboring Maidu settlements were

then called in to a council at the sawmill, and the result was a formal lease of some twelve square miles of land, for twenty years. The Maidu would receive $150 a year, payable on January 1, in flour, farming tools, and clothing, for the "common use and benefit of said tribe at the fair Market value." At the expiration of the term, the land would be returned. Sutter and Marshall had the "Privilage" of cutting timber and making a road from the mill to the fort, the right to erect a sawmill and to cultivate such land as they thought proper, and likewise to open mines and work them. The Indians reserved the right of residence on the tract excepting those parts "enclosed by Said Sutter and Marshall." Acting on this title, Sutter announced that he and Marshall would collect one-third of all the gold taken out on their property.

Ordinary secrets have a disturbing way of nagging their keepers until they are let out. But the secret of gold uses all the guile of the archvillain to wheedle and bully its release, and few men are strong enough to ignore its artifice.

Right after Sutter had exacted the promise of secrecy, Henry Bigler succumbed and wrote of the discovery to three of his brethren at work on the gristmill. He admonished them to keep the secret or, if they must tell, confide only in those who could be "trusted."

Sutter had trouble keeping the secret himself and, when he wrote next to General Vallejo, told him the news, prompting him to remark with characteristic grace to John Bidwell, who delivered the letter: "As the water flows through Sutter's mill-race, may the gold flow into his purse!"

About this same time, a native Californian who had somehow got wind of the discovery galloped into San Francisco with the report that some of Captain Sutter's men had found gold on the Rio de los Americanos. He had come in great haste by way of the Tule Cut-off, via the ranches back of Benicia, across Carquinez Straits, through Livermore Pass to San Jose, and up to San Francisco—"all in two days from the point of starting," just beyond Sutter's Fort.

Sutter was anxious to have official approval of the lease granted by the Indians, and he now sent Charles Bennett, a sawmill hand, to Monterey with a petition addressed to the interim governor and military commander, Colonel Richard B. Mason. Bennett was one of those who had agreed a few days before to Sutter's request that he keep the news of the gold discovery to himself, but he was taking with him in a buckskin bag six ounces he had picked up near the mill. By the time he reached Benicia the secret was already weighing heavily. There, in Von Pfister's store, he heard excited talk about the importance of a coal mine recently found near Mount Diablo.

"Coal!" Bennett snorted. "I have something here that will beat coal, and make this the greatest country in the world!" He took out his bag of gold dust and passed it around.

On reaching San Francisco (where he was to take a vessel for Monterey), he met Isaac Humphrey, a Georgia gold miner, and again the bag was produced. Humphrey told him this was gold of the finest quality, and he believed that the deposit was rich.

Several days later Humphrey appeared at the sawmill and earned the distinction of being the first professional miner to go there. He found that there was some talk about gold, but no one was mining, and the work on the mill was proceeding as usual. After prospecting with a pan and convincing himself that the diggings were rich, he made a rocker or cradle, and so became the first person to introduce "machinery" to the California mines.

According to Lieutenant William T. Sherman, who was present during most of the interview between Colonel Mason and Bennett, the mill hand showed his gold to the colonel, who called on Sherman for an opinion, knowing he was familiar with Georgia gold. Sherman bit one of the larger pieces and found that it retained its luster; he then called for a hatchet and beat it flat. There was no doubt that it was pure gold, but, as he says, "we attached little importance to the fact, for gold was known to exist at San Fernando . . . yet was not considered of much value."

Mason then asked Sherman to reply to Sutter, which he did, explaining that the United States government did not recognize the right of Indians to sell or lease their land to private individuals.

But the mill hands were content to respect Sutter's rights, pay the tithe, and look for gold only on Sundays or in their spare time as Marshall had requested. Then they would go down to the tailrace and, with their jack- and butcher knives, lift the gold out grain by grain from the bare rocks, or the seams and crevices. Tedious as this process was, they usually took out eight or ten dollars' worth.

It soon occurred to them that gold might lie in other places along the river, perhaps well beyond the claim. Two Sundays after Marshall's discovery, Henry Bigler and a friend crossed the river and, at a bar opposite the mill, took out ten dollars in gold in a short time. The next week Bigler went by himself half a mile down the river, found particles of gold exposed in the seams of some rocks, and picked up half an ounce.

Snow now prevented work on the mill, and the men were free to devote more time to gold hunting. The following Tuesday Bigler went back to the same place, but to discourage anyone from accompanying him, he took his gun on the pretext of duck hunting. He did not come back until nearly dark, and when his friends crowded around and asked to see his bag, he only looked wise and called for the scales. Then, unknotting his shirttail, he took out what he called his "yellow game," which weighed a good ounce and a half.

The questions then came fast: "How far away did you find it?" "Was it all in one place?" "Is there more?" "Can you find the place again?" He told them that he had found gold everywhere that bedrock cropped out.

Most of the men felt they ought to quit the mill and prospect full time. But when it came right down to it, no one was really ready yet to give up regular wages on the chance of doing better looking for gold. Gold fever had not infected these men, and they did not think in terms of fortunes, but this time was not far off.

Sutter now committed his crowning indiscretion by sending Jacob Wittmer, a garrulous ex-acrobat and fellow Swiss, to the sawmill with a load of provisions. Afterward he wished he had sent an Indian.

When he got there, several of the little Wimmer boys came running up to tell him that they had found gold; at this Jacob laughed loudly. But Mrs. Wimmer, who overheard and felt this was a slur on her children's veracity, came bustling up to say sharply: 'Well, you needn't laugh! It is true. We *have* found gold! Look here—what do you call that?" and she untied her handkerchief and showed him some flakes.

Later Wittmer heard all about the discovery from the hands, and he went into the tailrace and picked up a few pieces himself. Before he left for the fort, the Wimmer boys gave him more.

Jacob was ordinarily a temperate man, but on reaching the fort he decided to treat himself to a bottle of brandy. Walking into the newly opened store of C. C. Smith & Co. (Smith was a partner of the Mormon elder and entrepreneur Samuel Brannan), he asked for the desired article and put on the counter a little pile of gold.

"What is that?" Smith demanded suspiciously. "You know very well that liquor means money."

"But that is money! It's *gold*," Wittmer told him.

"Come now, that will do. I have no time for your little jokes."

"Well, go and ask the Cap about it, if you don't believe me," Wittmer retorted.

Smith picked up the little pile and took off in "hot haste" for Sutter's office. Bursting in, he announced angrily: "Your man Wittmer came to me just now and said this is gold," and he opened his hand. "Now of course I knew he lied, and told him so. . . ."

"Nevertheless, it *is* gold," Sutter interrupted. Later he explained: "I told him the truth—what could I do?"

It was impossible for Wittmer to keep any kind of secret, and he told everyone about all he had seen and heard at the sawmill. But as he had a reputation for exaggeration, no one took his story seriously until one day he showed a group of them some of the pieces he had picked up. The largest was the size of a pinhead, and several of the men laughed at the suggestion that this stuff was worth anything. Heinrich Lienhard, one of Sutter's assistants, who was standing by, suggested that they take the largest piece to the blacksmith shop and test it.

There was absolute silence, he recalls, as the men watched the tiny piece of heated metal expand under the smithy's hammer to over half an inch without breaking. When the realization struck them that the metal had been proven by this basic test, they lost their senses. Sober fellows like Lienhard went dancing around the anvil, shouting with joy, embracing one another, shaking hands, laughing, crying, yodeling. Little John Mouet, the tailor, shouted at the top of his lungs: "Gold! Gold! Gold! It's gold, boys! It's gold! We'll be all rich! Three cheers for the gold!"

The commotion was heard all over the fort, and people came running out to see what had happened.

As Sutter stepped out of his office, he saw Lienhard just leaving the smithy's (in a "dazed" state of mind, he remembers) and called him over.

"Well," he said to his young Swiss associate, "my secret I see has been discovered. Since we all expect to be rich, let's celebrate with a bottle of wine!"

In spite of Sutter's later protestations that from the moment of Marshall's discovery he was weighed down by ominous forebodings of impending disaster to his enterprises, it appears certain that his eyes, too, were dazzled by the luster of gold, and that he wove it generously in the fabric of his dreams for the future.

11

Exodus

ONE DAY in March 1848, Edward Charles Kemble, the nineteen-year-old editor of Samuel Brannan's newspaper, the *California Star*, stood watching Sutter's Indian and Kanaka crew land their launch at the foot of San Francisco's Clay Street. There were only a few passengers, all strangers. One man, "lean and nervous . . . black-eyed and bushy-bearded," lingered at the wharf, and the editor began questioning him about the activities at Sutter's Fort. But he didn't know "what was what, or which was which"; however, as Kemble was turning away to look elsewhere for news, the stranger said to him quietly: "If you come with me up to the store, I will show you something."

They walked in silence to the corner of Montgomery and Sacramento streets and stepped into the neat white frame building that housed the firm of Howard & Mellus, Merchants. The stranger then pulled out a greasy purse and from it a rag which he carefully unfolded to display a few thin yellow flakes.

"That there," he said in a low voice, "is gold, and I know it, and know where it comes from, and there's aplenty more in the same place, certain and sure!"

Kemble asked him where it came from, and he said Sutter's sawmill. The rag was passed around, but everyone in the store eyed the flakes suspiciously, and one man said with finality that it was only fool's gold.

That night the *Star* went to press without mention of gold having been found on the American River. It was left for its rival, the *Californian,* to print the first news of the discovery a few days later, in a brief, low-key paragraph. Whatever impact it might have had was deadened by the editor's generalization that gold had been found all over California. The public was generally reluctant to believe that gold in any quantity could have gone so long undiscovered.

But the story was different along the American River where men had the proof before them. By mid-March the sawmill was cutting two thousand feet of planks a day, but the hands were rapidly becoming infected with gold fever. The same was true at the fort and the gristmill, and from this time on Sutter's logbook records almost daily departures of this man or that to try his luck in the placer mines—the wagonwright, the smithy, the saddler, the gunsmith, the locksmith, the French baker, the tailor, the hatter, the cooper, the cook, the clerk, and even the doctor.

John Sinclair left two hundred acres of fine ripe wheat to look after itself and, taking the fifty Indians who were to have cut it, set out to reap an even richer harvest. He found Coloma, as the sawmill seat was to be called, already so crowded he went on to the American's North Fork, being the first person to mine there. Near what was later named Beal's Bar, he and his Indians, using only baskets for washing, took out $16,000 within a few weeks.

William Daylor, Jared Sheldon, and Perry McCoon, ranchers who had formerly worked for Sutter, went prospecting along the American's tributaries, and discovered in a little, dry gully south of Coloma a pocket from which they dug $17,000 in seven days.

This news brought men flocking there by the hundreds, and a camp sprang up that was called Old Dry Diggins; by the following year it had grown into a lively town that became noted for crime and vigilante punishment.

On a stream not far from Daylor's claim, Captain Charles Weber dug up a ten-and-a-half-pound nugget; and Claude

Chana, a French emigrant of 1846, on his way to Coloma from
Sicard's Ranch, discovered a deposit in a ravine near the North
Fork. This area proved so rich and extensive that a camp known
as North Fork Dry Diggins mushroomed there. It grew into a
permanent settlement that was later named Auburn by a group
of miners from Auburn, New York. It was told how men there
were taking out as much as $1,500 in a day, and of how five
carloads of dirt yielded one miner $16,000.

Accounts of these overnight fortunes were intoxicating, and
men dropped whatever they were doing and headed for the
river. Sutter says that in a matter of weeks he was left "with
only the sick and the lame behind." In retrospect he tended
to disparage his workers for their desertion, but he was not
deaf either to the siren call. As early as February he had set
a party of Indians under Heinrich Lienhard, to look for gold,
and later formed a company with Marshall, Isaac Humphrey,
and Peter Wimmer, which began mining at Coloma during the
first part of April.

One of the richest placers on the South Fork was found by
Wilford Hudson and Sidney Willis, two Mormons who had
learned of the discovery from Henry Bigler's letter. On hearing
the news they set off for Coloma, on the pretense of hunting
deer, and worked near the mill with fair success until March
2, when, in order to lend credence to their story of a hunt,
they started back to the gristmill. They followed the river
closely, keeping a sharp lookout for likely deposits. One afternoon they stopped to prospect at a bar near the confluence of
the forks, and the results of their trial washings were so promising, they hurried on to the fort to buy provisions and, with
admirable loyalty, shared their discovery with their brethren.
The bar was soon swarming with Mormons, and the hillside
above blossoming "with canvass tents and brush arbors."

Early in April, Sam Brannan, businessman extraordinary who
was the Mormon's spiritual and temporal leader in California,
hearing about these fabulous "lower mines," which had ful-

filled the promise and become heavy producers of fine-scale gold, came up from San Francisco to see for himself.

He had come to California in 1846, in the ship *Brooklyn*, bringing with him 238 colonists, mostly Mormons, and a stock of tools, a printing press, type, paper, and machinery for a gristmill, which had all proven useful and remunerative in the new land. Already he owned a newspaper, hotel, flour mill, and store.

Now seeing his "boys" taking out as much as $250 a day each, he made a preemptive claim in the name of the church and levied a tax, the "Lord's tithe," which, it developed, benefited Sam Brannan more than the Lord. However, it was paid regularly with little grumbling, until that July when Colonel Mason stopped by on an official visit. Then William S. Clark came up to ask: "Governor, what business has Sam Brannan to collect the tithes here?"

"Brannan has a perfect right to collect the tax, if you Mormons are fools enough to pay it," Mason replied.

"Then I, for one, won't pay any longer," Clark declared.

But Brannan had still better ways of collecting the gold from both Mormon and Gentile. His store at Sutter's Fort had already outgrown its quarters and would soon be moved into one of the large granaries there; and he was preparing to open a branch at Coloma and another at the Mormon diggings, along with a warehouse and a much-needed hotel. Later that year, after he bought out his partner C. C. Smith, he had a virtual monopoly in the valley. Trading at that time yielded profits of 200 percent over the San Francisco cost of merchandise. When his store at the fort began taking in $150,000 a month, Sam Brannan had no need to worry about tithes; he was well on his way to becoming one of California's first millionaires.

Accounts of the riches to be found along the American River made their way regularly to the towns, but the public was still unwilling to believe them and reluctant to chase a phantom. Editor Kemble voiced the general skepticism when he pronounced the gold discovery a "sham" and went to Coloma expressly to expose the placers as "a miserable fraud."

At sunrise on April 18, he, Major Reading, George McKinstry, and Sutter set out from the fort. Riding ahead were two Indians, José and Antonio, with extra saddlehorses and pack animals carrying provisions and camp gear. Sutter, "a very poor horseman," so Kemble noted, brought up the rear on the dependable Katy, firmly grasping the pommel and picking his way with anxious care over the rocky paths.

" 'Now den Katy—de oder foot!' " he could be heard expostulating from time to time. " 'God bless me, Katy—de oder foot, child!' "

On the second morning the party rode down the final hill into the "beautiful and romantic vale of Coloma"; Kemble noted that the river was "a perfect mountain torrent, thundering over its rocky bed with noisy violence."

The hands were idle, for the river, swollen by the spring thaw, had overflowed the dam, backed up in the race, and nearly surrounded the mill. Sutter introduced the party to Marshall who was "moodily whittling."

" 'These gentlemens have come to see der gold-mines, Mr. Marshall,' " Sutter said. On seeing Marshall's face cloud, Sutter explained that they were good friends.

But Marshall resented all visitors, for he expected to make a fortune from these placers and had no intention of encouraging a rush. Therefore, when Kemble asked him to point out the exact spot where he had found the gold, he picked up a chip of wood and glumly scratched an X on it with his knife. Then jabbing the point into the place where the lines intersected, jerked out the word, " 'Thar!' "

As for getting anything out of the crew, Kemble insisted that by comparison "opening oysters with a wooden toothpick would have been an easy task." One man " 'allowed' he didn't 'go much on its being gold, anyway.' " Another guessed Marshall was a 'little mite cracked' on the subject. In answer to the direct

question where the gold was found, the reply was, 'Oh, anywhere along the race or down by the river, where you've a
mind to try for it.' "

Reading, who had some experience washing gold, suggested
that he try his luck, and borrowing an Indian basket—"one of
those handsome, water-tight utensils" decorated with the gay
plumage of the red-wing—the party filed down to the millrace.

Hours passed, the sun grew hot, and Kemble, McKinstry,
and Sutter took shelter in the woods, "leaving the Major twirl-
ing and dipping his basket." Noontime came, and the Indian boys prepared lunch. Then, wrote Kemble, " 'remote,
unfriended, melancholy, slow,' approaches the sole representative of the mining interest in our party. He is greeted with a
quiet 'what success, Major?' and replies, 'not enough to buy a
drink.' "

"There can be no reality in such gold discoveries as these,"
observed Kemble and, opening his notebook to that page reserved for comments on the diggings, wrote the word HUM-
BUG in large letters.

Early in May, Sam Brannan made a flying trip to the lower
mines, by then called Mormon Diggings or Mormon Island, to
start preparations for the hotel, the warehouse, and the ferry
he planned to establish. All he needed now was more customers.

He filled a bottle with gold dust and flakes and went back
to San Francisco. Then, as he stepped ashore and started up
Clay Street, he took off his hat, and swinging it in one hand,
waved the bottle with the other, high above his head for all
to see.

"Gold! Gold! Gold from the American River!" he shouted.

All day he wandered around the town, calling attention
everywhere to the bottle of gold, like a hawker crying his wares.
The effect was strangely electric. The disbelievers were suddenly ready to drop everything and head for the river of El
Dorado.

"The inhabitants of the place seemed panic-struck and so

excited and in such a hurry to be off, that some of the mechanics left their work, not taking time even to take off their aprons," recalls one who was so aroused by Brannan's words he rushed off to buy up a stock of Indian baskets in which to wash his gold. Another man remembered that a "frenzy" seized him on hearing Brannan, and he had visions of such limitless wealth "the Rothschilds, Girards, and Astors appeared to me but poor people."

Stocks of blankets, boots, slouch hats, picks, shovels, crowbars, tin pans, buckets, bowls, bottles—even snuffboxes,—were swept from the merchants' shelves, and no more could be had except by import. Prices on these articles jumped tenfold and more.

The fever spared no one: the carpenter literally dropped his saw, the blacksmith his hammer, and the baker his loaf. Men hurried to dissolve partnerships and dispose of their property. Merchants and hotelkeepers locked their doors, while teachers, ministers, doctors, and judges deserted their schools, their flocks, their patients, and their courts. Thomas Larkin reported seeing the King of Hawaii's former attorney general standing in the river with a party of "his brethren of the long robe," washing gravel with an Indian basket, while farther downstream the French consul was diligently plying his shovel.

Sailors, forfeiting four years' pay, ran away from warships anchored in San Francisco and Monterey. A whole platoon of soldiers deserted the presidio at the capital, leaving only their colors behind. Henry Bee, the constable of San Jose, found himself in a plight when the fever hit him: he had ten prisoners in the lockup, two of them charged with murder. When he went to turn them over to the *alcalde*, he discovered that functionary had preceded him to the mines. Since there was no one else to whom he could legally deliver the prisoners, he took them with him and set them to work digging and washing gravel.

On May 20, Edward Kemble tried vainly to stem the tide with an editorial in which he declared that the "reputed wealth" of the mines was "a supurb take-in, as was ever got up to guzzle the gullible." Nine days later the *Star's* "divil" had rebelled, and the pressman was last seen in search of a pickax; two weeks later the paper suspended publication, and Kemble, the skeptic, followed the crowds to the American River, hunted for gold— and found it.

Many native Californians, like the venerable Luis Peralta, remained calm in the midst of this madness. He called in his family and said: "My sons, God has given this gold to the Americans. Had he desired us to have it, he would have given it to us ere now. Therefore do not go after it, but let others go. Plant your lands, and reap; these be your best gold-fields, for all must eat while they live."

On June 1, Thomas Larkin, confidential agent for the United States, made the first official report of the gold discovery. It was, he wrote James Buchanan, one of the most "astonishing excitements" ever to be brought to the government's attention, and he enclosed a few grains of gold. After a visit to Mormon Island, he wrote again, assuring Buchanan that the wealth of the gold regions had not been exaggerated.

A third report, written after further investigation, informed the secretary that gold was so plentiful and the deposits so extensive that five thousand workers, with a crude machine called a "cradle," could "daily obtain sufficient to pay the expenses of the war with Mexico." Some men, working with Indian labor, were counting their take at a dollar a minute. Two hundred thousand dollars had been dug out of the river in May, and double the amount in June. "I think now over half a million is the monthly estimate we can believe in."

These second and third reports, along with some official dispatches for the Secretary of the Navy, were given to Edward Fitzgerald Beale, a twenty-six-year-old naval lieutenant, to take on to Washington. Beale, a veteran of several hazardous overland journeys as a messenger, sailed on August 1 from La Paz aboard the flagship *Ohio,* bound for San Blas.

Dressed in a red shirt, leather trousers, and sombrero, the

dark-haired Beale hoped to pass for a Mexican on his overland ride to Vera Cruz. He carried an array of arms—four six-barreled pistols and a bowie knife—for the road was infested with ladrones. During his amazing ride, an exciting narrative in itself, through gales, torrential rains, floods, and avalanches, he was stopped three times by bandits. The resolution of the first group melted on sight of his small armory; the second he managed to outride, although they chased him for several hours and shot at him with their carbines. He gave the third the slip when he rode his horse down a cliff so steep they dared not follow.

At Vera Cruz he boarded the sloop-of-war *Germantown*, which put him ashore at Mobile, and from there he traveled uneventfully by stage and steamboat to Washington, arriving on September 16.

When he called on the Secretary of the Navy to deliver his dispatches, he found him having an after-dinner game of chess with the President, and took advantage of the informality of the meeting to show them the large gold nugget and collection of flakes he had brought on his own. He told them about the fortunes being made daily along the American River and said it was no exaggeration to predict that California was "destined to become the richest and most important territory on the continent." At this the President accused him jokingly of being "a real-estate and corner-lot boomer."

Beale talked enthusiastically about the new El Dorado and exhibited his gold specimens wherever he went. P. T. Barnum, just rising to fame, got wind of Beale's treasure and wrote him, offering to buy "the 8 lb. lump of California gold." If he did not wish to sell it, then would he allow Barnum to put it "on exhibition for a few weeks."

Beale turned down the offer and put the nugget on display at the Patent Office where crowds flocked to see it. The flakes he had made into an engagement ring for Mary Edward, who later became his wife.

A summary of Larkin's letters to Buchanan, published in the

Washington *Daily Union* soon after Beale's arrival, stimulated a fast-growing interest in the discovery, and by mid-October, Archibald H. Gillespie was writing: "The public in general are mad about California, & the late news respecting El placer has made many adventurers look towards that region. There are many solid people about to emigrate to California."

Still, the State Department made public no official report of the gold discovery.

California's military governor, Colonel Mason, found it hard to believe all he heard about the placers, and on June 17 set out to see for himself and make an official report to Roger Jones, the adjutant general. He took with him Lieutenant Sherman, an escort of four soldiers, and "a good outfit of horses and pack-mules." From San Francisco they crossed the bay to Sausalito and rode on from there to San Rafael, where they stopped for the night with its leading citizen, Don Timoteo Murphy, whose house was famed for hospitality. The next day's ride took them to Bodega, and the next to Sonoma, where they stayed with General Vallejo. From here they rode on to Rio de los Putos, going by way of Napa, Suisun, and Juan Vaca's rancho, and on July 2 came to the Sacramento River. They crossed in an Indian dugout canoe and set up camp on the pond behind the fort. Sutter sent them a freshly butchered beef and some mutton.

It was as though some pestilence had swept across the land through which they had come, Mason wrote. Farmhouses stood vacant, mills idle, towns deserted. Fields of ripe wheat were left for wandering horses and cattle to eat and trample, and crops of corn and beans, untended, wilted under the fierce mid-summer sun.

But at Sutter's all was bustle and business, and the talk was of nothing but *gold*.

Every storehouse and shed was crammed with merchandise; provisions, hardware and dry goods, whiskey and tobacco, and a hundred other things heaped in indiscriminate confusion. The dwelling of the hospitable proprietor, who had a word for everybody . . . was crowded with visitors. Launches were discharging their cargoes at the river; boatmen shouting and swearing; waggoners . . . whistling and hallooing, and cracking their whips at their straining horses, as they toiled along with heavily laden wagons to the different stores within the buildings; groups of horsemen . . . [were] riding to and fro, and crowds of people . . . moving about on foot.

"My ferry could hardly take care of all the people who crossed the river every day," Sutter wrote.

Those who could not find room within the fort camped outside its walls.

Samuel Kyburz, Sutter's former majordomo, had just taken over the main building and converted it into a hotel, paying Sutter $500 monthly rental; this and other rents within the fort were bringing him $2000 a month.

There was a constant ebb and flow, as of a great tide, Sherman recalled, as parties outfitted with the necessities moved excitedly upriver, confident of picking up at least $100 a day, while their places were taken by hordes of new arrivals, or by groups coming from the mines, eager to spend their newly gained riches. Gone forever were the days of leisurely hospitality and agrarian tranquility.

Preparations were under way for celebrating the first Fourth of July under American rule, and Sutter persuaded Colonel Mason to stay over. The day was greeted in a noisy manner with the firing of the old Russian cannons, which threatened to fly apart at each discharge and made some bystanders nervous.

Banquet tables were set up in the old armory, and the feast prepared by Kyburz was one that "would have done credit to any frontier town," Sherman thought. There was a good supply of excellent brandy and sauterne, bought from a French merchant captain, and a generous stock of *aguardiente*.

John Sinclair presided, and Charles Edward Pickett, who

listed his profession as "philosopher," was orator of the day. Pickett, a cousin of the future Confederate general, had recently opened a store at the fort and another at Coloma.

During dinner Sutter entertained his guests with stories of his service with Charles X. "Yes, gentlemen, during the fight at Grenoble, I received a bayonet wound in the leg. Our major, who happened to be standing nearby, seeing how the blood ran down over my white trousers, called, 'Captain Sutter is wounded! Take him where he can be treated.' But I refused, and went on fighting with my sword. . . ."

Mason's party left in the morning and, as Sherman remembered, after "twenty-five miles of as hot and dusty a ride as possible, we reached Mormon Island, where we made camp on a small knoll . . . and from it could overlook the busy scene. A few brush-huts nearby served as stores, boarding-houses, and for sleeping."

The next day found them at Coloma where they saw "upwards of 4000" miners at work. James Marshall, courteous and communicative, acted as their guide, taking them along the river to its junction with the North Fork, where they inspected Sinclair's rich claim. "Little stores were being opened at every point, where flour, bacon, etc., were sold; every thing being a dollar a pound."

Returning to the sawmill, they left Marshall and, fording the American, rode south to Old Dry Diggins where they saw the little gully from which Daylor and McCoon had dug their bonanza.

"Another small ravine was shown me," Mason wrote, "from which had been taken $12,000 worth of gold. Hundreds of similar ravines, to all appearance, are as yet untouched. I could not have credited these reports had I not seen in the abundance of the precious metal, evidence of their truth."

Every day new deposits of incredible wealth were being found. "We were quite bewildered by the fabulous tales of recent discoveries," Sherman added.

Lieutenant Lucian Loeser of the Third Artillery was selected to take Mason's report and a small Chinese tea caddy or chest, packed with $3,000 in gold, on to Washington. The governor had bought the gold from various sources; that nugget labeled "Specimen No. 9" had come from Editor Edward C. Kemble.

Loeser sailed from Monterey at the end of August aboard the chartered bark *La Lambayecana*, transferred at Payta, Peru, to an English steamer bound for Panama, and went on from there to Jamaica where he found a sailing vessel going to New Orleans. But he had so many delays and misadventures afloat and ashore, he did not reach Washington until December 7, two days after President Polk had delivered his annual message to Congress. However, a duplicate copy of the report had had better fortune and got through by November 22. Arriving on the heels of Larkin's dispatches it brought final confirmation, and the President felt free to include an announcement of the gold discovery in his message. He said, in part, that the accounts of the abundance of gold in California were "of such extraordinary character as would scarcely command belief, were they not corroborated by the authentic reports of officers in the public service, who have visited the mineral district, and derived the fact which they detail from personal observation."

Polk's message, which was widely published, gave foundation at last to those reports and rumors which had been almost too fabulous for belief. Then Lieutenant Loeser arrived with the tea caddy full of gold, bringing visual confirmation of the announcement. People jammed the War Office to stare at a two-ounce nugget put on display. Then came an announcement from the Philadelphia mint that the remaining specimens in the caddy were pure gold of the finest quality.

This was all that was needed. "The Eldorado of the old Spaniards is discovered at last!" announced the *New York Herald*.

Gold fever swept over the country from Maine to Mississippi, sparing few. In remote villages and populous cities men made ready to leave for California. "We are on the brink of an Age of Gold!" Horace Greeley predicted.

James Marshall's discovery was to precipitate the most extraordinary voluntary migration in modern times; to change the whole course of our western history, and to leave its impact upon the entire world. There had been nothing like it since the Crusades.

III

THE RIVER OF
EL DORADO

*Lola Montez
and
Lotta Crabtree*

12

The Golden Road

THE EYES of the world were now fixed on the American River, the river of El Dorado, and talk of its unbelievable riches was on nearly every tongue as trading vessels carried the news around the world. The accounts tended to grow with travel, so that in some lands men were led to believe that the bed of this marvelous river was paved with gold and its banks lined with pockets of large nuggets, just waiting to be picked up. Fabulous reports were given of the fortunes made in a day, of Mexicans picking out chunks of gold with their knives and returning to their homeland laden with wealth; of Indians throwing away their arrows and filling their quivers with gold dust. Such tales made men delirious, and, abandoning all else, they made hasty preparations to go. "When are you off?" became the most common greeting of the day.

The political climate gave impetus to the movement, for men's minds and lives were unsettled by those wars and revolutions that had been ravaging Europe and the British Isles. In other lands population pressures and poverty were the incentives. In the United States men had been made restless by the aquisition of vast unpopulated and inviting territory through the war with Mexico, and Marshall's discovery gave direction to the general westward trend.

The first excitement outside the United States was recorded in Honolulu when the schooner *Louise* of San Francisco put into port on June 17, 1848. Not only was she bringing news of the discovery at Coloma, but proof in the form of two pounds of gold.

"The fever rages here, and there is much preparation for emigration," a local merchant reported. In less than a month the first ship crowded with gold seekers had sailed, and others were fitting out. One impatient man, unable to get passage on the first ship and refusing to wait longer, set off in a whaleboat.

Before the news had time to reach Oregon overland, vessels from Honolulu brought it, and during that summer and fall, over two-thirds of Oregon's white population packed their big wagons and set off for the American River.

The news reached Canton that summer, and young men in and around the city were excited by these tales of a place where gold was harvested like a crop, and they made plans to sail to the fabulous *Gum San*, Land of Golden Mountains. The first few Chinese arrived in San Francisco that fall aboard a British steamer.

By October all of northern Mexico was in a ferment: "The mania that pervades the whole country, our camp included, is beyond all description of credulity," an army officer noted. "The whole state of Sonora is on the move."

The Atlantic world, which was to contribute the major portion of Argonauts, did not receive confirmation of the discovery in time to send any men that year, although, by mid-January 1849, five mining companies were registered in London and four in Paris, and nearly every European port had some ships fitting out.

By the time the President's message had circulated in the States, winter had set in, but the season was spent profitably in thousands of homes and communities, preparing for the great trek that coming spring.

One of the first things to be done was to organize a company for mutual protection on the journey—especially if going overland across the Plains, the Isthmus, or Mexico—for the joint purchase of outfits, and because it was believed that neither life nor property were safe in California unless men banded together.

The company was then named, often extravagantly, officers were elected, bylaws framed, a route decided on, a company song composed—for the Gold Rush was an odyssey of song—uniforms designed and ordered, for most groups were formed as military companies, and membership solicited. In these first companies great care was taken not only to enlist men of good character, but those who could contribute to the enterprise, like physicians, mineralogists, professional miners, and mechanics. Some of the larger groups had a chaplain and company lawyer.

Outfits included every conceivable article of utility and comfort: food and clothing enough to last a year; mining equipment of every sort; plows, harrows, and seeds; machinery for starting almost every trade; and merchandise to stock stores. Those who went by sea took deckloads of lumber, prefabricated houses of wood and sheet iron, printing presses, sawmills, and even small steamboats to navigate the river. One company going overland from Massachusetts took a coining press and dies for five- and ten-dollar gold pieces, to set up a private mint.

In every community the ordinary course of business was revolutionized. Bakers kept their ovens going night and day to turn out quantities of ship bread and biscuits. Manufacturers abandoned their regular lines and made special "California Goods." The Union India Rubber Company offered portable boats "for crossing the streams in the wild country," waterproof tents, blankets, boots, and clothing. There were "Californian Houses of the most substantial kind, built in sections," procurable at three days' notice. There were rifles, pistols, and bowie knives of every make and sort; special whistles for signaling in case of Indian attack; matches warranted "never to fail in rain or gale"; drugs and patent medicines that were sure cures for cholera morbus, typhoid, and fever-and-ague; and folding canvas stools to sit on while gathering nuggets.

The market was shortly flooded with a variety of pumps, dredges, mills, and washers, designed for gathering gold, the majority of them invented by persons knowing nothing about the properties of the metal, but a great deal about human nature. On the ship that brought one forty-niner, there were "all varieties and patterns" of these machines. "Some of them worked by a crank; others, more pretentious, having two cranks; whilst another . . . more economical and efficient, worked with a treadle. One variety was upright, requiring the miner to stand while using it; still another, the inventor . . . being of a more . . . humane temperament, was arranged in such a manner that the poor tired miner could sit in his arm chair and take his comfort as he worked it."

One washer that excited the envy of everyone on board was made like a large fanning mill, with sieves to sort the gold of a size for bottling, while consigning the larger chunks to a barrel. Although it required two men to operate it, it was expected that the greater part of their time would be spent in corking bottles and fitting heads to full barrels.

Then there was "Diving Armor," that was tried out several times on the American's Middle Fork, "but," it was reported, "the adventurous individual who donned the brazen helmet and braved the watery depths got no gold and when pulled up, was found nearer dead than alive."

One of the most useful articles a man could take along, and thousands of them were sold, was *The Emigrant's Hand-Book*, which instructed the novice in just how to put up a log shanty; how "in times of great scarcity" to make bread from wood; how to make cheese, "Labor-Saving Soap," "Cheap Candles," and "Spruce Beer"; how to cook pork and beans, make biscuits, corn bread, and slapjacks; how to care for cattle with the blain, and horses with swinney. And for man, every possible disease and accident, as well as those additional hazards of the Plains, gunshot and arrow wounds, and rattlesnake bites. In short, an answer to every question or situation that might arise.

As a final act before leaving, Argonauts were urged to insure their lives and have their daguerreotypes taken.

Those who came overland were the first to discover their folly in carrying so much equipment. One member of a Boston company that included two servants, four musicians, and six dogs, wrote his family from Fort Kearny: "We have thrown away 500 pounds of bread and bacon and large quantities of flour and beans. Wagons we abandoned or sold for a song. We are cooking dinner with fuel that was a brand new wagon when we left. . . . There is more clothing on the ground at Fort Kearny than would fill the largest store in Boston. It makes a man's heart sick to see the property scattered over the ground here."

Many of those who threw away food so recklessly were to face starvation before the journey's end. Reports of the high death rate and great suffering in crossing the plains that year reached San Francisco, and relief expeditions were outfitted, and stations that supplied water and food, and grass for animals were set up west of the final desert. By the next season, in addition to these charitable depots, enterprising traders had opened shops and eating houses which sold water at a dollar a gallon and whiskey at seventy-five cents a drink; flour at two dollars a pound, beans at one dollar, and served a full-course dinner for ten dollars.

Those going by sea did not realize how much excess baggage they were carrying until they reached San Francisco. Here they found freight charges so exorbitant and transportation so scarce, they simply abandoned everything they couldn't carry. The beaches were soon piled high with discarded trunks, chests, and valises filled with valuables—as well as the precious gold washers. "I saw . . . hundreds of huge bulky machines which would require, each one of them, a large ox-team to convey them to the mining regions," an Argonaut recalls.

Under favorable conditions the two-thousand-mile trip from Independence, Missouri, to Coloma might be covered in a hundred days, but conditions were seldom that favorable. A start could not be made until the prairie greened, which was late April or May, depending on the season. But by April 17, 1849, three thousand men from almost every city and state were already gathered at Independence, waiting for the grass; by the end of the month there were twenty thousand. Their encampment had all the appearance of a great fair to which throngs had flocked in their brightly painted wagons, many decked with colored banners bearing such slogans as "Ho! for the diggings!"

"Peddlers shouted their wares, dance halls and drinking saloons abounded, while the crowd of gamblers which ever attends a frontier settlement, relieved the unwary of their cash."

Not every man traveled with a wagon or cart. Many were going by horse or mule, others were walking with a pack animal or shouldering their loads, while one man, a Mr. Brookmire of Warren, Pennsylvania, attracted a good deal of attention as he pushed a wheelbarrow across the Plains. He was interviewed on reaching Coloma, and told the reporter that when "afflicted with the California fever" he had not enough money to buy a team, so had simply loaded his wheelbarrow "with 150 lbs. of provisions, besides his cooking utensils and baggage, and started from the States on his long journey. He was able to make greater headway than most of the teams, as he lost no time except for his meals and sleep. . . . At Salt Lake, he found the opportunity of joining a company then about starting; so he left his faithful hand-carriage by the side of the road and 'on he came a-whistling.' "

Some eighteen months later the "Wheelbarrow Man" made news again when he returned home with $15,000 in gold taken from the diggings along the American River.

The most popular Sierra crossing was by way of the pass Frémont had opened on his first trip into California, although once down the western face of the mountains, the gold seekers took an easier route to the river, following a trail blazed in the

summer of 1848 by a group of Mormons from the old Battall-
lion, on their way from Sutter's Fort, Mormon Island, and
Coloma, to Salt Lake.

Today this historic trail can still be followed by hunting out
the camps and landmarks along the way, almost every one with
some story behind it: Carson Spur, Silver Lake, Tragedy Springs,
Maiden's Grave, Corral Flat, Leek Spring, Sly Park, Pleasant
Valley, Hank's Exchange, Tiger Lily, and Diamond Springs
where the tide of Argonauts turned north to Old Dry Diggins
and Coloma.

All of these camps and way stations, along what came to be
called the Carson Emigrant Road, grew into thriving settlements, their prosperity based chiefly on supplying the destitute
overland traveler with everything—even baths. At some, gold
was discovered, which swelled their population and extended
their longevity. A twenty-five-pound nugget, the largest ever
found in what was to become El Dorado County, was taken
from the diggings at Diamond Springs. A number of these
camps managed to retain some later importance through lime
production, lumbering, and agriculture. A few exist today,
mainly on memories.

Although gold was found in all the other rivers that raced
down the western slopes of the Sierra, the American was the
magnet that continued to draw most of the men. It was "the
richest of the rivers, and from its bars and bed and the deep
gorges of its tributaries, flowed the golden stream that added
hundreds of millions to the wealth of the world in the first
few years following discovery," wrote an early chronicler. And
the men who came there called it El Dorado.

The Middle Fork proved the richest of all, having more bars
on it and several that earned the distinction of producing in
the millions of dollars. Mud Canyon and American Bar are
credited with $3 million apiece, and Horseshoe Bend, Green-
horn Slide, Volcano Bar, and Yankee Slide with runs ranging
down to $1 million each.

The Middle Fork was also famed for the Big Crevice, a lime-stone dyke filled with an ancient sediment rich in gold, which crosses the river diagonally at Murderer's Bar. Because of its depth (the bottom could never be found) and the difficulties and danger in working it—for the river had to be turned aside by flumes, and it was possible to control only two-thirds of the water—it was never thoroughly exploited. But the Big Crevice would always remain a favorite topic for campfire talk and speculation, for those who had worked in the pit reported that gold lay in handfuls on every side.

The first four hundred gold seekers out of the forty thousand who came from the States by sea in 1849 arrived at San Francisco, aboard the steamer *California*, on February 28. The day is reported as being bright and clear, and as the ship rounded Telegraph Hill, it "careened to the shore side, from the rush of passengers to get a look at the town." It was a gala occasion. Warships in the bay broke out their bunting and saluted the *California* with a twenty-one-gun broadside. Crowds of wintering miners and townspeople stood on the beach and cheered, while the throngs on deck shouted back and waved their handkerchiefs, and the band played patriotic airs. Before any of the passengers had time to get ashore, every crewman but one—an assistant engineer—was over the side and off to the mines.

From this time on the Coloma Road, marked out by Sutter's men in 1847 as a track to the sawmill, became the most traveled thoroughfare in the United States, packed solid with humanity. There were two ways to reach this historic road from San Francisco—by horseback and by boat, but the scarcity of horses and mules in the pueblo made the water route the more feasible.

In August 1849 some twelve thousand gold hunters were waiting impatiently for transportation to Sutter's *embarcadero*, although one Argonaut recalls that there were "not less than one hundred steamboats, schooners, brigs, sloops, lighters and whaleboats . . . carrying forward miners, their tools and their equipment." Those foresighted ones who had brought out their own little flat-bottomed steamboats fired them up and were soon off for Coloma. Some, less fortunate, who had neither boats nor the money for fare—which was based on the amount of baggage, and often ran as high as $200—in desperation put together coffin-shaped skiffs made from three boards, and started to row all the way.

Few of those who went by water failed to record their battles with the "bushels of voracious mosquitoes." Wrote one: "It seemed as if there were a stratum of swarming insect life ten feet over the surface of the earth. I corded my trousers tight to my bootlegs to keep them from pulling up, donned a thick coat, though the heat was intolerable, shielded my face and neck with handkerchiefs, and put on buckskin gloves, and in that condition parboiled and smothered. In spite of all precautions our faces were much swollen with the poison of numberless bites."

It was claimed that if a man raised his hat on a stick and then gently withdrew the prop, the hat would float in midair, buoyed by the swarms of mosquitoes that clung to it.

On the tree-lined banks above Sutter's embarcadero, an infant city now stood—Sacramento City, "the Metropolis of the Valley," as its backers promised. The first survey had been made in December 1848 while John Sutter was snowbound at Coloma. Sam Brannan, whose brainchild it was, planned to lay it out between the fort and the Sacramento riverfront. Sutter had long opposed building a town there because, as he said, the land except where his fort stood was low and subject to flooding with any abnormal rise in the American.

Taking advantage of his absence, Brannan had no trouble convincing John Sutter, Jr., who had joined his father the previous summer and taken over management of his business affairs, that this sale of land for city lots would provide a quick and certain revenue. The young man, who held his father's power of attorney, agreed, and the first lots were sold in January

1849; before the month was out, the first frame building had been put up. In February, Brannan built a store and moved his business from the fort. By June, the town could boast a hundred log cabins, countless calico shanties and tents, and the pretentious City Hotel, built in part from the frame of Sutter's gristmill, bought for $10,000 and rafted downriver.

On October 18, 1849, the Eagle Theatre, the first American theater to be built in California expressly for this purpose, opened on Front Street, two doors down from the City Hotel, with a professional performance (likewise a first) of *The Bandit Chief; or, Forest Spectre*. The metal-roofed canvas structure had cost $75,000, for the price of canvas was $1 a yard, and those ex-sailors who sewed it together were paid $16 a day.

Admission to the boxes was $3, and to the pit, $2; tickets were purchased by pouring gold dust into the treasurer's scales, at the bar. Entrance to the gallery was by means of a stepladder on the outside.

A press notice reads that on opening night the "dress circle was graced by quite a number of fine-looking, well-costumed ladies, the sight of whom was revivifying."

But the American River was no respecter of persons or places, and one night after a storm in the mountains it began to rise, and "before the first piece was over, the water commenced to make its appearance through the cracks of the floor and by the time the second piece had got fairly under way, so deep had the water become that the 'groundlings' were forced to stand on the benches." After two and a half months the Eagle closed because of "excessive wetness."

The Coloma Road was no longer a swath through the wilderness, for to either side of it were cities—paper cities for the most part—laid out by speculators who counted on their becoming bustling commercial centers for the mines.

After leaving the fort, the traveler came first to Boston, whose proprietor, Hiram Grimes, envisioned it soon rivaling its New England namesake. A passing Argonaut of 1849 noticed that it was already subdivided into lots that were selling quickly, and that large areas had been set aside for parks, schools, churches, and public buildings. It had the distinct advantage over its rivals of being on the north bank of the American, right along the road to the mines. But within a few years Boston was merely a memory.

On the opposite side of the river, a few miles east of the fort, was the town of Brighton. Since its chief proprietor was a sporting man, a racecourse was laid out and stables put up first of all. But Brighton did not fare as well as Boston; by 1852 it was abandoned, although its one hotel, the Five Mile House, remained a popular stopping place for a number of years more.

But this was an era of venture, and men were not easily daunted, so still another city, Norristown, was established just north of Brighton. And, as if this were not enough, one more, called Hoboken, a mile east of Brighton. The great flood of December 1852 gave Hoboken a promising start, for high water cut off Sacramento City from its mountain trade, and merchants in desperation moved their stores and warehouses to the new town. Steamboats made four round trips daily between cities, and during the first two weeks of trade, $80,000 in gold was shipped to Sacramento. Seventy business houses had been opened in Hoboken, and its backers saw its future well established.

For nearly two months the new settlement could claim a population of fifteen hundred. But then the rains stopped, the sun came out, the roads into Sacramento opened again, and Hoboken was soon deserted.

Cities were not the only attraction for wayfarers along this road. Every hollow and spreading tree, every spring and dell along both sides of the trace were marked with grogshops and eating houses, usually nothing more pretentious than a canvas or brush shelter adorned with a large and flamboyant sign announcing that this was The Willow Springs House, The Red

Mountain House, or The Rising Sun House. Later many of these became more permanent in structure, and a few may be found along this old route today.

For the first time in its history the United States became intensely speed conscious as men fretted about getting to the goldfields before they were exhausted. This impatience led to the building of the large fleet of clipper ships that was to rank the country first among maritime nations of the world.

Rufus Porter, a Massachusetts painter, musician, editor, founder of the *Scientific American*, and originator of many time- and labor-saving devices, had invented a power-driven airship, and exhibited a working model in 1847. With the coming of the Gold Rush he saw this as the answer for rapid transportation, and wrote a pamphlet expressly for Argonauts, describing in detail his "Aerial Transport," in which fifty passengers could be carried "pleasantly and safely from New York to California in three days." The fare was $50 including board. Among the safety devices provided were pontoons on the cabin and a parachute for every passenger.

But Porter was too far in advance of his time for the general public to take him seriously, and few men were farsighted enough to invest capital in his venture. R. Porter & Co. failed before the airship was finished.

By mid-January 1850 many companies were advertising express lines to take passengers to the California mines. Fare was $200, payable in advance; passengers were not expected to furnish any part of their outfit—except firearms. The most comfortable light spring wagons drawn by four surefooted mules would be used; drivers were experienced—all of them had crossed the plains at least once (one company made much of having a driver who had "performed a through trip seven times"). "Apply soon, if you want a pleasant trip to the Gold Region."

A few years later an extraordinary plan to expedite travel to California was promoted with Congress's blessing. Called the "Lightning Dromedary Express," it was scheduled to cover the distance in fifteen days. But the trails over the Arizona and Nevada deserts proved too rugged for the animals, and their personalities too complex for Americans to fathom. "Hi Jolly" (a corruption of Hadji Ali) and "Greek George," two drivers imported with them, turned out to be about the only men who could manage them. The experiment turned into a costly and dismal failure.

Sutter's position at the time of the gold discovery afforded him an unequaled opportunity to amass enormous wealth, and for a time the gold did flow freely into his hands. But then his luck changed, and every enterprise he undertook failed. Instead of reaping large profits from the land sold for Sacramento City lots, the agents he appointed to handle sales swindled him at every turn and founded fortunes for themselves. Sutterville, the town he had established and invested in so heavily, was soon eclipsed by Sam Brannan's new city, and in 1849 it was abandoned. The sawmill at Coloma closed down and the retail store he opened there, which should have brought him riches, foundered. He seemed either unable or unwilling to cope with the shrewd interlopers from the States, those "sharp-visaged Yankees, in straw hats and loose frocks," whose keen, competitive practices were foreign and distasteful to him. Like a man who feels he has outlived his time, he lost interest in the fort and neglected its affairs.

In March 1849, in an attempt to escape the new order, he moved from the fort. Taking along those Indians who had been with him since his arrival in the valley, his personal property and livestock, he and his son went to live at the Hock Farm which he had laid out along the Feather River in 1842, had planted to peach orchards and gardens, and named for the large village of Hok Indians on the land. In the "fine mansion" John Bidwell had built for him overlooking the river, he settled down to the life of a country squire and sent for the rest of his family to come from Switzerland.

More and more merchants seeing the business trend, moved from the fort to Sacramento City, which was fast fulfilling Brannan's prophecies and would ultimately become California's capital. Sutter's famous stronghold on the American River should have continued to be a bustling mart and stopping place for the thousands of men who took the Coloma Road. Instead it became a rendezvous for ruffians, a hideout for criminals, and "a gambling and drinking hell." Those rooms which had given shelter to so many destitute emigrants were infested with rats, fleas, lice, and other vermin, and the courtyard littered with broken wine and liquor bottles and trash of all kinds—even "bullock's heads with horns on 'em, fly-blown and decaying." By the fall of 1849 the fort's adobe walls, untended, were fast crumbling into dust, a fitting symbol for the fate of Sutter's empire, destined so soon to collapse.

But the river was unchanged. A gold seeker tramping along the Coloma Road that fall stopped to admire the purity of its waters—clear, sparkling, and swarming with fish—and to note the flocks of mallard, widgeon, and teal bobbing on its bright surface, and the number of deer and elk feeding in the riverside meadows. Above the chatter of the waterfowl he became suddenly aware of yet another wild sound and, looking up, saw clouds of geese heading south, cleaving the air with their cries. As he watched, they swooped down, and he could hear the whir of their wings and feel their wind as they settled among the tall reeds in the shallows and the waving grasses of the plains.

13

The Manner of Men They Were

THEY WERE nearly all young, and they came from all parts of the world. They arrived at the diggings full of hope and enthusiasm, expecting to stay just a short while and return home laden with riches. Some came in their patent leather boots, silk hats, and kid gloves; *they* expected to unfold their canvas stools beside the river and pick up nuggets by the pailful, without ever soiling their clothes.

All of them tried mining, some only for a day or two. Then, having seen the elephant, head and tail, they were ready to give up. "Mining is hard work and the constant exposure, severe; digging dirt, rolling heavy stones, rocking the cradle, and standing in cold water up to your knees in a scorching sun all day, is enough to kill anyone," a forty-niner reported to his wife. "Miners must have strength, patience, and perseverance or else they will not succeed."

But most of them kept at it, tramping along the river, prospecting at every bar and ravine, every tributary creek and wash, for mining was like a lottery, chancy and exciting: fortunes were made daily, and who knew when the pick might turn up a pocket of nuggets.

Those who left in disgust either went back home or found easier ways of making money. Most anything a man put his hand to paid well, and so they opened dry goods and grocery stores, butcher shops, saloons, gambling halls, bowling alleys,

hotels, boardinghouses, and restaurants; and they did teaming
and blacksmithing, and set up ferries at river crossings, using
the beds of wagons that had come over the plains, or old
ships' boats from vessels beached and deserted at Sacramento
City. It is of record that this business was so brisk, one ferry-
man on the American's Middle Fork cleared $60,000 in his
first year.

A few came up with more novel livelihoods, like the ingenious
party who made a tidy fortune producing what he called "Ex-
celsior Hair," derived from the coarse outer fibers of the soap-
plant bulb and sold as a substitute for horsehair in mattresses
and upholstery.

Gold seekers were a restless crew, incurable nomads, constantly on the move in search of El Dorado. Even those who
found paying claims spent more of their time prospecting for
still better ones than they did working what they had. No
breeze of rumor went unheeded, no tale of a rich strike was
too fantastic for belief. In the summer of 1849 they went
stampeding over the ridges to Truckee Lake where fabulously
rich placers were said to have been found, and the next season
they were chasing another will-o'-the-wisp—a mountain of
silver. But the most marvelous story of all in this marvelous land
was the discovery of Gold Lake, whose shores were literally
covered with pebbles of gold. Thousands of men abandoned
everything and flocked into the high Sierra where it was supposed to lie, some hundred miles northeast of the American.
Although the search was long and careful, for few were willing
to abandon such a prize, no one ever found it.

A miner at work on a paying claim near Coloma tells of his
reaction to the first reports of the wealth of the Middle Fork,
where gold "of the finest quality" was said to line the river
"in large pockets and huge bulky masses."

"One and two hundred dollars was not considered a great
day's labour, and now was the time to take advantage of its
pristine richness. The news was too blooming for me to with-

stand. I threw down my pickaxe, and leaving a half-wrought crevice for some other digger to work out, I packed up. . . ."

Into these new diggings they flocked from other camps—"almost one continuous stream of men," and every foot of ground was soon claimed. The riverbank or bar sprang to life with tents and brush shelters, and within a matter of weeks there was a camp, its meandering main street lined with stores, gambling saloons, boardinghouses (charge: one ounce per week); bowling alleys where a man might roll three balls for a quarter; and dance halls with squeaking violins.

Then over the ridges and down the steep trails the supply trains would come with jingling bells and brightly colored trappings. The canyons echoed with the cries of the Mexican muleteers, urging their animals on with "Upa! Mula! Arriba! Arriba!"

The miners built their first towns flimsily out of canvas and calico and basketwork brush, and with good reason, for as suddenly as it had risen, such a camp might one day stand empty, as miners, heeding tales of some new and richer strike, left it to a man. Then, as if by magic, such a deserted camp would come alive again with a new tide of gold seekers. Old working places were reopened, and the river canyon would echo once more with the ring of pick and crowbar, and the hum of voices.

Gamblers and saloonkeepers would pitch their round tents, and merchants set up their brush shelters. Rich new deposits were frequently found by this next flood of prospectors, sometimes extensive enough to give the settlement permanence. But many of these camps never experienced a rebirth, and in less than three years after the gold discovery it was noted that California seemed much older than its parent country because it already possessed so many ruins and deserted villages.

Bars and ravines that were supposed to be worked out had a way of proving rich again beyond the wildest dreams. An Irishman decided one day to try his luck in a ravine that had long been given up as worthless. Digging down some six feet, he struck a hard white clay which the gold could not penetrate. Washing this, he took out $100 the first day. The news spread, and the crowds poured in, and before the week was over some $15,000 had been taken out—with one lump that weighed twenty-eight ounces and was worth $448.

Ignorance of the geologic formation of the area led to belief in a Mother Lode that kept men always on the hunt. It was thought that the gold found in the river, thrown out in the old days of volcanic activity, was only a fraction of what still lay hidden somewhere in the heart of the Sierra, and each man hoped to be the first to find this treasure-house.

Reports of lost mines of untold wealth held them in thrall, and years were spent combing the wilderness for clues. On the North Fork American, two German prospectors found their fortune in a vein. After putting up a cabin, they set off for Iowa Hill to buy supplies. But on the way back they lost the trail in that maze of thickly forested ridges and rocky canyons, so typical of this region. Three weeks were spent hunting for the cabin, and in the end they turned up again at Iowa Hill. Here they told their story, and several parties volunteered to help them. Although the search went on for months, no one picked up the trail. The story of the Lost Cabin Mine became a part of the river's lore and kept men on a mad chase for years; but as far as is known, they never found it.

Few fortunes were made by those who were constantly at rumor's beck and call; most of them made little more than what it took to live at a time when a dozen sardines cost $35, and a fine-tooth comb, $6. Many of them panned as little as fifty cents a day, and some of these, experiencing hunger, sickness, and disappointment beyond endurance, took their lives. By the end of 1854 there were fourteen hundred recorded suicides. Others, unable to stand the strain of the constant excitement with its extremes in fortune, went insane. The hardy kept on roving, in semibeggary, gay and careless.

The thrill of discovery has been preserved in the journal of a miner working near the South Fork:

> Pick, shovel and bar did their duty, and I soon had a large rock in view. Getting down into the excavation . . . and seating myself upon the rock, I commenced a careful search for a crevice, and at last found one extending longitudinally. . . . It appeared to be filled with a hard, bluish clay and gravel, which I took out with my knife, and there at the bottom, strewn along the whole length of the rock, was bright yellow gold, in little pieces about the size and shape of a grain of barley. Eureka! Oh how my heart beat! I sat still and looked at it some minutes before I touched it, greedily drinking in the pleasure of gazing upon gold that was in my very grasp, and feeling a sort of independent bravado in allowing it to remain there. When my eyes were sufficiently feasted, I scooped it out with the point of my knife and an iron spoon. . . .

Weighing it at camp, he found that he was $31 richer.

Any miner finding a promising deposit made the most of it while he could, knowing that within twenty-four hours the secret was usually out. "The fox-hound's scent for its prey is not keener than that of a miner for gold," it was said. One prospector on the South Fork, who found a pocket that yielded $90 at the end of the first day, took every precaution to keep his discovery secret from his messmates. As far as he knew he had aroused no suspicions that night, and in the morning was careful to slip off before the others were awake. But close to noon, in looking out of his hole he saw that he was "surrounded by twenty good stout fellows all equipped with their implements of labour. I could say nothing . . . in three days the little ravine, which I had so fondly hoped would be my own . . . was turned completely upside down. About ten thousand dollars of gold dust was extracted from it, from which I realized a little over a thousand."

New diggings were sometimes discovered under odd circumstances. Once when a miner who was greatly respected by his fellows died, it was decided to give him a regular funeral. A prospector in a neighboring camp, who had the reputation of having been a "powerful" preacher in the States, was called in. After taking drinks all around, the funeral party filed out solemnly to the grave, dug just beyond camp. The coffin was lowered, the minister began an extempore prayer, and the mourners fell to their knees. But the parson having got under way could not seem to bring himself to a halt, and the prayer dragged on. At last, one of the company growing impatient, began idly fingering the earth. Suddenly he gasped, and a murmur of excitement ran through the crowd as others saw, too, that the earth was filled with shining flakes of gold. The preacher stopped, and looking down asked, "Boys, what's that?" Then stooping for a closer inspection, exclaimed: "Gold! and the richest kind of diggings! Congregation dismissed!"

The miner was removed from his grave and hastily buried elsewhere, and the funeral party, with the parson in the lead, hurried back to work the new placer.

Necromancy has long been associated with the search for gold, and many California miners used magical words and spells and devices that were believed infallible if worked with proper ceremonies. Most of the rites were practiced in secret, but many of the instruments saw the light. These were chiefly variations of magnets and pointers, one of the most popular being the hazel fork used to find water. In the hands of a qualified person it was supposed to pull down when passing over auriferous ground.

Other men had implicit faith in the potency of signs: good luck was sure to follow seeing the new moon over the left shoulder, or dreaming about finding a hen's nest full of eggs, or of killing a snake.

In the days of shaft mining, Cornishmen conjured up Tommy-knockers, those little people who tapped the walls and timbering with their tiny hammers to make sure they were sound. As long as the knocking was gentle, the miner knew he was safe, but as soon as it became loud and insistent, he had to keep a sharp lookout for cave-ins and falling rock.

The miner is pictured as uniform in dress: red flannel shirt, neckerchief of green, yellow, or blue; corduroy trousers stuffed into highwater boots; broad slouch hats called "wide-awakes," and beards and hair "emancipated from thralldom" and reveling in "long and bushy tufts."

But for the first year or two dress was as various as the faces: Englishmen in shooting coats; Yankees in black suits; New Yorkers and Southerners in the latest Paris fashions; mountaineers in fringed buckskin; sailors in sea clothes; frontier farmers in homespun shirts and long-tailed surtouts of frieze; Europeans in short jackets and tight trousers of many colors, armed with swords, and wearing all manner of headgear—red Polish caps edged with fur, blue Dutch caps with china knobs, peaked caps and square caps of red and green, and hunting hats with tufts of feathers in the band—Spaniards in ruffled shirts, velveteen trousers, and glazed hats; Mexicans in sombreros and striped serapes of red and black; Chinese, Malays, Moors, and turbaned Turks and Hindus, all in native dress.

Men from the States wore their clothes from home until they were in shreds, holding them together with patches. Trousers, which bore the brunt of abuse, were often so grotesquely metamorphosed, it required a strong memory to recall them in their pristine state. Flour sacks were a favorite recourse, after their contents had sustained the inner man. It has been told how "two gentlemen of respectability" lost their identities through the labels borne conspicuously on their trouser seats; they were known to the camp in all seriousness as "Genesee Mills" and "Eagle Brand." The patch on the seat was a badge of integrity, as well recognized and respected as the star of the Order of the Garter, it was claimed.

After the rags from home finally dissolved, men took to wearing anything that whim suggested, conventions having been so far flung aside that "no man could make his appearance sufficiently *bizarre* to attract any attention." A kind of foppery appeared among a certain class of diggers who sported "brilliant red shirts, boots with flaming tops, fancy-coloured hats, silver-handled bowie-knives, and rich silk sashes." But miners in general made a resolute stand against dandyism. It was excused in gamblers who adopted the Californian style of dress—ruffled white shirt, scarlet sash, shiny top boots, diamond studs, watch chain of "native gold specimens," and broad glazed hat with a tuft of feathers or a squirrel's tail tucked into the band, as a badge of their profession.

But every miner, whether he wore his patched clothes from home or allowed his fancy free reign, after a short stay in the diggings, acquired a manner that would have identified him anywhere in the world as the California gold seeker.

One distinguishing trait was vigor and exuberance. Like boys escaped from school and freed from all supervision and restraint, they yielded to impulse. Moderation was not a virtue consonant with the new environment. With a gay abandon, defying all precedents, they named their camps Rat-Trap Slide, Hell's Half Acre, Drunkard's Bar, Deadman's Hollow, Milk Punch Bar, and Hell-for-Noon City. The poet Bayard Taylor, touring the mines, was not amused; in his opinion these were "the most condemnable names which a beastly imagination ever invented. . . . What a field the future poets of California will have! Fancy one of them singing:

> When in Shirt-Tail cañon buds the grove,
> And larks are singing in Hell's Delight,
> To Ground Hog's Glory I'll come, my love,
> And sing at thy lattice by night!"

In no other part of the world, it is claimed, did men drink more deeply, gamble more heavily, or swear more mightily—attributes not limited to the adult population. Boys "from six upward" were to be seen "swaggering through the streets, begirt with scarlet sash, in exuberant collar and bosom, segar in mouth, uttering huge oaths, and occasionally treating men and boys at the bars."

When the mother of such an infant prodigy was asked why she did not keep her son from this "premature mannishness," she said that he washed his own gold and spent his earnings as he pleased. Further, every other boy in camp was doing the same, and it was impossible to stop one.

In a gambling saloon in Coloma one Sunday, a "curly-headed boy, whose mouth was little above the level of the bank," coolly threw down his full buckskin bag on the ace and announced in piping tones: "I'll break that bank or it'll break me!"

He then went on to play with all the skill of a veteran, and was soon raking in his winnings as carelessly as though the stacks of dollars were chips. As the pile of coin in front of him grew, he became the hero of the table, all other players regulating their bets by his. In the end he lost everything, and saw his well-filled purse stowed away with many others in a large Chinese box.

Whistling "O Californy," he turned his back on the scene and strutted out. One miner touched by this show of courage, followed him into the street, and offered him a part of his own purse. The boy looked around cautiously, and seeing no one near, said in a whisper: "Mum's the word; I believe you're a good egg! You want to know how much was in that bag? Well, I'll tell you; just four pounds of duck-shot mixed,—and—nothing more; what a swa'rin' and a cussin' when they open it!" and he turned and scampered off.

Argonauts as a class were devoid of sentimentality, as opposed to sentiment, and took delight in stripping their speech of what they called "tawdry finery." New idiom forged through intent or ignorance, and by the amalgamation of people from all parts of the Union, served to vitalize the language. Grotesque exaggeration or understatement, and awareness of the effect of anticlimax, gave their speech and storytelling a new impact and humor, as seen in the writings of Mark Twain, Dan De Quille, Bret Harte, and J. Ross Browne.

Even their toasts were typical: "Here's at you!" "Here's the hair off your head!" "Here's another nail in your coffin!"

Swearing reached heights and proportions of imaginative invention and prodigality never before attained. It was adopted as a fine art, and the miner aimed at preeminence. The character of a man was nowhere more clearly defined than in the quantity and quality of his oaths. Newcomers, unaccustomed to this strong language, were frequently misled as to the purport of a conversation and, supposing the participants to be furiously angry, expected them any moment to draw their knives and pistols and start killing one another.

Usually the first place of business to open in a new camp was the saloon, often nothing more pretentious than a keg set on blocks under a brush shelter. But as the camp grew, it became the most conspicuous place there. Every luxury connected with drinking was found in the diggings, and hardly a drink in the world was too rare or costly for importation.

No miner ever thought of drinking alone in a saloon and, on entering, looked around for friends, or strangers, whom he could call over to join him. After he had gathered at least twenty, and each was supplied with a glass, he would say, "Here's at you, gentlemen!" or perhaps "Here's another nail in your coffin!" and back would go the twenty heads, and down would go the Queen Charlottes, Stonewalls, Sulky Sangarees, Vox Populi, Deacons, Moral 'Suasions, and One-Eyed Joes.

Drinking was so general, even stores served liquor. On entering, one usually found the proprietor sitting on an empty keg at a rickety table playing seven-up with a customer for drinks; and yet everyone who was in the mines attests that there were no habitual drunkards.

Still, the temperance movement swept through the camps like an epidemic. Representatives were there as early as 1849 making converts, and the following year chapters of The Total Abstinence Society were opened. The Sons of Temperance came next and were soon boasting some twelve thousand members, including gold seekers who lived at Drunkard's Bar, Whiskey Hill, and Delirium Tremens. These were both national organizations. The Dashaway Association was California-born. Members took the pledge to "dash away" the use of alcoholic beverages. It became fashionable to join this society, and membership grew rapidly. The Dashaways were soon building halls and opening chapter rooms, presenting lavish "Moral Dramas," and persuading noted actors, musicians, and lecturers to appear in behalf of the cause.

The gambling hall was usually part of the saloon. The bar, with its glittering mirrors and rows of shiny bottles and glasses, stood against one wall, while scattered about the room were tables covered with blue or green baize, and comfortable chairs where miners could sit and smoke and drink, and play cards for money or liquor. One or two long tables in the middle of the room were presided over by professional gamblers.

Faro and monte were the most popular games, the former the favorite with systematic gamblers and heavy bettors. Stakes as high as $45,000 were sometimes placed on the turn of a single card. For those who preferred betting from fifty cents to five dollars, there was rondo, roulette, twenty-one, rouge-et-noir, and a number of small games played with dice and lumped together as "chuck-a-luck."

Mining proved the great leveler, crumbling all preconceived notions of class distinction. Since the work involved was physical rather than mental, the old superiority of headworkers over handworkers did not exist. There was never a question of dignity involved in the tasks men turned to. One distinguished judge drove an oxteam regularly between Sacramento and Coloma; a former senator built up a profitable business making gold rockers; an ex-governor played the fiddle in a gambling saloon; a noted French journalist turned bootblack, while a distinguished British scholar took up fishmongering, peddling fresh salmon from camp to camp. To work with the hands assumed the respectability of an older day when the country's founding fathers prided themselves on being farmers and artisans.

Although the miner was generally unsentimental, his heart was quickly touched, and his generosity was spontaneous, although because of his peculiar circumstances, appreciation of merits nearly always took a pecuniary form. Even professional gamblers were noted for magnanimity. The banker at the gaming table was instructed to keep a small tin cup in which to deposit all silver coins under a half-dollar. This small change was termed "chicken feed," and "when anybody came in looking hungry or thirsty, and seemingly in want of means . . . the banker would dive into the tin cup and take from it a dollar or more which he would hand to the stranger that he might get relief."

In September 1849, a Mrs. Stuart and her grown daughters (who were "the first young ladies to come to the mines") reached Old Dry Diggins. Mr. Stuart had died in crossing the Plains, and Mrs. Stuart, now finding herself destitute and "a stranger among strangers," decided she must find a way to return to their home in Illinois. Someone mentioned her plight in a gambling house, and the proprietor, "Lucky Bill," overhearing, said: "If Mrs. Stuart wishes to return East with her daughters, she shall go." He then passed his hat around among the gamblers in all the other houses; collecting $1,500, he soon had the Stuart family on its way home.

The miner was remarkable for his particular tenderness toward children, who remained a rarity in the mines for several years. At Georgetown, a thriving camp on the ridge south of the Middle Fork, the five-year-old daughter of a tavernkeeper so charmed the miners with her graces, her father's establishment proved a bonanza; it was crowded to the door each day by those who came as much to see the pretty child and listen to her prattle as they did to satisfy the inner man. As an expression of their regard they made up a purse and presented her with a pint of nuggets. Just the sight of a pretty, clean, well-mannered child would bring tears to their eyes, and many an appealing girl or boy would be followed in the streets and showered with gold or coin.

In the summer of 1848 a lad of sixteen came limping into a little ravine where some thirty miners were at work. The day was hot, and the boy tired, hungry, and penniless. He sat down to rest and watch them, his peaked face plainly telling his story. He was not unobserved. At last one of the miners, nodding toward him, said quietly to his companions: "Boys, I'll work one hour for that chap if you will." It was agreed, and at the end of an hour $100 in gold was poured into his handkerchief. Giving him a list of tools and supplies, they told him: "Now you go and buy these, and come back. We'll have a good claim staked out for you. But after that, son, you've got to paddle for yourself."

The relative ease with which a man might earn a good living or dig out gold made robbery almost unknown in the camps of 1848 and early 1849. It was easier to work than to steal. Further, the orderly element was in the majority, and the few scamps who were there were kept in line by swift and severe punishment for all offenses.

"I felt as secure in my tent with the curtain tied in front, as I had formerly with locked and bolted doors," Mrs. Sarah Royce was able to write of her camp near Old Dry Diggins. She tells of seeing buckskin purses of gold left lying in perfect safety beside the trail, while their owners worked down by the stream.

"We lie down at night with our goods scattered around and $3000 to $4000 in gold dust in a valise or box. It is much safer here than at home," a miner wrote his family. During the day this gold was left in camp, unguarded.

But among the hordes of gold seekers who began pouring in from the summer of 1849 onward, were "a parcel of the veriest rogues and ruffians" whose blemished reputations at home had sent them packing, and who saw in California's interregnum a fertile field for operations.

From this time on, every man, having to be prepared to defend himself or his property, went armed. By 1854, Californians had invested $6 million in bowie knives and pistols, and by then forty-two hundred murders had been committed. A pistol was never drawn in bravado; once in hand, a man had to use it quickly or expect to be laid low by his adversary's bullet.

Shooting on sight was much in vogue, and "I mistook you for another," a frequent and often anticlimactic apology to some innocent victim. In the absence of constituted authority, an armed man was expected to take care of himself.

Robbery was a far greater crime than murder in the eyes of men who had come to have a disproportionate regard for the material. The penalty for stealing a man's horse or his gold, or even a ham or a loaf of white sugar, was severe: a flogging, banishment, or death. To kill a man was another matter. A miner's right to avenge his wrongs, or defend himself or his property, was paramount, and many a murderer was freed by a miners' jury on a plea of "justifiable homicide."

The severe winter of 1849–1850 was in itself a social agent. Unbroken weeks of snow, rain, and river floods drove thousands of destitute miners out of the mountains and into the cities and towns. On January 9, 1850, the American's North Fork rose sixty feet and swept away flumes, dams, cabins, tents, food, blankets, everything and all, leaving hundreds of men homeless and hungry, and robbing them even of the means of livelihood. This devastation was repeated on all forks of the American, and on most of the other Sierran gold rivers.

Once the men got to town they found almost no work, and many took to stealing in order to survive. Of these, a good many made the discovery that a life of crime was far easier and more remunerative than mining, and they organized themselves into bands "with secret signs, passwords, and grips." When spring came and the diggings opened, these men flocked back to the rivers to rob sluice boxes, bullion trains, expressmen, storekeepers, and individual miners. Other bands found it more profitable to steal horses and cattle from the great herds that roamed the lands of Sutter and Sinclair and other pioneers. This larceny was carried on with as much system and enterprise as a legitimate business. In the spring of 1850, five men who had formed a company cleared $60,000 by supplying the Sacramento market with Sutter's beef.

The ever-moving current of life in the mines favored the criminal. The new arrival in camp was never questioned; his right to talk about himself or not was fully respected.

Most men knew each other only as Jim, or Pete, or Joe, or those nicknames given because of some physical characteristic or place of origin. Nearly every camp had its Big and Little Yank, its Scotty, Kentuck, Red, Dutch, Shorty, and Old and Young Pike.

It took months of intimacy to ask a partner his full name or anything about his past life. Still, unasked questions and unsatisfied curiosity were bound to nag, as this sly jingle implies:

> *O what was your name in the States?*
> *Was it Thompson, or Johnson, or Bates?*
> *Did you murder your wife*
> *And fly for your life?*
> *Say, what was your name in the States?*

Bell's Store
Coloma

14

Camp and Town

WITH THE COMING of the first rains in late October, the miner who had made a rich strike and had no thought of moving on for a while, usually put up a cabin with the help of his messmates. It was soon built from the materials at hand—stone, mud, or logs; the ground served as a floor, while the roof was made of most anything: clapboards, rough shakes, rawhide, brush, or canvas. One prospector tells of seeing roofs of "floursacks, cast-off shirts, and pantaloons, all sewed together like a homemade quilt."

Only with the fireplace and chimney was any care taken, for mining in the river meant wet clothes, and in winter a rousing fire was a necessity. Chimneys, too, were made from a variety of materials—stone, scraps of sheet iron, mud, wood, whiskey barrels, and even canvas.

Interior arrangements were kept simple. Bunks were made by nailing sacks or canvas from the walls to upright log frames; bracken or straw served as a comfortable and easily renewable mattress. A table fashioned from a few rough boards—or, in the case of those who had crossed the plains, from the tailgate of the wagon—was nailed to the wall. A bench, or blocks of wood, served as seats, while an open pickle or candle box that had rounded the Horn made an adequate cupboard in which to keep a few forks and spoons, tin plates and cups, and the cans of salt, pepper, and soda. A plank shelf held some old magazines and a book or two, a roll of paper, and pen and ink with which to correspond with the folks at home, and the indispensable flask and tobacco jar.

Pegs projecting from every convenient crack held bunches of onions and flitches of bacon, old boots, hats, and shirts. Above the fireplace hung the frying pan and coffeepot. In one corner stood the trusty rifle, and in another the sack of flour, bag of coffee beans, and water bucket.

The gold pan was the utensil of all work, serving also as mixing bowl, baking tin, and wash basin for clothes—and, occasionally, dishes. Dishes were washed only by the overnice, we are told. Sometimes a little hot coffee was poured over a plate to take off the last-formed grease, or it might be scoured with a handful of dry earth or a tuft of grass. But there was no time to wash up after breakfast, a forty-niner explains, and the workday was so long and everyone so hungry, supper could not be delayed to clean up. So dishes were left from meal to meal, each man consoling himself with the knowledge that he was eating only his own dirt.

Sunset brought the miners filing back to camp. Up from the river and out of the ravines they poured, gathering wood along the way for the kitchen fire, which in summer was lighted out-of-doors. Cooking was sometimes done turn-about for a week; at other times it fell to the lot of the best-natured man in the mess, the others chopping wood and toting water by way of offset.

One camp cook has described his summer kitchen set up under a spreading oak at Condemned Bar. On one limb hung a piece of preserved pork and a mackerel, "more salt than meat." From another dangled a corned rib of beef, a long-handled frying pan, a tea kettle, towel, and an old candle box holding the dishes. Notches in the trunk were handy places to stow the salt and pepper, beans, coffee, and flour, he found. The fireplace, the heart of his realm, consisted merely of "a big rock with two large stones for andirons."

There was little variety in the miner's diet: slapjacks, stewed beans, salt pork, and bread, served an average of twenty-one times a week. As a bit of a change, there might be flour dumplings boiled into an indigestible mass in plain water and eaten with molasses. Many a miner, after a brief stay "left California for his home with more dyspepsia than gold," it was remembered.

As to their bread, much has been written about it. At first every kind but good bread was made. Recalling that their mothers and wives put in soda, they put in soda in varying amounts with variable results; most of the time it tasted little better than "saleratus slightly corrected with flour." Some of them had brought along dried yeast, and tried leavened bread, but the result was just as disappointing.

Experience taught them that sourdough made the best and most reliable bread, so most camp cooks kept at hand a can of the bubbling flour and water mixture. When set in the sun this dough rose quickly, and when the soda was rightly proportioned, the bread was at least palatable.

Sourdough was stirred in the gold pan and shaped with the hands into a large flat cake. After it had risen, it was put in a frying pan and set in front of the fire to bake, being turned as soon as one side had browned. Sometimes a regular loaf was made. Then a hole about three feet square was dug and half-filled with stones, and a fire built in the bottom. By the time the wood had burned down to a bed of coals, the loaf was ready. The coals were raked aside, the loaf set in the gold pan was placed on the hot stones, and another gold pan turned over it. Then the whole was covered with live coals, hot ashes, and earth. "In this way is made a loaf that is as sweet as any that ever came out of the oven of the baker," one gold seeker remembers.

New Englanders used the same method for baking beans. Half a peck of soaked beans, one cup of molasses, and half a pound of salt pork were put into a covered iron pot, and smothered with coals and earth at bedtime. By morning they were "perfectly done and delicious, so good that half of the miners here are after the Yankee beans, or the mode of cooking them."

Slapjacks, for which the miner was famed, were made with either sour or straight dough, but with a little more water to make a thinner batter. He who could not turn his slapjack without the aid of a knife was considered a rank greenhorn. The proper way was to shuffle the cake about in the pan until loosened, then toss it in the air and catch it batterside down as it descended.

I once had a partner whose one dream of life it was to be able to turn a slapjack in this way [wrote Dan De Quille]. One day while in the cabin cooking slapjacks, he announced that he would turn one in the air or die. He was a man who weighed about one hundred and eighty pounds and had somehow got it into his head that in order to perform the feat successfully a great outlay of strength was required.

Taking hold of the handle of the frying-pan with both hands and getting out in the middle of the floor, where he could have plenty of room, he hustled the cake about in the pan until he found it was loose on all sides. He then squatted nearly to the floor and, giving it a mighty heave, sent the pancake flying upward. This done, he stood, frying-pan in hand, waiting for the cake to come down in order that he might catch it. But that pancake never came down; it stuck against the ceiling . . . as fast as a wafer on a love-letter!

A good many miners became expert cooks by practice, and necessity was responsible for some successful innovations.

Think of using a dry-goods box for an oven and baking a pig, or a shoulder of mutton in it! [wrote a forty-niner] No trick at all. Drive down a stake or two, and on them make a small scaffold, on which you place your roast; now build a very small fire of hard wood, at such a distance away that a moderate sized dry-goods box will cover it all, and your arrangements are complete. The fire will need replenishing once or twice, and in two or three hours, according to the size of your roast, you may take it out, done in a rich gold color, with a flavor unattainable by any other method.

Steaks were often broiled before the fire, he tells us, or smothered in a covering of dough and baked like a batch of biscuit, to make a delicious kind of meat pie.

After supper men gathered around the campfire to light up their pipes and talk about the latest rumors of rich strikes; or listen to the yarns of some grizzly-bear hunter or Indian fighter, or to the Münchhausen adventures of the old soldier who had been General Scott's right-hand man in Mexico and was responsible for the victory.

Other nights were given over to cards, singing, or music. Many men brought their instruments with them, "and often at night could be heard echoing from the ravines and cañons, the sounds of fiddle, flute, accordian, and clarionet." One young man who had brought his bugle climbed to the top of a hill above Old Dry Diggins on a moonlit night and gave the camp a long-remembered serenade with "Oft in the Stilly Night," "The Emigrant's Lament," and "The Star Spangled Banner."

Dancing to the fiddle was another popular pastime. The "Lancers" was the favorite with miners because it gave them the chance to dance with characteristic vigor and abandon. "To go through the 'Lancers' in such company was a very severe gymnastic exercise," observed one who had experienced it.

A few men of quieter disposition spent their evenings writing letters home, making entries in their journals, and reading, although reading material was scarce in 1849–1850. Men who had left home with collections of favorite books usually had to abandon them along the way to lighten the load. One prospector remembers that the only reading material he could turn up in the entire camp was an old *Farmer's Almanac,* for which he had to pay one dollar. During the winter he read it "through and through, forwards and backwards, sideways and upside down, and by spring had acquired such a knowledge of astronomical science, that I could locate the signs of the Zodiac blindfold, stand on my head and calculate an eclipse, [and] foretell the . . . weather for more than ten years ahead."

Once mail steamers began to come regularly they brought consignments of books, and the stores in San Francisco did a thriving trade, mainly in novels, which found a ready market with miners. With the coming of the mail ships, the expressman sprang into being and began bringing newspapers to the camps. There was hardly a gulch too remote for him, and miners felt that next to the trader who furnished sustenance, the expressman was most important. New York, Boston, and New Orleans papers published special "Steamer Editions," designed for California reading. In them were hundreds of items of local interest from all over the States, and men starved for home news read every word.

"Great was the excitement when the yell or horn of the expressman was heard as he was entering some mining camp, crying 'Here's your *Herald* and your *Tribune,* the *Delta* and the *Picayune!*'" Every shovel and pan was dropped as men ran to meet him.

Many miners wintered in camp to work their claims during those periods of sunny weather between storms, which are typical of the season in American River country. But when it did rain or snow, often for a week at a time, they were hard put for something to do. "This weather 'riles' our Yankee friends very much," an English gold hunter observed during a rainy spell. "They want the excitement of work, hunting a deer, hanging an Indian, or lynching a Sydney convict." Much of their time, he complained, was spent in "loafing" from cabin to cabin, "so no one is secure against intrusion." Playing cards for stakes, drinking, reading over old newspapers, and "speculating on the future results of gold-digging" were the chief amusements.

Christmas and the Fourth of July were the two holidays observed in nearly every camp. The New Englander, born in the shadow of Bunker Hill, greeted the dawn of Independence Day by firing off pistols and exploding powder charges in old stumps and logs. In some of the larger settlements, a military company was gotten together, and under the leadership of some Boston man marched through town with flying colors to the tune of "Yankee Doodle." An oration or two was always in order, and the celebration was concluded by blowing up a keg of black powder.

Christmas was a time when the joint efforts of several cooks turned out a rare feast. One miner tells how lucky he and his messmates were to collect a loin of grizzly bear meat, a haunch of venison, a slab of bacon, six bottles of wine, and two pounds of raisins. Each member of the mess then undertook the task he was best fitted for, one agreeing to roast the meats, another to boil the bacon, still another to make short- and sweet bread, and yet one more to make the dried apple pies. The chef d'œuvre of the feast was the plum pudding which a sea captain offered to make ship-fashion.

The chronicler was assigned "to rig out the table, and get the Sheffield in order. I managed my task admirably by means of the front and end boards of the waggon, making legs of willow sticks. . . . A purified waggon-sheet served the purposes of a tablecloth; and, if the cultery did not all match, it was matchless in its peculiar variety, a sufficiency being secured by supplying the carvers with bowie-knives and short swords, in lieu of the more legitimate instrument."

Sunday for the solitary prospector tucked away in Sunny South, Damascus, or Deadwood was usually spent in baking bread for the week, grinding a supply of coffee, washing and patching clothes, and hunting or fishing. But for most miners Sunday meant a trip to town to buy provisions for the week, get their letters from home, visit with friends, drink, gamble, and enjoy the excitement of the scene. There was no need "to dress up in 'store clothes' . . . The 'dress up' consisted of washing the face and hands, taking a fresh cud of fine cut (Mrs. Miller's brand), or donning a clay pipe well stocked," one of them recollected.

A Sunday in Coloma, as described by Charles B. Gillespie, a miner who wrote of what he saw there in 1849, was typical of all the other American River towns. The main street, he says, "was alive with crowds of moving men, passing and repassing, laughing, talking, and all appearing in the best of humor." They were from every land: "Antipodes of color, race, religion, language, government, condition, size, capability, strength and morals were there, within that small village in the mountains of California, all impressed with one purpose—impelled with but one desire."

He noted the continuous din: "Thimble-riggers, French monte dealers, or string-game tricksters were shouting at every corner: 'Six ounces, gentlemen, no one can tell where the little joker is!' or 'Bet on the jack, the jack's the winning card! . . .' or 'Here's the place to get your money back! The veritable string game! Here it goes! Three, six, twelve ounces no one can put his finger in the loop!' "

Rising above this clamor was the shrill voice of the downeast auctioneer, perched on a large box in front of a small booth, disposing of everything "at a bargain." The crowd around him was thick, for miners liked to buy everything at auction, even provisions.

" 'Here's a splendid pair of brand-new boots! cowhide, double-soled, triple-pegged, water-proof boots! The very thing for you, sir, fit your road-smashers exactly; just intended, cut out, made for your mud-splashers alone; going for only four ounces and a half—four and a half! and gone . . . walk up here and weigh out your dust.' "

Then the bargaining began at a furious rate for knives, pans, shovels, picks; hats and caps of every style; coffee, tea, sugar, bacon, flour, and liquors of all grades; within an hour's time the contents of the little grocery were distributed among the crowd.

Walking on up the street, Gillespie came to a large unfinished frame house, the sashless windows and the doorway packed with "a motley crowd." Pushing his way in, he saw a preacher "as ragged and hairy as myself, holding forth to an attentive audience. . . . He spoke well and . . . warmed everyone with his fine and impassioned delivery. He closed with a benediction but prefaced it by saying: 'There will be divine service in this house next Sabbath—if, in the meantime, I hear of no new diggin's!' "

Afterward the congregation filed out solemnly, the greater part directing their steps toward the saloon in the hotel across the street, where at "the gaudy and well-stocked bar . . . four spruce young fellows in shirt-sleeves and flowing collars" were mixing half a dozen drinks at once. Here, too, "there was a perfect babel of noises." At least seven languages were being spoken by the crowds lined up at the bar or standing around the monte and faro tables: "glasses were jingling, money was rattling, and, crowning all, two fiddlers in a distant corner were scraping furiously on their instruments, seemingly the presiding divinities of this variegated pandemonium!"

Shortly before noon the miners began to line up in front of the dining-room door. Just as twelve o'clock struck, it was opened, and with a shout some sixty to eighty men rushed in to scramble for places at the two long tables, covered with snowy cloths and well supplied with platters and bowls of beef, potatoes, beans, salt pork, bread, pickles, coffee, and tea. The unlucky ones had to turn back and take their places again outside the door. There were constant new arrivals, so the crowd waiting for the second table was fully as thick as before.

I saw that to dine at table number two, as I had intended, I must enter into the spirit of the thing, [wrote a British Argonaut] so I elbowed my way into the crowd, and secured a pretty good position behind a tall Kentuckian, who I knew would clear the way for me. . . . Being a stranger I did not know the lay of the tables . . . but immediately on entering, I caught sight of a good-looking roast of beef . . . at which I made a desperate charge. I was not so green as to lose time in trying to get my legs over the bench and sit down, and in so doing perhaps be crowded out altogether; but I seized a knife and fork, with which I took firm hold of my prize, and occupying as much space as possible with my elbows, I gradually insinuated myself into my seat. Without letting go of the beef, I then took a look round, and had the gratification of seeing about a dozen men leaving the room . . . it was a "grab game"—every man for himself.

Charles Gillespie says that after the edge of his appetite had in a measure been ground away, he took time to look up and down the table, and wondered how he happened among

such a collection of uncouth men. . . . There was not a single coat in the whole crowd, and certainly not over half a dozen vests, and neither neckties nor collars. But then, to make amends . . . there were any number and variety of fancy shirts, from the walnut-stained homespun of the Missourian to the embroidered blouse of the . . . Frenchman. . . . And yet many of these men were lawyers and physicians . . . farmers and mechanics from the "States," who now with their long beards and fierce mustaches looked anything else than the quiet citizens they were at home.

Sunday night usually found a miners' ball in progress. It was a strange sight to see a party of long-bearded men, in heavy boots, rough shirts, and slouch hats, their revolvers and bowie knives gleaming at their belts,

> going through the steps and figures of the dance with so much spirit and often with a great deal of grace, hearty enjoyment depicted on their dried-up sunburned faces . . . while a crowd of the same rough-looking customers stood around, cheering them on to greater efforts, and occasionally dancing a step or two, quietly on their own. . . .
>
> The absence of ladies was a difficulty which was very easily overcome, by a simple arrangement whereby it was understood that every gentleman who had a patch on a certain part of his inexpressibles should be considered a lady for the time being. These patches were rather fashionable, and were usually large squares of canvas, showing brightly on a dark ground, so that the "ladies" of the party were as conspicuous as if they had been surrounded by the usual quantity of white muslin.

Other miners tell of the "ladies" wearing handkerchiefs bound on their heads or tied about their arms.

The miner's rugged outdoor life suggests robust health. Actually, there was widespread sickness throughout the camps: pulmonary disorders that were often fatal; diarrhea and dysentery; malaria, scurvy, and periodic epidemics of cholera, which took many lives; rheumatism and sciatica, and numerous skin diseases. The origin of these ailments was in the main traceable to the long hours spent in the river, without adequate protection from the scorching sun; sleeping in wet clothes, for many had no other garments than what they wore daily; the abundance of mosquitoes; the steady diet of fat and salt meat; the lack of vegetables and fruit; and general unsanitary practices. Many men were known never to have undressed or put on clean clothing since leaving the States.

Poison oak was a further uncomfortable addition to life in the wilds and "caused great suffering from the itching and inflammation," one miner has written. Washing the skin with a tea made from grindelia or manzanita leaves and pounding the soap-plant bulb to a paste and applying it as a salve were common and helpful remedies, he says.

Good medical care was hard to find even though doctors were plentiful—or at least men who called themselves doctors. It has been remembered that they scrupulously avoided all hard work and, under the guise of being physicians, traveled from camp to camp with saddlebags packed with what one miner described as "a select assortment of cutlery either adapted for trade or surgical use" and a collection of small boxes and bottles containing calomel, castor oil, and blue mass pills, which were administered for every ailment, "skilfully alternated, and judiciously prescribed with regard to the hours of repetition."

A young miner, at work in the rich diggings at Ophir, took sick during the hard winter of 1849 and called in a Dr. Swan who had hung up his shingle in nearby Auburn. Since the doctor had to ride five miles to the camp, he made an initial charge of six ounces on arrival, to be paid in advance. At the end of the visit he presented his bill for $400, and took out his gold scales. The young man could pay him only $289.

The next summer Swan called to collect the rest of his fee, but the patient could pay him nothing for he had been ailing the whole time since and unable to work. On his return to Auburn, Swan filed suit.

A jury of miners, hearing the case, returned a verdict ordering Dr. Swan to pay the defendant $89 and the costs of the court, which amounted to $200.

Most men doctored themselves, we are told, with liberal

doses of castor oil, blue mass, and calomel which, bought at the trader's, cost one dollar a pill or a drop. For scurvy, a popular remedy was to bury the victim up to his chin. This disease was so prevalent, an entire camp would often be found underground, except for a man or two who acted as guard against attacks by coyotes or grizzlies. There has been no report on the efficacy of this treatment, but one certain cure, mentioned many times by those who had used it, was a decoction of spruce needles or bark, drunk regularly.

One young gold seeker, near death from scurvy, told of his miraculous recovery. His partner, out hunting, came on a patch of dry beans that had been spilled and taken root. He filled a bag with the new leaves and on coming back to camp boiled them for his friend. The sick man ate only the cooked greens for several days. "These seemed to operate magically, and in a week . . . I found myself able to walk." As soon as he was strong enough, he went on to Coloma, "and by living principally upon a vegetable diet, which I procured by paying three dollars a pound for potatoes, in a very short time I recovered."

Large doses of cayenne pepper were taken to cure diarrhea, while attacks of fever-and-ague were checked with such recipes as the following, printed by one gold seeker for the benefit of his fellows: "Twenty-five grains of blue pill, twenty-five grains of quinine, twelve grains of oil of black pepper, made into twelve pills; one to be taken every hour for six hours, on the morning of the fit; one every four hours, the following morning; the remaining two, at the same interval, on the third morning."

The miner did not always go to town on Sunday just to buy provisions for the week, get his mail, visit his friends, drink, gamble, or go to church. On the afternoon of January 20, 1849, the news flew up and down the river that five men had been arrested for robbery and attempted murder at Old Dry Diggins, that they had been tried by a miners' court, found guilty, and sentenced to be flogged that Sunday. One Argonaut who had been a reporter on the *New York Herald* before coming to

the goldfields, thought he should see lynch law in action and
followed the throng that set out from his camp.

When he reached town he found a huge crowd already
gathered around an oak tree where the flogging was taking
place. "A guard of a dozen men, with loaded rifles pointed at
the prisoners, stood ready to fire in case of an attempt being
made to escape."

After the sentence had been carried out, further charges of
robbery and attempted murder committed the previous fall
were preferred against three of the prisoners, a Chilean, a
Mexican, and a Frenchman, and a trial was held in the middle
of the main street by a crowd of two hundred men who had
organized themselves into a jury and appointed a *pro tempore*
judge. The accused were too weak from their recent punishment to attend.

The charges, writes the *Herald* man, amounted to nothing
more "than an attempt at robbery and murder; no overt act
being even alleged." But the general opinion was that they
were "bad men" and "ought to be got rid of."

At the end of thirty minutes the judge put to vote the question of whether they had been found guilty; the affirmative
was universal. When he asked next what the punishment
should be, "a brutal-looking fellow . . . cried out 'Hang them!' "
and the proposition was seconded.

The reporter was shocked and, mounting a stump, started to
protest against such a course. "But the crowd, by this time excited by frequent and deep potations of liquor from a neighboring groggery, would listen to nothing contrary to their brutal
desires, and even threatened to hang me if I did not immediately desist from any further remarks." Convinced these were
not idle threats, and seeing the utter uselessness of further
argument, he stepped down, and prepared "to witness the hor-
rible tragedy."

Another thirty minutes were allowed the prisoners to prepare for death. Meanwhile three ropes were attached to the

stout limb of an oak. Then, the half-hour being up, the men were brought out, stood in a wagon, and the nooses fitted.

"No time was given them for explanation. They tried vainly to speak, but none of them understanding English, they were obliged to employ their native tongues, which but few of those assembled understood. Vainly they called for interpreters, but their cries were drowned by the yells of a now infuriated mob."

With this execution the name of Old Dry Diggins was changed to Hangtown, a name it continued to deserve for several years more.

With the admission of California into the Union in September 1850, and the establishment of law courts and other supposedly civilizing influences, these executions turned into extravaganzas that drew thousands of spectators in holiday mood. The double hanging on November 13, 1854, of the first men convicted of murder in the District Court of El Dorado County, brought to Coloma, the county seat, such crowds as it had not seen since the first days of the Gold Rush. From early dawn every road leading there was "thronged with one continued line or mass of people on foot, on horseback, in wagons and carts," reports an old chronicle. Hours before the appointed time, the streets were one "dense mass of human beings, while the hillsides were covered with thousands more." Some six to eight thousand had turned out for the spectacle.

But the most bizarre execution to take place along the river in the 1850s was the hanging of Dr. J. B. Crane and Mickey Free. Free was a notorious criminal, a member of a gang that specialized in the robbery and murder of Chinese, although he had been convicted for killing an Occidental tavernkeeper.

Crane's crime was less prosaic, for he had in a fit of passion murdered the girl he loved. He was the teacher at the little school in Ringgold Creek and had fallen in love with one of his older pupils, Susan Newnham. Old accounts tell how he proposed repeatedly, was constantly refused, but remained "ever hopeful." It was his habit to walk home with her after class,

an attention she did not discourage, and one afternoon as they
neared her house, he asked her again to marry him. What she
said will never be known, but her words so excited the doctor's
rage or jealousy that he whipped out his pistol and killed her.

The entire countryside was aroused; posses scoured the hills
and ravines up and down the river for many days without finding a trace of their man. Later it was learned that he had buried
himself under a heavy carpet of dead leaves and branches deep
in the woods.

Then one morning he was seen sitting beside the path that
led to Susan's door. The constable was called, and when he
came the doctor submitted quietly to arrest.

Word of his return soon spread, and an angry mob of several
hundred armed men, intent on lynching, gave chase. Overtaking the constable, they snatched the prisoner away, carried
him off to a lonely cabin, locked him in, and selected a judge
and jury. Before the trial was half over the sheriff of El Dorado
County came galloping up the glen with a small band of
deputies and citizens who held the crowd at bay with their
guns, knocked in the door, and whisked the doctor away to
the stout stone jail at Coloma.

The courtroom was packed each day during the trial with
spectators eager for lurid details, but there were none. It was
only mildly shocking to learn that the doctor had a wife and
several children in Kentucky. He made no attempt to deny his
guilt or defend his act. All he would say was that he had killed
Susan Newnham because he loved her. As the poet wrote,

> The man had killed the thing he loved,
> And so he had to die.

Dr. Crane was sentenced to hang on October 26, 1855.

The incorrigible Mickey Free, already sentenced, was passing
his time in jail writing his "confessions," which were printed
serially, under the title *The Life of Mickey Free,* by Coloma's
Empire County Argus, and peddled on the streets.

Both cases received so much publicity, execution day brought out the throngs. The Hangtown brass band and fire company rode over to Coloma to form a kind of military guard. Five thousand people pressed around the gallows, and thousands more covered the slopes beyond. The band played and the crowd cheered.

On the scaffold Dr. Crane asked permission to sing one stanza of a poem he had written in jail and set to a popular tune of the day. Permission was given and, while the band played softly, the doctor sang:

> *Come friends and relations, I bid you adieu,*
> *The grave is now open to welcome me through.*
> *No valley of shadow do I see on the road,*
> *But angels are waiting to take me to God.*

The miners were pleased and asked for more. He then sang other verses written in a similar vein. There was hardly a dry eye in the crowd, and they demanded an encore. Crane obliged with another song. The people shouted and called for still another, but at this point the executioner stepped up to fix the noose. As the trap was sprung, Crane shouted, "Here I come, Susan!" Many a leathery miner bawled aloud.

Mickey Free, awaiting his turn, had been walking up and down with an air of jaunty nonchalance, carelessly munching peanuts. Not to be outdone, he too gave the crowd a song when he mounted the platform. Then, cocking his hat at a rakish angle over one eye, he defiantly danced a jig on the trap.

15

"California for the Americans!"

THE MINER's noted generosity and bluff tenderness was reserved for his fellow Americans. For every other people, except perhaps the English, there was a stubborn intolerance. All foreigners were regarded as interlopers who had no right to come to California and pick up gold, the mines belonging to the Americans as their God-given property.

All crimes for which the Indians could not be blamed were attributed to Spaniards, Mexicans, and South Americans (lumped together as one people, and called "Greasers") because they were more numerous than any other foreign miner and were as a people, polite, obliging, and less likely to stand up for their rights. Much of this hard feeling (aside from an innate bigotry and misguided concept of natural superiority) arose from envy, for these Mexicans and Spainards were nearly all experienced miners and therefore successful.

An English gold seeker tells how in his camp a large group of newly arrived Americans applied to the Chileans and Mexicans for instruction and advice on mining methods, "which they gave them with cheerful alacrity; but as soon as Jonathan got an inkling of the system, he, with peculiar bad taste and ungenerous feeling, organized a crusade against these obliging strangers, and chased them off the creek at the pistol's mouth."

In an attempt to exclude all foreigners from the mines and force those already there to leave, the first state legislature passed the Foreign Miners' Tax, which exacted twenty dollars monthly from every non-American engaged in mining. The immediate result was injury to many camps made up largely of South Americans, Europeans, and men from the British Isles, and the driving of hundreds of penniless foreigners to San Francisco. While scamps and rogues from other lands were not kept out by the threat of taxation, "many a cautious, sober, intelligent foreigner might be warned away by the exorbitant tax, as well as by the hostility that it indicated," observes the philosopher Josiah Royce in his study of California's social evolution. And it had the effect of making those foreigners who were in the mines surly, suspicious, resentful, and ready for the worst.

Trouble was immediate. "The French got up a perfect revolution, and a war nearly broke out . . . while murders were committed daily," one miner has recalled. War did break out among the Mexicans and South Americans when men from the States tried to force them all out of one of the larger camps. The bloodshed and killing that took place engendered lasting bitterness, driving many of the victims of this intolerance to seek revenge upon those Americans who had refused to give them an equal chance, and forcing others to take up a life of crime in order to live.

In one camp, an Irishman known as Jack, resenting the tax collector's question of whether he was an American citizen, retorted hotly: "It's none of your damned business!" To which the collector, bristling with guns and officiousness, replied: "I'll show you whether it's any of my damned business or not!"

Drawing one of his revolvers, the officer started to dismount. Jack ran to his tent and by the time the collector had reached the ground, stood ready to meet him with a pistol.

"I'll give you as good as you can send!" Jack challenged. The officer cocked his gun. At this juncture Jack's partner, an American, stepped in and, by fast talking, made peace.

But peacemaking was rare; in dozens of cases foreigners shot it out with the law, often with fatal results; and tax collectors became such frequent victims of ambuscades and sniping, they took to traveling with bodyguards. The second legislature repealed the act, but it had already done untold harm.

By 1850 the exodus from China to the fabulous *Gum San* was well under way, and some four thousand Chinese sailed into San Francisco. They were treated with deference and given a prominent place in the "grand celebration" for California's admission into the Union. They were referred to officially as "our Chinese fellow-citizens," and the governor spoke of them as "one of the most worthy classes of our newly adopted citizens." Their immigration was encouraged, for they were found to be honest, sober, dependable, and industrious. There was a marked shortage of common laborers, and these Orientals proved adaptable and faithful workers in the mines, in hotels, on ranches, and as domestic servants.

In 1852, eighteen thousand Chinese passed through the Golden Gate, most of them bound for the mines. They came off the ships wearing all their clothes, layer upon layer, and carrying bundles of tools and blankets wrapped in matting. In these bundles some were bringing little packets of seeds of a favorite tree, the *Ailanthus altissima*, to plant and make the wild, strange land more homelike. Today, these handsome trees are found in nearly every camp along the river, standing as mute monuments to a gentle people long since moved on.

They kept to themselves in the diggings, well out of the way of the aggressive whites. By systematic labor, perseverance, and frugality, they began to prosper. Even though they confined themselves to abandoned and worked-out claims, they took out more gold than their roving Anglo neighbors.

Then the early charitable feeling changed, and all the animosity heaped upon other foreigners was suddenly transferred to the Chinese. Later another Foreign Miners' Tax was passed with the Orientals in mind and levied on them almost exclusively. This "exorbitant swindle" as Mark Twain termed it, was often "repeated once or twice on the same victim in the course of the same month," but "John Chinaman" was patient and peace-loving, and paid as many times as asked, without a murmur.

Mass meetings were held to "check this Asiatic inundation that threatens to roll over the State."

Resolved: That no Asiatic . . . shall be permitted to mine in this district either for himself or for others. . . .

Resolved: That a Committee of Vigilance, consisting of twenty, be appointed, whose business it shall be to see that the above resolution is carried out . . . and endeavor to secure a thorough and efficient organization of miners, for the purpose of protecting themselves from this influx of degraded inhabitants from China. . . .

"California for the Americans! The Chinese must go!" became the battle cry. Infuriated mobs stoned them, robbed and murdered them without compunction, hung them by their queues to trees and lampposts, bullied and browbeat them, and blamed them for every crime.

"A . . . Chinaman . . . is a great convenience to everybody—even the worst class of white men, for he bears most of their sins, suffering fines for their petty thefts, imprisonment for their robberies, and death for their murders. Any white man can swear a Chinaman's life away in the courts, but no Chinaman can testify against a white man," wrote Mark Twain in utmost seriousness.

During the panic of 1854 when thousands of miners flocked to the cities seeking work, they found the labor market glutted and held the Chinese responsible. "Human leeches, sucking the very life-blood of this country!" editors stormed. The governor called on the legislature to prevent further immigration, and an entry tax was imposed. The hostility extended even to children, who were encouraged by their elders to stone the Chinese or insult them at every opportunity.

Anti-Chinese riots occurred in Coloma, Auburn, and every

other camp along the American where there was a large Chinese settlement. In 1859 feeling ran so high among the miners, the governor was forced to call out the militia to put down riots.

In the gold towns the Chinese were herded into their own quarter to live, which they must have preferred from the standpoint of personal safety. These self-sustaining communities became bits of transplanted homeland where language, customs, and culture were perpetuated.

Of all the American River towns, Auburn probably had the largest Chinese settlement, numbering ten thousand at its peak, it is said. Today, just a few Chinese families, descendants of pioneer miners, merchants, and farmers, live there. Old Chinatown, crowded with exotic sights and smells, is no more. Until recently the Joss House had survived, watched over by members of the local Yue family who had established a haven there for Chinese travelers who might stop overnight and get a meal, without cost. But this final relic of Gold Rush days has fallen a victim to vandals who have stripped it of its Buddha and other statues, its paintings, its brass and pewterware, its lanterns, silk hangings, and intricately carved altars of scarlet and gold.

During the Civil War attention was focused on getting the gold out of the mines and into Union coffers to keep the government from going bankrupt. Towns along the river were drilling volunteer companies to be sent to the field, and little thought was given to the "Chinese Menace." But with the return of peace it became a vital question again, and state politicians made it a leading issue. In 1871 Governor Booth was elected on an anti-Chinese platform.

Hostility and prejudice were carried over well into the present century, and there are Chinese living along the river today who remember only too vividly being segregated in school and, because they were bright and studious, being hurt by thoughtless teachers who, in trying to spur Anglo pupils

to better efforts, would say, "Now, you're not going to let that
Chinese girl [or boy] best you, are you?"

It may be said in dubious defense of the miners that they
did not massacre the Chinese wholesale. That treatment was
reserved for the peaceful Indians who were not even considered
worthy of mass-meeting resolutions or legislation, but were
killed without provocation at every possible opportunity.

The Anglo-Americans, inheritors of the traditions and prejudices of two centuries of border warfare, brought to California an implacable hatred of the Indian that made no distinction between tribes or individuals. Contemptuously they called
them "Digger" Indians, classed them with vermin, and began
ruthlessly exterminating them. In American River country,
Maidu villages came to be regarded as excellent targets for
rifle practice, a Sunday's recreation; or they were destroyed
wholesale by fire and mass murder, no quarter being given even
to women and young children. Since an Indian's life was considered worthless, no American was ever brought to trial for
killing one, and because an Indian had no civil or legal rights,
and could not testify in court, anything he possessed could be
taken or destroyed on any pretext.

The American system of colonization had no place for the
native, who was rigidly excluded from its social order. If he
could, on his own initiative, subsist within the alien framework,
there was nothing to prevent him. But if he came into any
conflict with the system, then he must be eliminated. Nor was
there any hope of a blood bond to alleviate the low regard in
which the Indian was held, for intermarriage was censured, and
the offspring relegated to the same rank as the native parent.

With the discovery of gold, thousands of Anglo-Americans
penetrated the most remote corners of Maidu territory, subject-
ing the occupants of the entire area to a sudden and nearly
total inundation. "A population perfectly strange to them . . .
has taken possession of their former homes . . . and cut them
off from all means of subsistence," denying them even "the
right of working here, or, of staying upon the spot which was

once their own," wrote Dr. Oliver Wozencraft, a member of the United States Indian Commission in 1850.

Those Indians who escaped the white man's rifle were killed in numbers by disease, starvation, and whiskey. Cattle, horses, and sheep trampled and grazed away the more delicate herbage which was an important food source, while mining operations, fires, and lumbering destroyed their hunting and fishing grounds, burned down their acorn groves, and killed those shrubs and plants used for baskets, netting, cordage, and other practical purposes.

"Driven from their homes and the land of their fathers, they fled like hunted beasts to inaccessible and desolate spots and secret lairs," one historian has written.

As early as 1849 a miner at Coloma noted that "now a redskin is scarcely seen in the inhabited portions of the northern mining region. Their *rancherias* are deserted, the graves of their ancestors are left to be desecrated by the white man's footprint, and they are gone. . . ."

The wonder is that any survived. Even the very government agencies set up to protect them took shameless advantage. The history of those agencies, wrote J. Ross Browne, an early inspector for the Department of Indian Affairs, "is a melancholy record of neglect and cruelty, and the part taken by public men in high position, in wresting from them the very means of subsistence, is one of which any other than professional politicians would be ashamed." Every year, "numbers of them perished from neglect and disease, and some from absolute starvation," Browne continued. "As often as they tried the reservations, sad experience taught them that these were institutions for the benefit of white men, not Indians."

By consulting early mission records it has been possible to set the number of Maidu at 9,000 for the year 1770; the census of 1910 gave a count of 1,100. A tribal historian estimates that there are now only 700–900 Maidu left in California; of these, a small number are still living in American River country.

Today, many of these Maidu are taking a keen interest in

their heritage, are proud of being Indian, and are anxious to perpetuate customs and culture.

At least one ancient and important Maidu ceremony has been revived. This is the Bear Dance, which for some years now has been held each June on the Mankin Ranch near Janesville. Then, Maidu from all over northern California gather to take part in this sacred rite that expresses thankfulness for survival through the past winter.

Considering the Anglo-American's general contempt for the native populations of California, it is surprising to find so many Spanish and Indian place-names retained and given. The meaning and origin of most of the Indian names have unfortunately been lost, for by the time any serious study of their significance was undertaken, most of those who could have explained them had been destroyed.

These Indian names of towns, counties, mountains, lakes, and rivers are almost all that remain to remind a newer people of the ancient culture that once flourished here, and preceded their coming by uncounted centuries.

16

Thespians Along the River

NEARLY EVERY mining camp along the river soon had a theater. Some, like Coloma and Rattlesnake Bar and Georgetown, put up substantial buildings dedicated as "histrionic temples"; others converted empty stores, or on performance night simply set up a stage and hung a curtain in some dance hall, gambling saloon, or hotel parlor.

The first entertainments were made up entirely of local talent, and ranged from *Box and Cox* to Shakespeare. Because of the scarcity of women, their parts were taken by "the most effiminate-looking members of the company," reports a miner-turned-actor, which in the case of Shakespeare was perpetuating Elizabethan tradition. Many of these troupes were blessed with talent and took to the road, with varying fortunes.

One company that had been making a successful tour of the other camps rode into Mud Springs, then a populous town, on a fine April day in the early 1850s. The avant-courier, who had preceded them with his pastepot, had done his job well, and every rock, tree, awning post, and dry-goods box was plastered with notices. In expectation of a large audience the troupe rented the biggest hall in town, fitted it up without thought to expense, and hired an orchestra of three, whose pay, given in advance, about emptied the purse. "But we knew it would be filled by the rush for seats that evening," one of the actors recalls, so "we went to our hotel in fine feather and ate a hearty supper."

When they got up from the table they were alarmed to find that it was raining; however, "we assured ourselves with the belief that it would prove only an April shower." But this was no passing cloud; by the time they reached the theater "the rain had increased in violence and was coming down in sheets." Their spirits drooped as they listened to it beating ominously on the tin roof "like a shower of bullets."

An hour went by and it was still pouring. The door was standing open, but so far only one man had ventured out in the storm. Thirty minutes past the hour for the curtain to go up, and there was still only an audience of one. The actors talked it over and decided to go on with the show unless their solitary customer demanded his money back.

When approached he proved "a good-natured fellow, and . . . seemed to be delighted with the idea that he could have the performance all to himself. I told the two accordeons and the fiddle to tune up and . . . went on stage to dress."

The novelty of the situation inspired the actors to a top performance, which was fully appreciated.

I had never before played to a more enthusiastic audience. The man was delighted with everything we said or did—guffawed outright at every hit, and in the most serious parts of the scenes we gave from "Venice Preserved" and "The Wife," he fairly shed tears. . . . And when the curtain dropped on the last scene and I dressed and went out to him, I asked him how he had liked the performance. He declared it was the best he had ever seen, and said he would come every night. When we started for the hotel, I took the whole audience out and treated it, notwithstanding to do so consumed all the money that had come into the treasury.

The next morning they were off to Hangtown. Their precarious financial condition prevented a stop at Diamond Springs, depriving the good people there "of a taste of the legitimate drama as presented by 'two eminent American tragedians.'"

At Hangtown they joined forces with "Miss" Eldridge and her husband, whose troupe, having made an unsuccessful tour, "had been thinned by desertion." They filled out the company with volunteers and put on *Hamlet* for several nights to full houses. Then, their exchequers replenished, the combination broke up.

Even after the coming of those companies of dedicated professionals from the States who penetrated the wilderness with their New York and London successes, these local troupes still played to crowded houses, filling in the long stretches between the professionals' visits.

McKean Buchanan, who had been a levee cotton broker in New Orleans when "he startled the South with his advent as a tragedian," was one of the first to play the gold towns. He arrived in the early 1850s, organized a small company of "the finest artists on the Pacific Coast," so his handbills stated, and set out from Folsom one day in May to enlighten the mining camps "with illustrations of the drama, as it had never been seen before, and would never be seen again."

They traveled with a carriage that held ten, and a four-mule team with a baggage wagon; were six weeks on the road, covered seven hundred miles, and played some forty camps, most of them along the forks of the American River.

"Little Jimmy" Griffiths was one actor with the troupe long remembered for his versatility: he served as property man, scene shifter, wardrobe keeper, and played three or four important roles besides. It was Jimmy, too, who sat in the back of the wagon and thumped the bass drum to announce their entry into town—except when Buchanan took it into his head to beat it himself. When one of his actors asked him why he stooped to this "unnecessary lowering of his dignity," his answer was: "Leman, my dear boy, you don't see the thing clear. It makes capital . . . when the miners see me beating the drum they'll say, 'See, there's Buchanan, the great tragedian, beating the drum; how odd! Let's all go and see him to-night.' "

The company met with enthusiastic response wherever it went until it came to Yankee Jim's, which was either aesthetically barren or highly critical. After playing several nights to virtually empty houses, Buchanan announced for all to hear that "the braying of an *ass* could call into existence a better town than Yankee Jim's." And they heard, and the incensed citizenry replied: "If the *ass* but spoke he would be a better actor than McKean Buchanan." But "Buck" had the final word: "Oh, that this town had but one neck, that I might sever it at a blow!"

In another remote camp where the only available hall was a large room on the second floor of a canvas shanty, a stage was improvised by laying boards across two billiard tables tied together. A pair of windows that opened onto a shed roof at the rear was the only means of getting on and off stage. Playing anything heroic on this stage was impossible, but the audience seemed to enjoy even more the novelty of seeing Julia, the heroine of Knowles' *The Hunchback*, pushed in through a window by Master Walter, for her entrance and lowered unceremoniously to the shed roof for her exits. "There was a deal of fun if not tragic fitness" to it, Leman observed. He has recalled how often, when playing on such a makeshift stage, Buchanan "knocked 'Bosworth Field' all to pieces in his frantic tragedy of the fifth act of Richard III, for want of room to get on and off."

He remembered, too, the day the mules ran away with the baggage wagon and tore in "a go as you please style" down a steep hill on the divide between the North and Middle forks,

scattering the wardrobe on the greasewood and manzanita bushes from the top to the bottom, a mile and a half distance, with perfect impartiality. Miss Vaux's skirts were dangling from one bush, Jimmy Griffiths' russet boots and doublet from another, while Buck's trunk, being the largest and heaviest, had burst and scattered all his regal finery in the dust of the road. . . .

Any other man than Buchanan would have abandoned the
idea of playing that night, for it was dark before we reached
the hotel; but he . . . never lost a night.

Someone was sent back with a lantern to retrieve the cos-
tumes, and the curtain (made on the spot of four blue blankets
basted together) was raised. Then Buchanan made a rousing
speech to the audience, explaining the mishap—"and after
the performance won enough at poker to repair damages."

Dan Virgil Gates was another noted performer who toured
the mines. A monologuist, he was famed for impersonations
of "celebrated orators and actors." He traveled alone, riding a
wiry brown mule over the mountain trails, and acting as his
own advance agent. One Sunday morning he came into Michigan Bluff, ringing "a deep-toned bell," and pulled up in front
of the Sierra Nevada House. When enough of a crowd had
gathered, he announced that D. V. Gates would have the honor
of presenting "an oratorical and theatrical performance" that
night at the hotel. Tickets were one dollar; ladies would be
admitted free.

"A good performance, gentlemen, or your money shall be
refunded." No one asked for his money back—it was a good
show. Gates gave them masterful impersonations of Henry
Clay, Daniel Webster, "the eccentric John Randolph"; Mac-
ready and Kean, Forrest, Booth, and Buchanan. Then for
variety's sake, and as "a sure cure for the blues," he gave
imitations of "lovesick damsels" and "stagestruck youths," and
rounded off the evening with a scene in a country school.

It was in the mining camps and towns of California that
nineteen-year-old Edwin Booth gained his first acting experience playing everything from leading roles in Shakespeare to
a banjo-plucking minstrel, a bit he did between acts during
his father's performances.

Nearly all the best actors, singers, musicians, dancers, and
lecturers came to the gold towns, enduring the discomforts of
travel through wild and broken mountains, in storms and floods

and unbearable heat, over roads that were often no better than trails, putting up with the inconveniences of makeshift halls and stages and primitive living conditions. But these tours were profitable. Walter Leman says that when he was trouping with the beautiful Julia Dean, it was a rare thing "to play anywhere, even in the roughest mining camp, to less than three hundred dollars a night." Then, if an actor or company pleased, after the show the stage would be covered with buckskin bags of gold, each containing what the generous donor thought was a proper testimonial of appreciation. And it was also the custom for miners to hold benefit nights for women performers of exceptional beauty or talent who captured their hearts, and to present them with large purses of choice nuggets.

Beyond the money to be made, there was that challenge which delights every good performer: demanding and responsive audiences. Any trouper who misunderstood this and thought he could get by with what miners called "claptrap theatrical grinders," and second-rate acting, risked bombardment with rotten vegetables.

Once, during a performance of *Richard III*, a self-styled "Master tragedian" playing the lead was tearing his emotions to shreds. The miners soon had his measure, and when in the first act Richard lays bare his breast and begs Lady Anne to stab him, the audience as one man shouted their opinion of the actor with the urgent advice: "Kill him! God damn him; kill him!"

Editors fumed over those "many impositions in the shape of theatricals" that played the camps. They made it plain that "the good people of the mountains" had not always lived there, that they all had at some time lived in civilized country, and that beneath those unkempt exteriors were many men of learning and discrimination.

Ole Bull, the famed Norwegian violinist, thought he was among Philistines when he toured the mines, and confined his programs to the humdrum pieces of the parlor fiddler. To his

surprise his reception was cool. One critic wrote that he admired his skill but "detested his music."

Miners in general demanded quality, but they also expected
variety, and billings of the day indicate that they got it. There
was Mrs. Hayne in *Camille*; the Chapman family in farces and
melodramas; Misha Hauser, a violinist; Jacobs the Wizard;
The John Potter Company giving *Hamlet* and *Richelieu;* "The
Fire King" who consumed "live coals, blazing sealing-wax
[and] melted lead"; mimes; French ballet troupes; and men-
ageries. There were Mr. and Mrs. Barney Williams, famous im-
personators of Irish and Down East Yankees; and Frank S.
Chanfrau, creator of "Mose, the Bowery B-hoy," the big-hearted
Irish fire laddie who was the idol of New York theatergoers.
There were child prodigies playing the title roles in *Hamlet,
The Merchant of Venice,* and *Richard III,* or dancing hoe-
downs and shuffles in blackface. There were lecturers—Josh
Billings, Bayard Taylor, and Mark Twain; and there were cir-
cuses—Joseph Andrew Rowe of North Carolina having pio-
neered the field when he came in 1849 with his celebrated
equestrian acts, clowns, and strong men.

The novelty of the troupes of Chinese actors, musicians, and
jugglers, who toured for the entertainment of their own people,
attracted many Occidentals. Newspapers devoted columns to
explaining the complexities of plots for their readers. Most
editors were favorably impressed, and at least one suggested
that Western playwrights might profit from a study of the
"hieroglyphic books of the Celestial Thespians."

But Chinese music was another matter. One Auburn editor
advised those who planned to attend to first get "their ears
brushed with sheet iron." It was a general complaint that the
orchestra accompanied the entire play. "Imagine a room in
which one man is mending pots, another filing a saw, another
hammering boards, another beating a gong, and two boys
trying to tune fiddles, and you will have some idea of . . . their
grand efforts in the music line."

Of the many child entertainers then trouping, the one who took the American River camps by storm was Lotta Crabtree, pretty and dainty, with bronze curls, bright eyes, and an infectious laugh. She was the daughter of a New York bookseller–turned–gold seeker, one of those luckless fellows whose fate it would always be to abandon a claim just before the pocket of nuggets was turned up. Instead of discouraging him, these near-strikes spurred him to greater efforts, and picturing his prospects rosily, he wrote for his wife and little girl to join him at Grass Valley, over the ridge from Auburn. Here were rich placers, turning out thousands of dollars daily, and the inexhaustible quartz mines that were to produce in the millions.

But the hapless John Crabtree was no sharer in these riches. He was still on the trail of his El Dorado when Mary Ann and young Lotta arrived, and, although it might be around the next bend, until he found it he proposed keeping a boardinghouse and letting his wife run it while he prospected farther afield.

One summer day not long after Mrs. Crabtree had come to Grass Valley, Lola Montez rolled up in the Marysville stage, bringing with her her new husband, Patrick Purdy Hull, and her maid, Periwinkle. She had been on tour, giving gold seekers the chance to see the famous Spider Dance that had chilled and shocked audiences everywhere.

But now she was ready to retire with Pat to some quiet mountain town and turn to domesticity, she said. She looked around Grass Valley, liked its cosmopolitan air, and announced that she would stay. She bought a little house set among Lombardy poplars, three doors down from the Crabtrees, wrote to Ludwig I of Bavaria for furnishings from her villa at Munich, began enlarging the cottage, and planting the garden to roses, lilacs, and mock orange.

Everyone knew the story of Lola Montez, Countess of Landsfeldt, Baroness Rosenthal, and Canoness of the Order of St. Theresa, titles conferred on her by Ludwig whose mistress she was said to have been, although she staunchly denied it. True or not, it is a part of history that this nineteenth-century Pompadour virtually ruled Bavaria, and that her liberal sympathies during the revolution of 1848 precipitated Ludwig's abdication and her own banishment.

She was born Dolores Eliza Rosanna Gilbert, of Irish parents, although when she took her stage name she insisted there was reason for it since she was related to the Montalvos of Spain. She encouraged the romantic rumor that she was a natural daughter of Byron, and offstage wore simple black dresses with rolling white collars that set off her finely chiseled profile, intellectual brow, and dark curls, and lent credence to the tale.

The scheming of an ambitious, unscrupulous mother had made her childhood miserable. After being deserted by a scamp who had married her in her teens, she managed to collect a succession of husbands and lovers; for a time she was the mistress of Liszt and Dumas. But her one real love seems to have been Alexandre Henri Dujarier, literary critic for *La Presse,* whom she was to have married in the spring of 1845. His unexpected death in a duel was a blow from which she never recovered.

Now she was married to Pat Hull, a witty and urbane San Francisco editor and raconteur. She was drawn to him, she said, because he reminded her of Dujarier, and had married him because he could tell a story better than anyone else she had ever known.

That fall the shipment arrived from Munich. Everything she had asked for was there: the ebony drawing-room pieces inlaid with mother-of-pearl and upholstered in crimson; the console tables with nine-foot gold mirrors; the swan bed with its brocade drapery, and the gilded boudoir table and chest painted with flowers and shepherdesses. She and Periwinkle soon had the house in order, and Lola was then ready to hold her first salon.

These gatherings drew to her house all the touring performers, the wits, poets, editors, painters, mining magnates, politicians, and the most interesting men in Grass Valley—among
them two nephews of the great Victor Hugo.

"Sometimes the genial spirits would protract their meetings
until daybreak. Every new song, every neat story that was
read or heard, every bit of eloquence or scrap of humor that
any of the young men came across, was preserved for the salon,"
it is recalled. "There was champagne, brandy, and wine. . . .
Cake, fruit, and occasionally a pudding or a Spanish dish comprised the edibles, and every one smoked," Lola puffing cigars
like a western George Sand. Occasionally she danced. Once
when Ole Bull was there, she dressed up as a Spanish Gypsy
and danced to his fiddling.

But her private life was not all joy and laughter. Pat Hull had
a temper as hair-trigger and violent as her own, and the climax
of their stormy marriage took place when one of Lola's two
pet grizzlies bit him in the leg. Pat pulled out his pistol and
shot the bear dead. Lola sued for divorce.

The children of Grass Valley were always welcome at Lola's
cottage. It was one of the paradoxes of her complex personality
that she could romp with them and be one of them. On their
birthdays and at Christmas she gave them parties, and treats
between times.

There was one pretty child among the ones racing in and
out who attracted her special interest. This was Lotta Crabtree, whose mother had been one of the first women in town
to accept and defend Lola. Although Mrs. Crabtree hardly ever
allowed Lotta out of her sight, she did not mind how often she
ran over to Lola's house, or how long she stayed. Lola, in turn,
was delighted to have the child's company, and the woman
who was known as a "tigress" and the little girl became close
friends. Lola taught her to ride and would go dashing through
the streets and over the hills with Lotta on a pony at her side.
The child had a good ear for music, a sweet voice, and nimble

feet, so Lola taught her to sing ballads and dance *jotas* and
flings. Lotta was soon spending almost as much time with Lola
as she was at home, often going back to the house at night with
her mother, to listen to music or watch some actor put on a
skit in the parlor.

Mary Ann Crabtree herself had a talent for mimicry and a
modest flair for acting, so she was sympathetic with the profession and ambitious for her daughter, since child performers
were at the peak of popularity, and Lola had said many times
that Lotta should go to Paris.

But before Mrs. Crabtree had time to get Lotta started along
the path she saw opening for her, John Crabtree sent for them
to join him at far-off Rabbit Creek; new rich diggings were
being opened there, and he was so sure of a fortune this time,
Mary Ann shut up the boardinghouse, and packed in by mule
to the new camp. But once again riches were for others, and
Mary Ann had to open another boardinghouse.

There was a versatile young Italian at Rabbit Creek who
went by the name of Mart Taylor: a tall man with long black
hair, piercing dark eyes, and "an Oriental grace of figure and
cast of countenance." He was a cobbler by trade, a musician
and dancer by avocation, and owner of the local gambling
saloon and theater. He and little Lotta soon struck up a fast
friendship, and he taught her his stock of jigs and reels.

She had begun to attract favorable local attention with a
few performances by the time Dr. "Yankee" Robinson, a stroll-
ing player and manager, rode into town with his young actress-
daughter, Sue. He heard about Lotta and asked to see her.
With a billiard table for a stage and little Miss Robinson grinding the hand organ, she danced with grace and fire a *cracov-
ienne* Lola had taught her. He might have hired her if he and
Mart Taylor had not had words over the rental of the theater.
Robinson thought he was asking too much, so he hired a dance
hall across the street. Angered, Taylor decided to get even by
putting on a show of his own, starring Lotta.

Mrs. Crabtree, who at one time had made a living with her needle, hastily stitched together a long-tailed green coat, knee breeches, and a tall green hat for Lotta, while Taylor cobbled her a pair of brogans. Like one of Ireland's little people, she skipped on stage that night, to dance jigs and reels.

"She always had a way of laughing when she danced, hard enough to achieve by design when every breath counts, but natural for her. She seemed tireless, a tiny bubbling fountain of fun and quick life. On the rough stage . . . in the midst of smoke and shadows she danced again and again; every other number was forgotten." Then she came out in a white dress with puffed sleeves and round neck, and "sang a plaintive, innocent ballad, looking like a pretty little red-haired doll.

"The . . . room was shaken with excitement. Money rained upon the stage: quarters, half dollars, huge Mexican dollars, a fifty-dollar gold slug, a scattering of nuggets."

After this success, the next step was to organize a small traveling company. During the winter Mart Taylor taught Lotta more songs and rounded up a fiddler—he himself played the guitar; Mrs. Crabtree mastered the intricacies of the triangle, and under the name of Miss Arabella prepared to give impersonations. By late spring they were ready to start. A note, a pot of beans, and several loaves of fresh bread were left behind for Crabtree, who was in pursuit of some new mirage.

They played one-night stands in smoke-filled barrooms, in stores among the barrels of pork and sacks of flour and piles of mining tools, in tents and calico shanties, the stage made of a few boards set on trestles, candles stuck in bottles for footlights. And they risked their lives, traveling through the mountains during the spring thaw. Once, on their way to Auburn in February, they found the American in flood, and the approach to the main bridge washed away. As the stage-coach plunged into the muddy torrent and sped across the span, timbers creaked and shivered. Just as it reached the farther shore and got safely on the road, the bridge toppled in.

At the entrance to each new town Taylor would ride ahead to whistle and sing and beat a drum. He alone was arresting enough to have drawn a crowd if miners had not seen Lotta following on her little mule. Children were still rare enough to assure the company a rousing success everywhere. "The singing and dancing of little Lotta was admirable, and took our hearts by storm" was a sentiment repeated in many a notice.

For the final number she always appeared in her white dress and sang a plaintive song, and the miners would shower her with coin and nuggets in such profusion she was often frightened, and her mother was obliged to come out and gather them up in a basket. Later Lotta learned to turn the picking up of gold and coin into a comic bit, when with a saucy fling of her curls she would kick off her shoe and run about filling it, or she would drop the money into an old hat that had no bottom.

During the years she toured the gold towns—and she played them all, up and down the American—she kept adding to her repertoire. In Hangtown, Mart Taylor met a breakdown dancer who was willing to teach her the soft-shoe technique. Someone in the company suggested she do this in blackface, so she learned to play the banjo and sing plantation songs; for the sailor's hornpipe she mastered the snare drum. With every song that she romped through there was pantomime or bold mimicry. For audiences craving variety, they got it in the one small person of Lotta.

Within a few years she had surpassed all her rivals and was being given top billings. By then few entertainers of any age could match her varied repertoire.

Unlike other child stars who waned on reaching maturity, Lotta went on to become a full-fledged actress, working with such celebrities as E. H. Sothern and Mrs. John Drew. Eventually she was to have her own company.

She became the idol of thousands of young men all over the country, who would stand patiently outside the theater waiting to get a glimpse of her as she and her mother sped out the stage door. Yet with all the adulation she remained unspoiled. Throughout her long career, she retained a childlike innocence and freshness and never lost her vivacity or youthful appearance.

As she went on to meet spectacular success in New York, Boston, Philadelphia, and London, critics sought to explain the magnetism that captivated audiences everywhere. "Witchery" was the best they could do, and called her "a child of Nature."

Lotta came to San Francisco again and again for engagements and to spend brief holidays, and she went back to visit the gold camps where she had played as a little girl. She gave San Franciscans an ornate drinking fountain—"Lotta's Fountain" they called it—which still stands on Market Street, bravely defying the snarls of traffic.

Lotta retired from the stage in 1891, when she was forty-four and at the peak of her popularity. Although her personal vogue might have continued for years, for at fifty she looked only half her age and had lost none of her vivacity, it was a timely decision. She could already see the coming changes in taste, and knew it would not be too long before her romping comedies would be outmoded.

Thanks to her mother's wise investments and thrifty management, they could count their wealth in the millions. Lotta had never married, and so the two, after the years of hard work and the early privations, settled down to enjoy their riches. They traveled some, although travel was no novelty, and they spent long months at the spacious country house they had built in the New Jersey hills. Here Lotta often presented whole scenes from her plays for the entertainment of a wide circle of friends; and here she kept a string of racehorses, indulging her childhood fondness for swift horses and riding. She took up painting, and made many portraits of herself costumed for her favorite roles. Two younger brothers (for Crabtree had over the years drifted in and out of Mary Ann's life) frequently joined their travels and, because they shared many of Lotta's interests, spent considerable time at the New Jersey home.

In 1905 Mrs. Crabtree died, and Lotta's brother Ashworth came to live with her. But not too many years later he died, and Lotta was alone, for her other brother had lost his life at sea, and Crabtree had passed away while in England. Lotta and her mother had made few intimate friends, and life for the former idol of millions became essentially solitary. She insisted that she never missed the theater, and yet she was to say during those lonely years, "I want to go away where there are many people. I cannot exist without many around me." Perhaps to satisfy this need she moved into a suite in her own hotel in Boston. Summers she spent in Gloucester, painting pictures of the landscape and still more portraits of herself, always dressed for some part.

In 1924 Lotta died in Boston. Over half her great fortune was given to a foundation for the relief of needy veterans of World War I. Nearly all the rest of her money went to provide funds to aid actors and students of music and agriculture, to care for jaded horses and stray dogs, and to promote laws against vivisection. There were only a few personal bequests.

During her long career, Californians had followed her triumphs closely, possessively, and the local papers in telling of her latest successes spoke of her as "our Lotta." She was truly their own, and that wonderful vitality, hoydenish humor, and boisterous freedom that characterized her acting and won her the world's acclaim were as distinctly products of the diggings as the glittering nuggets with which the miners had showered her.

17

Last Chance

IN THE SUMMER of 1850 a small party of prospectors worked their way through that maze of narrow gorges and steep wooded canyons where the Middle Fork of the North Fork flows, a wild and beautiful country that is still largely inaccessible except on foot. Climbing to the top of a ridge, they stopped to prospect at the end of a promontory that juts high above the river. Here they found deposits so rich they stayed on to work them far longer than they ought, lingering, in fact, until there was nothing more to eat. Then one of them who was a good shot, and was anxious to protract this enchanting process of getting rich, offered to try his luck at hunting—but it had to be good luck for there was only one bullet left.

"This is our last chance to make a grubstake, boys," he said as he tramped off into the woods.

Sometime during the afternoon he came back to camp with a large buck—and so the new diggings were called Last Chance. Two years later it was a thriving settlement with stores, hotels, gambling saloons, a church, and a Sons of Temperance Hall.

It was close to noon on a December day in 1857 when Allen Grosh and Richard Bucke crawled painfully across the snow to a cluster of cabins occupied by a group of Mexican miners. The two young men had eaten nothing in four days, and their legs were frozen well above the knees. The night before, when they stopped to camp in a hollow near the river, young Bucke had said: "Let us make our bed for the last time, for we shall never leave this place."

Although Grosh's strength was failing fast, he replied staunchly, "No, we will get somewhere yet."

Their sleep that night was tortured with strange visions, and Richard Bucke, starving, had disturbing dreams of feasting on quail and other delicacies. In the morning he was surprised to find that they were still alive, although when they came to walk, they were both so weak they had to crawl on their hands and knees much of the way. It took them all morning to cover three-quarters of a mile.

Around eleven o'clock that day Grosh told his companion he had heard a dog bark, but Bucke, who had heard nothing, was afraid Allen was beginning to imagine things. In a short while, however, they came to a mining ditch with water in it and, following it, saw the cabins ahead.

"There is smoke," Allen said feebly, and Bucke looked up to see a thin blue thread rising from one of the chimneys.

When they reached the cabins, they were near collapse. The Mexicans, realizing that the two must have better care than they were able to give them, lifted them gently onto sleds and pulled them up the ridge to the town of Last Chance. Here a miner named Hamilton took them in, put them to bed, and gave them food.

"Our troubles are over," Bucke murmured gratefully. Actually they had just begun.

In March 1849, Ethan Allen Grosh, then twenty-four, and his younger brother, Hosea Ballou, daguerreotypists, left their Pennsylvania home with a company heading for the goldfields. They were the sons of the Reverend Aaron B. Grosh, a Universalist clergyman and editor of some note, and they had been well educated. Their party went to California by way of Tampico and Mazatlán, and wherever they stopped for any length of time, the Groshes set up their camera and darkroom and took pictures of the local notables: in Tampico they made daguerreotypes of the Mexican hero General La Vega.

But Hosea contracted malaria and dysentery along the way, and when the company reached San Francisco that August, he was too sick to go on to the placers. It took Allen several weeks of careful nursing to bring him back to health, supporting them meanwhile, probably, by making daguerreotypes. By the time enough money had been put aside to buy their outfit, the mining season had closed, and it was nearly summer again before they got on their way to Mud Springs.

Like hundreds of others they had come to make a quick fortune and go back home; but unlike many others they were better prepared, for they had considerable knowledge of chemistry and metallurgy and had brought equipment to test and assay ore.

They prospected along the American's South Fork, and made $2,000 above expenses that first season; later they lost it all in a vain effort to flume the river aside so they could wash the rich gravel of its bed. Alternating good and bad luck became the pattern of their lives over the next few years.

In 1851 they heard reports of the riches to be found in Gold Cañon, Nevada (then Utah), and made a quick trip to look around. Two years later they went back to prospect more thoroughly. Those already in the canyon had found gold enough to justify its name, but all the ore was mixed either with a rock that was variously violet-blue, indigo, and greenish-black, or with some "dark gray mass" that "resembled thin sheet lead, broken very fine." And lead the miners supposed it all to be, and threw it away in disgust. But the Groshes were curious and took samples back to California to test. It proved to be silver.

They continued to work along the American, looking for gold-bearing quartz, and "trying to get a couple of hundred dollars together," as Allen wrote his father, so they could return to Gold Cañon which they felt certain was equally rich in silver. But it was not until 1856 that they were able to get back there. This time, Allen reported, they found "two veins of silver at the forks of Gold Cañon. . . . One of these veins is a perfect monster." And, he added, they had "hopes amounting to certainty of veins crossing the cañon at two other points."

By organizing a company among their California friends, they gathered enough capital to return to Gold Cañon the following May, when they located a number of claims, discovered more silver veins, and made further tests. The ore was unbelievably rich: "Our first assay was one half ounce of rock; the result was $3,500 of silver to the ton. . . . We are very sanguine of ultimate success," Allen told his father.

By fall the future looked bright. Then, on August 19, as they were preparing to leave for California to raise more money, Hosea, in doing some final work at Gold Hill, ran a pick into the hollow of his left foot. There was no doctor in camp, and the boys had trouble finding "a few simple lotions . . . to poultice the wound." For a time it seemed to respond to "water treatment," but then quite suddenly gangrene set in, and on September 2, Hosea died. It was a crushing blow to Allen.

"In the first burst of my sorrow I complained bitterly of the dispensation which deprived me of what I held most dear of all the world, and I thought it most hard that he should be called away just as we had fair hopes of realizing what we had labored for so hard and for so many years," he told his father in a letter describing Hosea's accident, death, and burial in remote Gold Cañon. Three days later he wrote again to say that he missed Hosea so much, he was at times "strongly tempted to abandon everything and leave the country forever, cowardly as such a course would be." Later he decided to carry on for his father's sake.

After Hosea's death he was more anxious than ever to leave for California, but had to stay in the canyon long enough to wash sufficient gold to pay the funeral expenses. By then it was mid-November, and although he knew it was foolhardy to attempt a crossing of the Sierra this late in the season, he was determined not to winter in the lonely cabin filled with poignant memories. A friend, Richard Maurice Bucke, a young Canadian prospector, offered to go with him.

Before leaving, Allen made up a waterproof packet containing ore samples from the silver claims, a diagram of the veins, and his assay books. The rest of his papers, maps, and books he boxed up to be left in his stone cabin, in care of H. T. P. Comstock, a trapper and mountain man, known to his intimates as "Old Pancake."

On the afternoon of November 20, Allen Grosh and Richard Bucke started off on what was known as the Washoe Trail, with a donkey to carry their baggage. That night they camped just below the eastern summit of the Carson Range, and in the morning pushed on over and down to the shore of Lake Tahoe which they followed until dark. That night it rained, and snow fell on the peaks.

The Washoe Trail, which was opened in 1849, skirted the northeastern shore of Tahoe until it came to where the Truckee River exits from the lake. The trail then ran north down the right bank of the river for eight miles, crossed it, and followed westerly along Squaw Creek into Squaw Valley; from there it led over the western summit to Fork House, where the trail divided, one branch leading to Michigan Bluff, another to Last Chance, and a third to Iowa Hill.

The two men traveled all of the twenty-second in a rainstorm that brought still deeper snowpacks to the mountaintops. Oppressed by the necessity for haste, they tried to cross the western summit that same afternoon after reaching the valley. But as Bucke has written: "We soon came to snow, then lost the trail, hunted for it until it began to get dark, and then turned back to Squaw valley, lit a fire, had supper, dried ourselves as well as we could . . . and lay down by our fire until morning."

During the night it turned colder and by morning it was snowing in the valley. This day they tried again to get over the divide; they not only lost the trail, but found the drifts too deep for their donkey to press through and had to turn back once more to their old camp.

Snow was still falling the next morning, and important decisions had to be made concerning their future. To go back at this point seemed to them as dangerous as to go on, or to stay where they were until spring. They considered returning to the Truckee River and following it out of the mountains, but knowing nothing about its course, they were afraid it might prove impassable. There was no choice but to press on.

They were already out of provisions and, since they could not take the donkey with them, decided to kill him for food.

November 27–28 saw them making two more vain efforts to reach the summit and being driven back each time to their camp. It began to seem as though Squaw Valley had them locked in an icy prison.

But November 29 was a "fine, bright day," and they started out with hope. By climbing from point to point through waist-deep drifts, and pulling themselves up by bushes and outcropping rocks, they finally reached the summit.

They hurried down the steep western slope into the canyon of the Middle Fork American and that night came to an empty cabin used in summer by cattlemen. Bucke, who had been over this trail before and had stopped with the cattlemen in passing, counted on finding provisions there. But the cupboard was empty. Someone had broken that unwritten law of the mountains: always leave a little for the next comer.

Then a new storm broke, and although they were only about thirty miles from the settlement of Robinson's Flat, they knew it would be impossible to keep to the trail on these thickly wooded ridges unless it was clear enough to see the tree blazes. They stayed in the cabin two days, waiting for the storm to pass, husbanding their dwindling supply of donkey meat.

December 2 was "a beautiful, bright morning," so they started on, but the snow was so deep in places they kept losing the trail. Toward sundown they lost it completely and found themselves traveling in a circle, following with rising hopes those fresh tracks they thought belonged to others.

"Then we knew that our only chance of life was to find shelter immediately." To conserve their strength, Bucke says, they threw away many things: the gun that was wet and rusty and no longer fired, and Allen's packet of ore samples and papers. Other sources say that Allen put the packet in the hollow of a fallen tree, blocked the opening with a rock, and drew a rough cross on the bark with his knife. "We kept nothing but our blankets, a butcher's knife, and a tin cup in which was the miserable remains of our meat, and ran for our lives."

At the bottom of the ridge they came to a little ravine that was sheltered from the bitter wind they had been fighting all day. Several days before they had thrown away their matches, by then wet and useless, and had been lighting the campfire by a flash of powder from the gun. Now this was gone, too, and to keep from freezing to death during the night, they made burrows under the snow and crawled into them to lie until morning. They "slept very little" for the warmth of their bodies melted the snow above them and soaked them to the skin.

It was useless to climb back to the top of the ridge and try to find the trail, so the next day they kept to the ravine, knowing it would lead them to the river. That night they ate their last meat, "which amounted to not more than two or three mouthfuls apiece." Around noon the following day, December 4, they reached the North Fork of the Middle Fork, and followed it until dark, keeping a sharp lookout for muddy creeks, a sign that miners were working nearby. But the streams were all disappointingly clear, and they saw no sign of habitation.

In the morning they were extremely weak. "We did not feel hungry, but we had a sinking feeling much worse than hunger." That afternoon Bucke sat down, "exhausted and despairing," and proposed they give up and die right there. But Allen told him firmly, "No, we will keep on going as long as we can walk." The next afternoon they were at Last Chance.

In Hamilton's cabin they were warm and dry for the first time since leaving Lake Tahoe, but they could not sleep, and everything they ate made them sick. Gangrene had already set in. Then they grew delirious, and the miners sent out of the mountains for a doctor.

Allen, who was in a coma most of the time, died twelve days later—December 19, 1857—and was buried in the cemetery at Last Chance. With him went the secret of the location of that great silver vein that was to become famed as the Comstock Lode. For two more years men would keep on throwing away the despised blue and gray rock mixed so thickly with the gold, until a man named Stone decided to have it assayed. The results of that assay started the stampede to Washoe.

Richard Bucke survived the crude amputation of one leg and part of the other foot. As soon as he was able to travel, he left Last Chance for San Francisco, hobbling to the door of a friend, Alpheus Bull, who helped him get back to his home in Canada. After he had completely recovered, he went on to Europe to study medicine, and became one of the Dominion's most noted neurologists. Some years later he had a headstone put up over the grave of his friend at Last Chance, a marker that still stands among others in the quiet old cemetery of that remote ghost town.

A few miles from the place where Allen Grosh either hid or threw away his precious packet stands a little-known group of Big Trees, *Sequoiadendron gigantium*, "the noblest of a noble race," as the botanist Sir Joseph Hooker described the largest of all trees growing in the California Sierra. They are so old, "thousands of them still living had already counted their years by tens of centuries when Columbus set sail from Spain," John Muir has noted. "As far as man is concerned they are the same yesterday, to-day, and forever, emblems of permanence."

Once these trees were numerous, with many species flourishing in the now desolate Arctic wastes and in the interior of North America. Today they are limited to an area covering about fifty square miles on the western slopes of the Sierra Nevada.

This northernmost group, consisting of six living trees and two that fell during the heavy winter of 1861–1862, was discovered by Joe Matlock, a miner who was hunting deer one day in 1855. The largest tree is about ten feet in diameter and

two hundred and twenty-five feet tall, while the second largest, although smaller in diameter, is almost nine feet taller.

So exquisitely and finely balanced are even the mightiest of
these monarchs of the woods in all their proportions . . . there
is never anything overgrown or monstrous-looking about them
[Muir wrote]. The great age of these noble trees is even more
wonderful than their huge size, standing bravely up, millennium in, millennium out, to all that fortune may bring them,
triumphant over tempest and fire and time, fruitful and
beautiful, giving food and shelter to multitudes of small fleet-
ing creatures dependent on their bounty.

These giants stand on Duncan Ridge above the North Fork
of the Middle Fork American. A little stream edged with ferns,
azalea, western dogwood, and mountain alder flows through
the grove. Its channel is partially underground, yet its voice
can be heard distinctly, carried to the surface like a haunting
echo, through small well-like openings, lined with moss.
Glimpses of its sparkle can be caught as it flashes past the larger
holes.

Since no natural reproduction was observed in this grove,
seedling Sequoiadendron have been planted by civic groups,
from time to time since the 1920s. Most of these young trees
have unfortunately suffered from competition with the surrounding undergrowth or have been damaged or killed by bears.
More successful plantings have been made in recent years under
the supervision of the United States Forest Service which now
protects this group of rare trees, and sixty-one surrounding
acres of virgin sugar pine, white fir, and incense cedar.

"I never saw a Big Tree that had died a natural death,"
observed John Muir, "barring accidents they seem to be immortal. . . ."

18

"The Pirate of the Placers"

RICHARD BARTER was his name, and he was born in Quebec, the son of a British colonel and his pretty, high-spirited French wife. When the colonel died, Richard and an elder brother emigrated to Oregon with their sister and her husband.

But the Barter boys were not content to settle down to farming in the Willamette Valley, when nearly every day they heard some new tale of the fortunes to be made in California. So off they set for the goldfields one spring morning in 1850, full of enthusiasm and hope. They promised to be back in a few months with gold enough to make the whole family rich.

It did not take them long to discover that nuggets were not picked up by the pailful at Rattlesnake Bar—or anywhere else along the American River, for that matter. By the end of the first season the elder Barter was ready to return to Oregon, but not Dick, who had a mind of his own. He had come to the river to make a fortune and he was going to stay.

A headstrong, reckless youth of seventeen left on his own for the first time in an untamed mining camp was likely to be drawn to the petty heroes of the diggings: the dandy, the braggart, the gambler, the roisterer, even the small-time thief, all of whom seemed to be getting the most out of life.

It was into such company that Dick Barter drifted, and it was among them that he somehow made enemies, so that when a local merchant reported the theft of some clothing from his store, they started the rumor that Dick was the thief. He was arrested and tried in Auburn, but evidence being scanty, he was acquitted. Later it was learned that he had been falsely accused.

But his enemies were not content to let matters stand, and a few months later he was charged with another crime, a more serious one: horse stealing. For this offense men were often hanged first, and questions asked afterward. There was sufficient incriminating evidence this time to convict Dick, and he was sentenced to serve two years in the state prison. But as had happened before, it was found that certain men at Rattlesnake Bar had perjured themselves. Then the stolen animal turned up, and the man who had taken him confessed, so Dick was released before his sentence could be carried out. Shortly afterward, his record was cleared officially.

But he knew there were some who believed the original charge was true and that he had somehow got out of it. To escape their suspicious glances and put himself beyond the reach of his enemies, he moved on to Shasta, to make a new start under the name of Dick Woods.

For two years he lived quietly, keeping to himself. Although he had no better luck than before in finding gold, he stuck at it, for mining was a gamble, as everyone knew, and his rich strike might turn up tomorrow.

Then one day a man who had known him at Rattlesnake Bar drifted into camp and recognized him. Dick did not need to be told what had happened; it was obvious from the changed attitude of his comrades that the old slanders had been repeated.

"An Ishmaelite," he now called himself. Feeling that he could not succeed by fair means, his spirit rebelled.

"I left Rattlesnake Bar with the intention of leading a better life, but my conviction hounded me at every turn until I could stand it no longer," he explained. He decided to become an outlaw.

"I have been driven to it. Hereafter my hand is turned against everybody, for everybody's is against me."

He started out his new career by holding up a stagecoach on a lonely mountain road. He said to the driver, just before he faded into the night, "If anyone asks who robbed you, say it was 'Rattlesnake Dick.' " Later he called himself "The Pirate of the Placers."

Dick Barter was a dashing figure. In dress he was something of a dandy, looking more like a member of the gentry of the green cloth than a highwayman. One who knew him writes that he was tall, slender, muscular, and broad-shouldered; "his form was almost a paragon of manly beauty." His walk "displayed that supple, springing motion peculiar to the Indian." The handsome face with its regular features, the slim neck, the silky black hair, and the flashing eyes "that betrayed every passion that animated his mind" made the heart of every woman who saw him beat faster.

By robbing stages, lonely travelers, and sluice boxes, Dick worked his way south to his old haunts, determined to make those enemies who had driven him beyond the pale take notice. He roamed the countryside from Rattlesnake Bar to Folsom, working alone until the summer of 1856, when he got together his first gang.

About three miles from Auburn, on the Folsom Road, stood a wayside station called the Mountaineer House, kept by Jack Phillips, a dubious character who encouraged the roughest gentry of the road to use his tavern as a rendezvous. Tom Bell, a noted desperado, whose band numbered in the hundreds and who was the scourge of the country from the American River as far north as Oregon, made this inn his headquarters. Phillips was in a position to help Dick recruit men, and a choice lot they turned out to be: there was George Skinner, known also as Walker and Williams, who had been twice sentenced to the penitentiary and was now free only because he had escaped; his brother Cyrus, who likewise had broken out of state prison; a horse thief known as "Big Dolph" Newton; a small-time robber named William T. Carter; and a Mexican of unrecorded talents, "Nickanora" Romero.

With these five, Dick launched into a campaign of wide-spread larceny that took him through Placer and Nevada counties. Nothing was safe: cabins and stores were looted, sluice boxes emptied of their flakes, individual miners relieved of their full bags of dust, stages and bullion trains held up. The miners were aroused; posses were formed to hunt the outlaws down, but a well-timed warning from a confederate like Jack Phillips who always kept a sharp eye on the movements of the law, and Dick and his men went into hiding in some remote canyon until things cooled down.

Late in the summer of 1856, Dick's big chance came. He was about to stage the largest holdup California had ever seen. He would make those small fry on Rattlesnake Bar take notice.

He had learned that a shipment of $80,000 in bullion was coming out of the mountain mines near Yreka. A convoy of twenty men would be guarding the mule train, but Dick believed that a small well-armed party, acting quickly and with precision, could surprise and overpower them and make off with the gold. There was just one problem: the mules would all be bearing the Wells, Fargo & Company brand. To escape recognition, it would be necessary to transfer the gold to other animals. But Dick had it all worked out.

Skinner, Newton, Romero, and Carter were to lie in wait for the train on the Trinity Mountain road, a lonely and remote stretch in the wilderness. Dick and Cyrus would meanwhile pick up mules in the Auburn area and drive them to the hills at night to a designated meeting place.

Skinner and his companions carried out their part of the plan smoothly. They lay in the thicket until the train came abreast of them, when "they sprang suddenly among the convoy, and with weapons drawn and cocked, commanded them to stop. The action was so sudden, the demeanor of the robbers so fierce, that the men in the train could not resist," an old chronicler related. The guards were tied to nearby trees, the gold unloaded, and Skinner and his men took off with it to the rendezvous.

It was a spot well-chosen, in the heart of another thicket, and here they lay hidden all that night and the next day, waiting for Dick and Cyrus to come with the mules. But they never came. By the third morning it was obvious that something had gone wrong with the other part of the plan, and Skinner decided they must get out of there as soon as possible with the gold.

But the $80,000 in gold was more than they could pack on their backs the 130-odd miles they had to go. Half the amount was as much as they could carry, so Skinner buried the rest, to be picked up another time.

Meanwhile, the twenty guards had broken loose and, hurrying down to the settlements, raised a hue and cry. Jack Barkley, a Wells, Fargo detective, got together a band of five armed citizens and started in pursuit of the robbers. He wisely made no attempt to comb the wilderness, but set out instead for the Mountaineer House.

It was to the Mountaineer House that George Skinner and his party went. After getting there and hiding the gold in a ravine near the headwaters of Clear Creek, they took horses and started back to Auburn to find out what had happened to Dick and Cyrus.

Just a few miles up the road they met Jack Barkley, and both sides started firing at once. At the first shots four members of the posse decamped, leaving the detective and one citizen to fight it out.

For a few minutes the battle was hot, Barkley firing away with two Navy revolvers and his companion shooting as fast as he could reload. It was soon over. George Skinner was killed, and Big Dolph Newton and Romero wounded. Romero made off through the trees but was captured after he plunged into the American River and attempted to swim across. Carter laid down his gun and surrendered.

All three were tried at Auburn and sentenced to ten years in prison. Later Carter was pardoned after he gave information that led to the recovery of the $40,000 hidden at Clear Creek.

As to the other half lying on the slopes of Trinity Mountain, he could tell them nothing, for George Skinner had buried it himself and kept its location secret and now Skinner was dead. That $40,000 in gold is doubtless still there, for no record or rumor exists of anyone's ever having found it.

Dick and Cyrus's failure to keep their mountain rendezvous was soon explained: they had been caught stealing the mules and clapped in the Auburn jail. But Dick had no intention of languishing there, and one night his chance came when a keeper accidentally left a key in a locked door. Slipping his arm through the bars, Dick turned the key, and he and Cyrus vanished in the dark, each to go his own way.

Dick boldly boarded a stage for Folsom, and at Sacramento took the riverboat to San Francisco to recruit a new gang. But for Cyrus it was jail again when he was found the next morning hiding in the brush. This time it took him four years to find a way out. Then, feeling that California was not the best place for him, he took off for Montana, where a vigilance committee strung him up for his first offense.

In San Francisco, Dick met several men of wavering morals —George Taylor, Aleck Wright, Billy Dickson, and Jim Driscoll—all willing to join him. They soon returned to the mines, for the city's climate was a poor one for men of this sort. James King of William, the crusading editor of the *Bulletin*, had been recently shot on the street, and San Franciscans were demanding immediate punishment of the murderer, as well as a general cleanup of the city's underworld. Since the elected officials could not be counted on to do the job, the Second Vigilance Committee had been formed.

Rattlesnake Bar became the headquarters for Dick's new band, and again they roamed the country up and down all forks of the American. Sometimes they worked as a unit, at other times individually or in pairs, but Dick is credited with planning most of the robberies they committed.

For two years he did well, and it seemed as though he might

continue his lawless career as long as he pleased without ever being caught, for the river country teemed with desperadoes who had been swept out of San Francisco, and the lawmen couldn't keep up—some of them didn't even try.

But this could not be said of John C. Boggs, sheriff of Placer County, the one officer most feared and hated by the outlaws of the foothills because of his daring and tenacity, and the fact that he nearly always caught his man. It was said that he bore a charmed life, and some highwaymen regarded him superstitiously, for as many times as he shot it out with these desperate men, he always escaped unharmed while those right beside him were often killed.

Rattlesnake Dick was at the top of Boggs' list. He and Dick were avowed enemies, each determined to get the other. Dick's hatred of the sheriff harked back to those early days on the Bar when he had been wrongly accused and, he claimed, Boggs had sworn falsely against him. Dick never forgave him, and now they played a grim game of hide-and-seek, which neither won.

A good number of times Boggs caught up and put Dick in jail, but he never stayed long. It was said that there wasn't a jail in two counties that could hold Rattlesnake Dick. Even when they loaded him with irons, he still found a way out and, once beyond the walls, managed to get help and escape. Sometimes he left the country for a while; other times he simply hid out in the tangled wilderness of the North Fork.

There were several occasions when Boggs congratulated himself that the bird was finally caught, but each time he returned empty-handed, and at least once was made to play the fool.

One day during the fall of 1858 he learned that Dick and George Taylor were aboard the stagecoach going to Folsom, and thinking to capture both outlaws at once, he set out from Auburn armed with a derringer, a warrant, and a complement of handcuffs. He waited for the stage on Harmon Hill, and when it came, ordered the driver to stop. Then, addressing Dick and Taylor who were riding outside, he invited them to step down. Both men began vigorously denying their identity, and Taylor, demanding his authority, asked to see the warrant.

Boggs seems to have been momentarily thrown off guard, for without thinking he began fumbling in his pocket for the paper. The highwaymen took this moment to open fire with their revolvers, and Boggs, brought to his senses, returned fire with his derringer. But his aim was also bad, and Dick and Taylor, unhurt, slipped down from the coach and struck off through the woods upriver. A contemporary report states that Boggs' face wore "a woeful expression" on his return to Auburn with his "wristless handcuffs, his unserved warrant, and his empty derringer."

But Dick's good luck was bound to run out. One by one the outlaws who roamed the river country were being shot, hanged, or sent to the penitentiary. The dread Tom Bell had been lynched, and his gang of cutthroats broken up. The old rendezvous at the Mountaineer House was no more, for Jack Phillips had been sent to prison for harboring highwaymen and murderers. Jim Driscoll, one of Dick's own men, was serving a long term for having held up the stage that ran from Rattlesnake to Folsom and making off with $6,000 from the Wells, Fargo strongbox.

Relentlessly, methodically, Sheriff Boggs kept on Dick's trail, tripping up other members of his gang, arresting his confederates, frustrating his plans, pressing him ever closer, and forcing him to take rash chances. It was a fight to the finish now.

The night of July 11, 1859, was cloudless, with a bright moon. Around eight thirty a man knocked at the door of George Martin, Placer County's deputy tax collector, and when he answered, told him that Rattlesnake Dick and a companion had just been seen riding through Auburn, heading toward the Illinoistown road. Why the stranger had brought this news to Martin rather than the sheriff remains a mystery, unless he too had reason to avoid the law. But Martin did not stop to ask. Mounting his horse he galloped off to the jail and told Undersheriff George Johnston and Deputy William Crutcher what he had just heard. The three set out in pursuit.

About a mile from town they caught up with two horsemen, and Johnston, who was riding ahead, called on them to halt. One of the riders turned in his saddle to ask who they were, and there was barely time to see that it was Dick before he fired his revolver; the bullet shattered Johnston's left hand and cut the bridle rein. Dick's companion fired an instant later, and George Martin dropped from his horse, dead.

For a few moments it looked as though the outlaws might get away without the pursuing party firing a shot, for Crutcher had dismounted to look after Martin, and Johnston with one useless hand and no rein was having all he could do to control his badly frightened horse. But just as Dick and his henchman wheeled to make their escape, Johnston managed to let fly one shot, and Crutcher another. They saw Dick reel in his saddle and almost fall, but then straighten up and gallop off.

It would have been rash for Crutcher to think of giving chase alone. Leaving Johnston to watch beside Martin's body, the deputy rode into Auburn for help. Searching parties were organized and scoured the countryside the rest of that night without finding a trace of the two highwaymen. But they learned something about them from a man and his wife who lived beside the Illinoistown road. Earlier in the evening, two men had ridden past at a furious rate; in the bright moonlight they saw plainly that one was swaying in his saddle and the other was supporting him.

The next morning as the Iowa Hill stage was approaching the Junction House, just outside Auburn, the driver and passengers were startled to see a corpse beside the road. The body was fully clothed and partly covered with a saddle blanket. The driver got down and, looking at the dead man closely, identified him as Rattlesnake Dick. A quick examination disclosed that he had been shot through twice, from breast to back and side to side. Either wound would have been ultimately fatal, but immediate death had been caused by a third bullet through the brain.

In Dick's gloved right hand was a pistol; his left clutched a scrap of paper on which was scrawled in pencil: "Rattlesnake Dick dies but never surrenders, as all true Britons do!" On the back was written: "If J. Boggs is dead, I am satisfied." This was thought to mean that Dick had mistaken George Martin for his old enemy.

His body was taken by wagon to Auburn, where, after studying the evidence, the sheriff announced that he had taken his own life. But there were those who thought otherwise, for it was known that Dick had repeatedly told his men that if he ever got into a tight fix from which he couldn't escape, they were to put a bullet through his brain and get away themselves. Now, knowing that he was mortally wounded and that capture was sure, he gave the word to his comrade to kill him.

About a month later Dick's horse was found near Grass Valley, alive, but with a bullet hole in its neck. Two shots only had been fired that fatal night of July 11 by the sheriff's men, and the wounds in Dick's body bore this out. Who then had fired the shot that hit the horse?

Dick was buried in the clothes he wore at the time of his death: "fine black pants, light-colored vest, a drab merino coat, and kid gloves."

"Thus ended the career of one of the boldest villains that ever stopped a stage or rifled a treasure-box," a writer of the day observed.

Bold, surely, but not entirely villainous. In the pocket of Dick's coat was found a letter written by a younger sister from their home in Quebec. It was dated four months earlier. She addresses him as "My Dear, Dear Brother" and speaks of him as "the guide of my infant joys, the long-lost friend of my childhood." She begs him to write, for she has so many things of interest to tell him. She has heard some of the worst, and she has "grieved, but never despaired"; she prays that he will be "restored to the paths of rectitude." She signs herself "your own most affectionate sister, Harriet Barter."

There was surely a great deal more good in Rattlesnake Dick, The Pirate of the Placers, than the record indicates.

19

The Discoverer's Fate

As COLOMA became deluged with humanity, James Marshall began to have his troubles with those men who refused to respect his claims, who looked on his horses and cattle as public property, and who ran off with tools and lumber from the sawmill. Many of these adventurers, especially the immigrants from Oregon, harbored uncompromising hostility toward the peaceful Maidu of the area and killed them at every opportunity.

Marshall, who had always lived on friendly terms with his Indian neighbors and employed many of them at the mill, spoke out against these injustices. In June 1849, he had to fly for his life when he attempted to save eleven innocent Maidu from execution at the hands of a mob. He spent that summer and fall prospecting along the Middle and North forks but, having little success, returned to winter in Coloma.

As the discoverer of gold, he was looked on by some men with a kind of awe and credited with supernatural powers. Many suspected that he had knowledge of the Mother Lode, and these men began to shadow him. Others tried to coax him into showing them where rich placers lay, or to lead them into the mountains and point out the source of all the gold. Still others tried to bully him by saying: "You found it once, you can find it again. Show us!" On one occasion a group threatened to hang him to the nearest tree unless he shared his knowledge.

"To save him," wrote a friend, "I procured a horse, and with this he escaped."

He had always been eccentric. Now, as a result of these un-
fortunate experiences, he grew misanthropic and querulous.
He had been born with a caul, and as a boy had seen visions.
As a young man he came to believe in communication with the
spirit world, and now he delved more deeply into this realm.
In obedience to their promptings, he spent the next four years
tramping up the canyons and over the ridges along all forks of
the American, carrying a forty-pound pack on his back, and
"living on China rice alone," as he wrote. He searched every
bar and ravine, hoping to be led by the voices to rich diggings.
Although the treasure continued to elude him, he did not
blame the spirits: "I wandered under some fatal influence, a
curse."

Around the middle of September 1850, four Ohioans rode into
Burke's Station, just north of Antoine Canyon where Marshall
was prospecting. They had with them seventy-five pounds of
gold dust which they claimed to have dug out of a nearby
ravine in only a few days. This news raced from camp to camp,
and men were soon off to hunt for the "Ohio Diggins." Among
them was a group that included Marshall.

For fully two months men combed the area without finding
a clue, and with the approach of winter most of them gave up
in disgust. But Marshall and a companion, Jonathan Favorite,
stayed on to continue the search.

One day in late November, while following a dim trail, the
two men came out of the woods onto a beautiful oak-covered
plateau between the North and Middle forks. Here they saw
signs of former occupancy and, with this first bit of encouragement, set up camp beside a spring.

In the morning, while exploring the surrounding coppice,
Marshall discovered a mochila (a removable leather cover that
fitted over the saddle), which prompted him and Favorite to
make a thorough search. What they found was not pleasant:
four men who had been murdered and four horses shot through
their heads. It was evident from the position of the bodies that
the men had been surprised as they sat around the campfire.

Marshall then recalled that while he was at Kelsey's Diggings that spring, four Spaniards, heading for the North Fork, had left camp with considerable gold dust. Later he heard that they had gone to Todd's Valley, left their treasure with an acquaintance, James Williams, a storekeeper there, and had then gone on to prospect higher in the mountains.

What Marshall did not know was that some time in August Williams was called away and that, before he left, he sent word to the Spaniards to come for their gold, which they had done, taking it with them to their camp in the mountains.

From the condition of the bodies it was apparent that the men had been killed about the first of September, and from the shreds of clothing and horse accouterments, that they were Spanish. This then, was the grim secret of the Ohio Diggins.

In the spring of 1857, Marshall returned to Coloma. He bought fifteen acres of hillside land for fifteen dollars and planted it to grape cuttings. While he waited for the vines to mature, he turned once more to carpentry, filling orders for household furniture, waterwheels, miner's rockers, and coffins.

But Marshall was not destined to succeed. With the years, his infirmities of disposition increased, and he grew still more moody and suspicious. He became slovenly in dress and habits. His clothes, described as "dingy and brown," hung loosely on his bony frame, tobacco juice yellowed his beard and stained his shirt front, and he began to spend more time in the saloons.

"A drinking man but not a drunkard," recalls the poet Edwin Markham who taught school in Coloma for six years before going on to Hangtown, where he wrote the first lines of "The Man with the Hoe." Marshall "dealt in volumes of vapory talk," and could frequently be seen on the village street, like the Ancient Mariner, "holding some neighbor with his glittering eye."

He liked Markham and one day loaned him "a queer manuscript from his pen, which purported to be a communication from the spirits." Later he gave him "a strange volume on

'Biblical Archeology', one that included an elaborate discourse
on the Hierophants of Baalbek and Persepolis."

The poet has described Marshall's "grim little cabin":

> It was a dingy hut, some twelve feet square, made of logs
> and picked-up lumber; and it was typical of thousands of
> miners' cabins scattered through the hills in the early days. . . .
> In one corner was a cracked and greasy stove; at one wall
> was a grim narrow bunk for sleeping; in the center was a
> grease-marked, melancholy table; and looking sadly on all
> the spectacle were three or four tottering and disheartened
> chairs. There were also one or two sad little windows that
> the dust darkened and the flies haunted.

Here Marshall brooded. He had come to think of himself as
the most deserving man in California, and the most aggrieved.
He liked to point out how Edmund H. Hargraves, the discoverer of gold in Australia, had been rewarded with a gift of
$75,000 by an appreciative government, and a pension of $1,250
a year, while he, Marshall, had received no official recognition
at all.

Some ten years later he left Coloma and settled in Kelsey's
Diggings, where on the advice of spirits he invested his meager
savings in two gold mines. They brought him small returns,
but he refused all offers to sell, for the voices had told him
they were rich. The voices were right, for had they been properly developed they would have been heavy producers. In order
to live, he ran a blacksmith shop in conjunction with his carpentry.

In 1874, the state, after many proddings and much delay,
granted him a pension of $200 a month for two years. On its
renewal it was reduced to $100, but at the end of the next two
years it was discontinued. By then stories of Marshall's thrift-
lessness had reached official ears. It was told how he loaned
money without security and made no attempts to collect it; how
he and his drinking cronies would wait on the steps of Tom

Allen's Pioneer Saloon for the mail to bring his check, and when it came how they would flock inside where Marshall treated them all to rounds of drinks.

Continuation of the pension was considered again in 1878 and might have been passed had Marshall not attended the hearings in Sacramento. One afternoon as he took his seat in the Assembly Chamber, a flask of brandy slipped out of his pocket and fell to the floor with a crash. All eyes turned toward the sound of shattering glass and immediately recognized the shabby old man who sat there glowering.

Marshall went home, if possible more bitter than ever. From then on he was entirely dependent on his own earnings and the charity of his Kelsey neighbors who saw to it that he always had enough to eat.

Around six o'clock on the morning of August 10, 1885, James Wilson Marshall, then seventy-five, was found dead in his little house. He was lying on his cot, fully dressed, his battered old hat pulled down over his eyes. It was thought that he had gone outside to start the day's work, for the front door stood open. Then, not feeling well, he had gone back inside and stretched out on his bed.

As with many men, more importance was attached to him dead than alive. Within hours of his passing, a controversy was raging over the most fitting burial place for the man who, it was suddenly realized, had by his discovery unlocked the vast treasure-house and opened the gates for that tide of immigration that had founded an empire in the Far West.

The Society of California Pioneers thought he should be laid to rest with honors in the Capitol grounds at Sacramento and sent a delegation to Kelsey to make this request. But the townspeople there disagreed, pointing out that he ought to be buried in the village where he had spent his last years. At this point the citizens of Coloma spoke up to insist that the only fit place was near the site of the discovery that had made his name known around the world.

Some of his Kelsey friends had heard him say he wanted to be buried there, for he had come to dislike Coloma. But then there were men in Coloma who had heard him say: "I want to be buried on top of that hill," and he had pointed to his old vineyard on the slopes above the river. To add substance to this claim, there were others who knew that when he sold this land he had reserved a plot for his grave, and they recalled his saying that he wanted to look down forever on the place where he had discovered gold. A few of his drinking companions remembered that he had told them he wanted to be up there so he could look down on the town and watch the "boys" in the saloons.

In the end Coloma won out, and on the morning of August 12 Marshall's body was taken there by wagon. The Society of California Pioneers and the Native Sons of the Golden West took charge of the funeral. Services were held in the little white Episcopal church built at the bottom of the slope below Marshall's old cabin. There was a sermon by his friend the Reverend Charles C. Pierce and a eulogy by the lawyer-orator George Blanchard.

Then the coffin was carried up through the fragrant piney woods to the sunny hilltop. Jays flew scolding as the men crashed through the chaparral. Pausing on the summit to catch their breath, the funeral party stood silent beside the open grave. In the hot stillness a flycatcher sang his thin sweet notes, and a quail called insistently and clearly in the thickets beyond.

Below was the hurrying river, sparkling in the golden light of late afternoon. Along its osier-lined left bank was the site of James Marshall's greatest moment, no longer distinguishable, for the river had long since reclaimed its own.

20

The Great River Road

"Now GENTLEMEN, all aboard! All aboard for Brighton, Mormon Island, Mud Springs, and Hangtown! Here's your stage for Hangtown in seven hours. Just three seats left. Who's agoin'?" a runner for the Pioneer Line was bellowing in front of Sacramento's main stage-hotel.

The street was a solid mass of four- and six-horse vehicles of many kinds, the elegant Concord coach conspicuous among more humble mud and light-spring-wagons. On each stage was painted in bold letters the name of the towns to which it ran, but, taking no chances, drivers were also exhorting the crowd to hurry up and board for this place or that.

Of the throngs milling about in front of the hotel and struggling through the maze of wagons, only half were passengers, the rest runners, ever on the alert for some man who might betray the slightest appearance of indecision. A British gold seeker, already in his seat, watched with interest as a runner pounced upon such a man, seized him by the arm, dragged him through the crowd of stages, and started to bundle him into a coach bound for Nevada City before the poor fellow could make it clear that it was to Coloma he wanted to go. Keeping a firm hold on him, his captor then called to a brother runner collecting passengers for Coloma: "Oh, Bill! Oh, Bill!—where the hell are you?"

"Hullo!" shouted Bill from across the street.

"Here's a man for Coloma!" bellowed the other still clutching his prize lest he escape before Bill can take him in hand.

Apparently, mused the Briton, if a hundred men wanted to go anywhere, it took a hundred others to dispatch them. There was certainly no danger of anyone's being left behind, but the strong possibility that some timid man happening by would be shipped off to parts unknown before he could collect his wits and speak up.

After all the stages were full, the drivers settled themselves, gathered up their reins, cracked their whips, swore at the horses, and the solid mass began to dissolve. The grooms cleared the way, the passengers cheered, and they were off, those teams in front starting at a gallop, and as soon as there was room, all racing in a body until they were out of town. Then they began to spread in various directions and, as one passenger bound for Hangtown tells it, "in a few minutes I found myself one of a small isolated community, which four splendid horses were galloping over the plains like mad. No hedges, no ditches, no houses, no road in fact—it was a vast open plain, as smooth as a calm ocean."

They made a straight course of it across the valley for thirty miles, catching glimpses of the river as they sped along, changing horses at the numerous stations, and threading their way in and out of the strings of wagons laden with supplies for the mines and the trains of mules staggering under barrels of gin, brandy, and flour, all churning up clouds of suffocating dust.

With the ascent of the first range of hills the track grew narrow and rough, pitted with deep ruts, strewn with large rocks and stumps, and interwoven with a tracery of gnarled roots. To anyone not used to such a road an upset seemed sure, but confidence was inspired (in some passengers, but by no means all) by observing

the coolness and dexterity of the driver as he circumvented every obstacle, but without going one inch farther than necessary out of his way to save us from perdition.

With his right foot he managed the break, and, clawing the reins with both hands, he swayed his body from side to

side to preserve his equilibrium, as now on the right pair of
wheels, now on the left, he cut the "outside edge" round a
stump or a rock; and when coming to a spot where he was
going to execute a difficult manoeuvre on a piece of road
which slanted violently down to one side, he trimmed the
waggon as one would a small boat in a squall. . . .

"Hard up to the right!" (or left), he would shout, and all
the insiders would loll their heads and bodies out on that side
to preserve the balance.

This danger past, the whip would coolly light up a cigar
and, lashing his snorting horses to a run, dash on to the next
stump, boulder, or craggy chasm.

Thirty more miles of this sort of driving and there was Hangtown, the end of the line, where passengers scrambled out, con-
gratulating themselves on their arrival all in one piece.

In 1848, Colonel John Calhoun Johnson, an early transmoun-
tain mail carrier, opened up a trail that reduced the distance
over the Sierra to less than a hundred miles. Going east, he
had followed the canyon of the South Fork American and,
above its headwaters at Tom Audrain's, found a pass (now
called Johnson Pass) from which he dropped into Lake Valley.
There he forded the Upper Truckee River, crossed Luther
Pass, traversed Hope Valley to the canyon of the West Carson
River, and following it, reached Mormon Station (presently
Genoa).

Major George Chorpenning was awarded the government
contract to carry letters weekly between Hangtown and Salt
Lake City, and ran his first "Jackass Mail" over "Johnson's Cut-
off" in 1851. He left on May 1 and arrived at Salt Lake on
June 6, with the first mail to reach the Great Basin via the
Johnson Pass. But sixteen days had been spent in fighting his
way over the snow-packed summits.

Several years later a young Norwegian, John A. Thompson
(born John Tostensen), read a news item about Chorpenning's

trials in getting the mails over the Sierra in winter, and a solution occurred to him. As a boy in Norway he had, like everyone else, made his way about in winter on skis. Although he had not seen any since he was ten, he was certain that, if he could make himself a pair, this would end the problem.

He had crossed the Plains in 1851, to try his luck gold mining at Hangtown, Coon Hollow, and Kelsey's Diggings, but like so many others he was disappointed, and turned in disgust to farming along Putah Creek, in the Sacramento Valley.

He now set about making skis from the valley oaks that grew on his ranch. When finished they were ten feet long and, being of green wood, weighed twenty-four pounds, heavy by later standards, but then Thompson has been described as "a man of giant strength," "of splendid physique, standing six feet in his stockings, and weighing 180 pounds"—a handsome man, with "blonde hair and beard . . . fair skin and blue eyes . . ."

He took his skis to Hangtown to try them out and was soon feeling so confident he held a public exhibition. These were the first skis to be seen in California, and people called them Norwegian snowshoes or Norwegian skates.

Those who watched him fly down the slopes predicted he would dash his brains out against a tree or plunge to death over a cliff. His old friends begged him to give it up; but instead, he announced that he was ready to carry the mail across the mountains.

He made his first trip in January 1856, covering the hundred miles from Hangtown to Carson Valley in three days. On his return he found himself hailed as a wonder—and already regarded as a necessity.

"Snowshoe" Thompson they called him, and he soon became a fixed institution, carrying the mails for twenty winters. He never delayed his departure on account of a storm, but kept a regular schedule. It was said many times as he started off into the teeth of a blizzard that he would not be seen again until his body was found after the spring thaw.

He carried no arms, because of excess weight, and took along neither overcoat nor blankets. "The heavy pack on my back, and my vigorous exercise kept me warm," he told a friend. The weight of these mail sacks was usually sixty to eighty pounds, but there were times when they weighed more than a hundred.

Whenever he stopped for a few hours' sleep (he required little), he would build a good warm fire, pile pine boughs thickly on the snow, and stretch out on them with his feet toward the flames and his head pillowed on the mailsack. He did not always sleep in the open. At Cottage Rock, below Strawberry, he had a favorite small dry cave where he slept whenever he could conveniently pass that way. And sometimes in storms he would take shelter in a deserted cabin buried in the drifts, often having to enter by way of the chimney.

All he carried for food was a small packet of jerked beef or dry sausage and a few hard crackers stuffed into the front of his shirt, never anything that had to be cooked, for his meals were often taken on the run. For drink he simply scooped up a handful of snow.

Thompson kept to no regular path, but rather to a general direction, being guided, as he explained, by "the prevailing course of the winds, the trees and rocks, the formations and configurations of the mountains, and the stars in the heavens." Occasionally when traveling at night he would be caught in a blizzard so heavy he could not see to go on. Then he would climb to the top of some large flat rock, which the winds swept free of snow, and there keep up a dance until daybreak. Near one pass that was subject to blizzards, for years a certain rock was pointed out as the spot where Snowshoe Thompson had jigged away many a night to keep from freezing.

He was never lost. "I can't be lost! I've got something in here" he explained, tapping his forehead, "that keeps me right. I have found many persons who were lost—dozens of men. . . . There is no danger of getting lost in a narrow range of mountains like the Sierras, if a man has his wits about him."

He was much more than a mail carrier, being a sort of un-

official ambassador to both sides of the mountains, bringing
the latest news and gossip, reporting on weather and depth of
snow in the passes, executing special commissions, and undertaking missions of mercy. It was Thompson who took to the
assayer, wrapped in a piece of checked shirting, samples of
that puzzling "blue stuff" that turned out to be the rich silver
ore of the Comstock Lode; he who shopped in Sacramento for
a "peep-stone" for Eilly Orrum, the "Washoe Seeress"; he who
packed in the type that was to print the famed *Territorial Enterprise*, the journal on which young Sam Clemens got his start.
The list is long.

Thompson got very little pay for what he did. "Two years
he carried the United States mail when there was no contract
for that service, and he got nothing"; there was nothing either
for those winters when he helped George Chorpenning, for
Chorpenning failed. "First and last, he did a vast deal of work
for nothing. Some seasons our overland mail would not have
reached California during the whole winter, had not Thompson
turned out on his snow-shoes and carried the sack across the
mountains," wrote Dan De Quille.

With the constant increase in overland travel to California
from 1850 onward, the demand for improved, all-year roads
over the Sierra became loud and insistent. After much agitation
and pressure, the state legislature at length passed a bill au-
thorizing the survey and construction of such a road. However,
no appropriations were voted, and the surveys had to be paid
for by popular subscription. After the surveyor-general had
made his recommendation of Johnson's Cut-off, money for
building the road had to be raised by those counties to be most
benefited.

There was immense local enthusiasm for the project, especially in Hangtown (by this time Placerville), which foresaw
a bright future as a great staging center. A Board of Wagon
Road Directors was formed and, in July 1857, seven of them
made a trial run of the route in a six-horse Concord coach fur-

nished by the Pioneer Stage Company, with Jared B. Crandall, one of the owners, in the driver's seat.

Although this road had been the path of the great overland migration, it was still a rudely broken track, hardly fit for mud wagons even in summer. Within two days after this first crossing by the directors, contracts were let to grade and level it, and ten days later Crandall announced the opening of a weekly stage service between Placerville and Genoa.

But within a year the whole enterprise seemed doomed; no money could be raised for repair or maintenance and the road was rapidly becoming impassable. The melting of each winter's snows washed it partially away, and what remained was deeply furrowed by the countless streams that sought outlet in the river.

Then came news of the greatest silver strike north of Mexico, and the cry that had been "Gold!" was now "Silver! Silver in Washoe! Beds of it ten thousand feet deep! Acres of it! Miles of it!" as men prepared to leave California for the Comstock, the Ophir, the Central, and the Choller mines.

But when the vanguard reached Placerville in March 1860, they found the great movement checked by the snow blockades and the hundreds of tons of freight that clogged the streets. The gambling saloons were filled to overflowing with men practicing for Washoe; clothing stores were placarded with notices offering goods at "ruinous sacrifices" to Washoe miners; forwarding houses and express offices were crammed with boxes and bales marked for Washoe; grocery stores were making up bundles and bags for the Washoe trade. "The newspapers were full of Washoe. In short, there was nothing but Washoe to be seen, heard, or thought of"—and yet no way to get there.

But the halt was only temporary. Pressed on by the incoming tide, and impelled by the desire to get there first, the advance guard toiled up the mountains and over the pass. Mule trains and sleds carried the necessary food, blankets, and tools, or men packed them on their backs.

"Improve the road!" was the cry. It was "literally lined with broken-down stages, wagons, and carts, presenting every variety of aspect, from the general smash-up to the ordinary capsize . . . loads of dry-goods and whiskey-barrels lay wallowing in the general wreck of matter. . . . Whole trains of pack-mules struggled frantically to make the transit from one dry point to another; 'burros', heavily laden, were frequently buried up to the neck, and had to be hauled out by main force. . . ."

The Wagon Road Directors were helpless. The best they could do was turn it into a toll road. Companies contracted to operate sections as turnpikes and be responsible for their repair and upkeep. A small army of laborers was set to work blasting boulders, grading and leveling, filling ruts, planking bogs, building bridges, and widening turnouts. The narrow, dangerous trail shortly became a broad, compact, well-graded highway. When snowdrifts blocked passage, well-equipped parties of men and horses went out from every toll station to clear the way, while in summer watering carts passed up and down in an effort to lay the dust. Around $5,000 was spent on each mile of the road's 101 miles.

But a tollhouse proved more lucrative than a gold mine. Receipts for the ten-mile stretch from Strawberry Flat to the western summit ran from $40,000 to $70,000 a year. An actual count kept during three weeks in August 1864 at George Swan's Upper Toll House at Slippery Ford recorded passage of 6,667 men on foot, 833 horsemen, 3,164 stage passengers, 5,000 pack animals, 2,564 teams, 4,649 head of cattle and flocks of uncounted turkeys afoot bound for the tables of Washoe miners.

In the beginning, freighting was limited to four- and six-mule teams, but as the grades were lowered and the road improved, ten-, twelve-, and even sixteen-mule trains become common. They stretched for miles in unbroken procession. If a teamster had for some reason to fall out of line, it took him hours to regain a place.

In 1861, 25,000 passengers traveled on the Pioneer Stage Line, and Jared Crandall had to put twelve Concord coaches on the run to handle them all. "From daybreak to sunset this sierran caravan traversed the mountain passes in long files," wrote a chronicler of the day. "Bells jangled, whips cracked, drivers shouted and swore, mules tugged and snorted, horses pranced, lumbering carts creaked and swayed, and mail-coaches rattled down the grades at full speed, threading the slow-moving lines which parted to give them free passage." Packers, traders, teamsters, vaqueros, peddlers, and bearded miners tramped through the dust or mud.

Overland Pony Express riders clattered over this route during their brief day. On April 3, 1860, the first westbound pony left St. Joseph, Missouri, and ten days later Sam Hamilton came flying through Placerville "amid the waving of flags, the firing of guns, and the hurrah of the multitude which lined the sides of the road to witness the important event." But after some 150 round trips made during eighteen months, the transcontinental telegraph outmoded this romantic service, and the ephemeral pony was gone.

Within weeks after the start of the rush to Washoe, tent and shanty booths offering board, lodgings, and liquor were as common as "blackberries in June" in every ravine and gulch all the way to the summit. A traveler, describing one of these tents ("not more than ten feet square"), related that the public bedroom (next to the bar) was lacking "beds, bedding, chairs, tables, and washstands"; its only amenities, he added, were "a piece of looking-glass nailed against the window-frame, and the general comb and tooth-brush hanging by strings from a neighboring post."

But these temporary structures were soon replaced by "good and substantial taverns, well-supplied with provisions, beds, fleas, bugs, etc., to say nothing of the essential article of whisky. . . ."

Three, Five, Six, Nine, Ten Mile House; Sportsman's Hall, which in its day had stabling for five hundred horses; Thirteen Mile House; Pacific House, where tradition holds Mark Twain,

Horace Greeley, and Josh Billings stopped; Whitehall; Sol
Perrin's; Sugar Loaf House; Dick Yarnold's; Dirty Mike's, "a
ruinously delapidated frame shanty," where the plates were
washed but once or twice a week; Mother Weltie's, Log Cabin
No. 2; What Cheer House; Strawberry, "known the length and
breadth of the land as the best stopping place"; Slippery Ford;
Phillips'; and Tom Audrain's are a few of the better known of
the ninety-three inns that marked nearly every mile of the high-
road.

The scheduled time by Concord from Virginia City to Sacramento was soon cut to eighteen hours, and special express
coaches with relays of horses were able to reduce the trip to
twelve and a half hours. Drivers were expected to rival Jehu
and did not disappoint passengers, who were often outraged
at the jolting, but were the first to complain when the stage
was slowed to a snail's pace up a grade.

"Do many people get killed on this route?" a Washoe-bound
passenger, seated on the box with the driver, asked as the stage
"made a sudden lurch in the dark and bowled along the edge
of a fearful precipice."

"Nary a kill that I know of," the whip responded. "Some
drivers mashes 'em once in a while, but that's only whisky or
bad drivin'. Last summer a few stages went over the grade,
but nobody was hurt bad—only a few legs 'n arms broken.
Them was opposition stages. Pioneer stages as a genr'l thing,
travels on the road . . . our company's very strict; they won't
keep drivers . . . that gets drunk and mashes up stages. . . .
'Twon't pay; 'tain't a good investment for man nor beast. A
stage is worth more'n two thousand dollars, and legs cost heavy
besides. . . ."

"How in the world can you see your way through this dust?"

"Smell it. Fact is, I've traveled over these mountains so often
I can tell where the road is by the sound of the wheels. When
they rattle I'm on hard ground; when they don't rattle I gen'-
r'lly look over the side to see where she's a-going."

Still, no driver could foresee when some grizzly would charge across the road in front of his stage, as one did on a fine May night in 1864, causing the lead horses to rear and back in terror, breaking the pole, and sending the badly frightened passengers leaping out and off in all directions, some in their scurry tumbling and hurting themselves.

The stage driver was the captain of his craft and autocrat of the road at all times. He was the

> best liked and most honored personage in the country through which he took his right of way. . . . His orders were obeyed with the greatest celerity, and he was always the first to be saluted by the wayfarer, the passenger, the hostler, the postmaster, and the man at the door of the wayside inn. He was a general favorite with the women who lived along his route, earning the privilege of greeting them by their first names, and chucking the young ones under the chin,

recalled one who knew all the early drivers well.

Their average pay was $300 a month, and much of it was spent on the fine-fitting suits, tailor-made of the best materials, the boots, gauntlets, and hats—"cream-white, half stiff and half slouch," which distinguished them as dashing figures. No one ever thought of offering such a lordly personage a tip, but a hat, a pair of boots or gloves, silk handkerchiefs, or good cigars were always acceptable.

Many of these knights of the lash were teetotalers; others occasionally "spreed it" when off the run; and there were still others who couldn't keep their teams on the grades unless they took "a couple of fingers" at every inn, and joined the "outsides" moderately often between changes.

The most famous of all the drivers on the great river road was Hank Monk. He was below average height, wore no whiskers, and lacked that "dandy-robust way" of his brother jehus. He sported the fine boots, gauntlets, and hat, but when it came to suits, Hank preferred common corduroy, "of the true tobacco-juice tint," one of his friends remembers. When on the road, he mended his clothes with copper harness rivets, not being much of a hand with needle and thread, and it is said that in the 1870s, Levi Strauss, a San Francisco clothing manufacturer, learning of Hank's ingenious makeshift, adopted it for overalls.

Still Hank Monk was a favorite with women passengers who enjoyed the little jokes he played on them and relished his yarns. One of the best liked was a supposed Indian legend attached to the towering granite cliff called Lover's Leap, looming above Strawberry. It might even have been Hank who was responsible for the story of how Strawberry got its name.

Irad Fuller Berry, who kept the inn and toll station, was a shrewd man of business and soon grew very rich. "His dinners were excellent; his suppers without reproach; his beds as good as any on the road . . . and altogether he was a popular and flourishing Berry," observed a traveler of the day. But it did not take the teamsters long to discover that he sometimes mixed straw with the hay he sold, charging, of course, hay prices. This was nothing out of their pockets, but they took great pride in keeping their mules in top condition and fed them only the choicest oats, barley, and hay. And these drivers grew angry and complained loudly, and began calling him "old *straw*-Berry." The name was soon attached to his hostelry, and it has been known as Strawberry ever since.

Hank Monk was not opposed to taking a little liquor aboard now and then, and at least once had more than was good for him. On this occasion, runs the story, he became so fuddled he gave his horses whiskey and watered himself, becoming sober enough by accident to handle his inebriated team. But this was perhaps a slander, for it was his boast that he had never injured a passenger during twenty years of driving over the Sierra.

At ten o'clock on the night of July 19, 1858, Hank Monk brought the first overland mail into Placerville, the western terminus for the Central Overland Route. There was a small crowd waiting to cheer him, and William Cary illuminated his

new hotel in honor of the event; but the hour was so late the
real celebration was reserved for the next evening when "a
grand jubilee" was held in the town plaza. There were bonfires,
band music, and many speeches, received with "vehement
cheers." The climax to the entertainment was provided by a
"Dr. Pettit, who sent a beautiful balloon into the ethereal regions."

But Hank Monk's lasting fame stems from his having driven
Horace Greeley on a wild ride from Carson City to Placerville,
almost exactly a year later. The famous editor, following his
own advice, had gone west as an advocate for the contemplated
transcontinental railroad, and to see for himself California's
potential—which overwhelmed him. It was not Greeley's account of that ride but those spirited and humorous ones written
by Artemus Ward, Dan De Quille, and Mark Twain that made
Hank immortal. The essentials of the tale are the same in all
versions: Greeley on stepping into the stage told Hank Monk
that he had an engagement to lecture in Placerville, and was

> very anxious to go through quick. Hank Monk cracked his
> whip and started off at an awful pace. The coach bounced up
> and down in such a terrific way that it jolted all the buttons
> off of Horace's coat, and finally shot his head clean through
> the roof of the stage, and then he yelled at Hank Monk and
> begged him to go easier—said he warn't in as much of a hurry
> as he was awhile ago. But Hank Monk said, "Keep your seat,
> Horace, and I'll get you there on time"—and you bet he did,
> too, what was left of him!

This "most laughable anecdote," as Mark Twain termed it,
made its way around the world and was even set to music. "The
Hank Monk Schottishe," a popular piece in its day, had on its
cover a drawing of a stagecoach going pell-mell, with the
legend: "Keep your seat, Horace, I'll get you thar on time."
There were many who affirmed that it was Hank Monk who
made Horace Greeley famous.

The humorists had not stretched the truth. The proprietor of the Cary House remembered clearly that the top of the stage that brought the noted editor to his door was broken in three places, that Greeley's hat was knocked in, and that the horses were covered with foam. "What was left of him" hobbled out of Hank's coach and into the hotel barroom where a reception committee discovered him and hustled him off to a banquet in his honor. In responding to the numerous toasts that night, he is said to have risen from a couch rather than a chair.

The next day he sent a dispatch to the *Tribune,* giving his readers a tame account of his ride but ending on a strong note of advice: "I cannot conscientiously recommend the route I have traveled to summer tourists in quest of pleasure, but it is a balm for the many bruises to know that I am at last in CALI-FORNIA."

The enigma of all the select whips of the Sierra run was Charley Parkhurst. "One-Eyed Charley" they called him because early in his career a horse had kicked him in the face and blinded one eye. Those who knew him said that he was compactly built and broad shouldered, sun-browned and beardless, with even, pleasant features which were at times moved by a warm smile. His voice was high-pitched but strong. He was considered by the fraternity to be one of the boys, although reticent about his affairs and never a hand with the ladies no matter how trim the bodice or pretty the face. He smoked, chewed, drank moderately, and played cards for cigars and drinks.

Only once did anyone see Charley betray strong emotions. Then a highwayman had poked a pistol into his ribs and told him to throw down the box. Charley was angry. "I wasn't expecting this," he said. "But the next time you try and stop me, I'll be ready for you!"

And the next time, he was. When the leader of the road agents yelled "Halt!" Charley whipped out a pistol and shot him dead, then, applying the lash to his horses, escaped. Charley was never stopped again.

He was equally cool in the face of other dangers. Once when he was crossing a bridge at the time of a freshet, the structure began to sway and rock in the churn of water. Feeling it about to give way, Charley laid on the whip and went dashing over, reaching the other shore just as the planks and timbers crashed into the river.

It was at the close of the 1860s, after twenty years on the road, that Charley Parkhurst stepped down from the box for the last time, to open a stage station and saloon on the highway between Watsonville and Santa Cruz. A few years later he went into the cattle business, but after a time, feeling that he had worked hard enough, he retired to a modest cottage near Seven Mile House, right on the Watsonville road where he could keep an eye on passing coaches and hear their familiar rattle and jingle. He lived there quietly, well known to his neighbors as a pleasant, elderly little man who preferred to keep to himself.

On December 29, 1879, Charles Dudley Parkhurst, a native of New Hampshire, and registered voter of the State of California, died. Friends who came in to prepare his body for the funeral suffered a rude shock. Charley, the celebrated whip of the Sierra, the dashing driver, the fearless foe of highwaymen, was a woman—said to be the first woman ever to vote in the United States.

With the transportation of so much Comstock bullion over this road, stage robbery became a flourishing industry. Masked desperadoes, well armed and well trained in their duties, posted themselves at strategic points and attacked so suddenly, resistance was nearly hopeless. If a driver refused to obey the order to halt, one well-aimed bullet saved him the trouble, for his horses would not move with a dead or dying animal in the traces. The passengers would step out meekly enough in the face of an ominous row of shotguns and stand silently in line, their hands above their heads, while one of the robbers adroitly relieved them of their money, watches, and jewelry. Meanwhile, the Wells, Fargo strongbox was pried open; or if the treasure were in a safe, a well-applied blast of powder tore it apart. When all the valuables had been taken, passengers and coach were allowed to go on; lives were not in danger unless resistance was offered.

Between nine and ten o'clock on the night of June 30, 1864, the most bizarre and famous robbery on this road took place on the narrow grade a few miles above Sportsman's Hall, to be known ever after as Bullion Bend. Eight men armed with pistols and shotguns stepped suddenly out of the gloom and called on Ned Blair to bring his stage to a halt. They held his leaders and demanded the express box.

"I have none," he replied fearlessly.

"Then throw down the bullion!"

"Come and get it!" he challenged.

While the others covered Blair with their guns, two of their men climbed up and removed eight heavy sacks of silver. Blair had something more to say: they were not to molest his passengers. They assured him, politely enough, they were only interested in what belonged to Wells, Fargo.

Just then another coach was heard approaching. The driver, Charley Watson, seeing Blair's stage stopped, supposed he had had an accident, and pulled up to help him. In an instant two highwaymen had him covered with their guns and ordered him to deliver the bullion and express. He handed them three sacks of silver and a small strongbox.

True to their word, they did not rob the passengers but instead asked them to pass the hat and take up a collection for the Southern cause. Then just before riding off, the leader handed Watson a slip of paper that read:

> This is to certify that I have received from Wells, Fargo & Co. the sum of $——— cash, for the purpose of outfitting recruits enlisted in California for the Confederate States Army.
>
> (signed) R. Henry Ingram
Capt. Com'g. Co., C.S.A.

June, 1864

As soon as the drivers reached Placerville, they reported the robbery to Sheriff Rogers. Taking his deputy, Joseph Staples, constables Van Eaton and George Ranney, two policemen, and Charley Watson, he set off in pursuit around daylight.

At Thirteen Mile House, Rogers arrested two men; Watson had recognized one of them. The landlord told the officers that the two had knocked at his door sometime after midnight, asking permission to sleep in his stable since they had no money to pay for a bed. He told them they were welcome to sleep upstairs in the house, and they accepted the offer. He had thought it strange that they kept their hats drawn down over their eyes while they talked with him.

Deputy Staples and Van Eaton and Ranney had by this time tracked the other men to the head of Pleasant Valley, on the old emigrant road. Van Eaton was sent back to report to the sheriff that they had picked up the trail, leaving the others to ride on to Somerset House on the Grizzly Flat road, to ask the landlady if she had any guests.

"Why, yes," she told them, "there are six men asleep in the room at the head of the stairs."

Staples rushed up and, bursting open the door, leveled his gun and shouted: "You are my prisoners!"

A shot rang out and Staples slumped to the floor, dead. Another shot, and Ranney fell beside him, badly wounded. Taking the officers' money, watches, arms, and horses, the highwaymen vanished without a trace.

Many months passed before the trail was picked up again, some two hundred miles away, and a number of arrests were made. The leader turned out to be a former law officer from the South, and his men Confederate soldiers—or, this is what they said.

Today's traveler over this historic highway, once an Indian trail, can hunt out some of the old landmarks and recapture a breath of its romantic past. In among the asters and mimulus on the shoulder stand a number of granite milestones which told

of the great robbery; beyond is a promontory where early travelers caught their first view of the river threading its way at the
bottom of the wooded gorge.

The canyon of the South Fork with its vast forests, tumbling
waterfalls, flowery meadows and banks, and, in the higher
reaches, bald domes and windswept granite peaks covered in
season with snow, is one of spectacular beauty. Although the
Placerville road remains a much-traveled route over the Sierra,
that part which winds close to the river is but a two-lane track
through this enchanting wilderness, grown more scenic with
time, for under the protection of the Forest Service, a heavy
mantle of second-growth timber and chaparral now covers the
scars of early-day logging and mining rubble.

This is the only fork of the American where a road follows
along its banks for miles, allowing the traveler to observe it
closely at all seasons and listen to its year-round song of haste
and urgency; marvel at summer's play of sun and shadow on
gold-green waters and winter's deep mantle of white; mark the
foam and splash of its cascades; note the bubbles racing over
its surface like flotillas, and wonder at the deceptive phenome-
non of the plunging rapids, when the river seems to have turned
back. The lower waters, apparently defiant of this impelling
hurry and boldly challenging the onward rush, appear to be
struggling upriver, slipping and sliding like bands of horsemen
scaling a mountain of glass.

21

The Fall of Sutter's Empire

MANY OF THOSE very Americans whom Sutter had urged to settle in the Sacramento Valley and help build up his empire, whom he had welcomed with open arms and befriended after their arrival, were the ones who in the end cheated him at every turn, squatted on his lands, stole his horses, butchered his cattle, sheep, and hogs for the market, raided his orchards and gardens, and cut down those fine stands of oaks and sycamores which were among his last valuable assets. They had the audacity to set up a lumberyard on his property, and when Sutter protested and tried to salvage some of this fortune in timber for himself, they vengefully set fire to his woodpiles, knowing that he had no redress since they controlled the local courts. Sutter became so disgusted and disheartened that in 1850 he turned over all his real property, aside from the Hock Farm, to a firm of land agents for $6,000, and the right to one-sixth of the proceeds from sale or lease. As it turned out, this was the only money he ever received for those vast acreages. "I understood little about business and was foolish enough to have faith in men who cheated me on every side," he was to write. "I was the victim of every swindler that came along."

When both of Sutter's land grants (New Helvetia and Sobrante) were confirmed by the United States District Court, a whole boatload of his friends steamed up the river to congratulate him. "They were treated to the most cheer that the land could raise, and the costliest wines flowed freely as water." But

Sutter's jubilation was short-lived, for the federal law passed in 1851 to settle private land claims in California was so constructed that every case won by a claimant in the lower courts was automatically appealed—at the defendant's expense. Within two years Sutter spent $100,000 on lawyers' fees, witnesses, and interest on the loans. To defray these costs, he was forced to mortgage parcel after parcel of the Hock Farm.

Sutter's personal life was no less troubled. His eldest son and namesake, who had come to the fort in 1848, had been shocked when he discovered the true state of his father's affairs. "I saw myself how everything went on," he wrote. "Anything belonging to my father was at everybody's disposal." He was a witness to the drunken orgies that were an established pattern at the fort, and observed the dissolute habits and dishonest practices of those who lived there and were closest to his father. He was capable and conscientious, and set about at once to try and salvage his father's fortune and bring order into his chaotic life. But his efforts only served to estrange his parent who became bitterly resentful of the son's presence. Designing cronies of the old man, afraid of losing their control and forfeiting their opportunities to cheat him, did everything they could to widen the breach. They filled Sutter's ears with so many malicious lies about his son he came to hate him, and one day, in a towering rage over some new evidence of supposed rascality on his son's part, he took out a pistol to kill him.

By July 1850 they had become implacable enemies, and the young man, unnerved by the endless quarreling, and suffering fevers and fits of blindness as a result, sailed from California for the eastern states. But while waiting for a ship at Acapulco, he fell in love with a young Mexican woman, married her, and went into the import and export business there.

That January, Sutter's wife, his daughter Eliza, and two younger sons, Emil and Alphons, had arrived from Switzerland, expecting to find Sutter the richest and most influential man in California. In anticipation of their exalted station they had put

on airs, according to Heinrich Lienhard, who had been sent to
Europe to escort them to San Francisco. He found them unbear-
ably conceited, rude, and petty. Only Eliza had inherited in
part her father's good looks and charm, although she lacked
his polish. The boys were without any of their father's good
qualities, while Mrs. Sutter, overworked and prematurely aged,
tended to be harsh, grim, and penurious. Nor were their dis-
positions improved any when they finally discovered Sutter's
real position, and the time came when sons were forced to work
in the gardens and orchards, and mother and daughter attend to
household and kitchen tasks.

None of the children had received the advantages of much
education or training, for the debts their father had left behind
when he escaped to the New World had entirely consumed
their mother's generous inheritance. For sixteen years she and
her children had been forced to depend on the charity of her
sisters.

Not too many months after their arrival, Sutter discovered a
budding love affair between his daughter and George Engler,
a talented young Swiss of good family whom he had hired to
give piano lessons to his youngest and favorite son. Sutter was
furious, for in his opinion Engler was aspiring far above his
station. "*My children* can marry into the finest families of Philadelphia and New York, if they choose," he once told Lienhard.
Accordingly, Engler was summarily dismissed and forbidden to
write Eliza or come near the place again. Lienhard recalled:
"Old Sutter was in a highly excited state, and talked so harshly
to his daughter that she tried to commit suicide. . . ."

Then suddenly one winter day two years later, Engler, who
was then working in Sacramento, received an urgent letter from
Eliza asking him to come at once to the Hock Farm. He packed
his belongings and left on the next steamer. Not long afterward
there were rumors afloat that old Sutter had finally consented
to the marriage.

On March 21, 1852, the wedding took place at the Hock Farm.

For the last time Sutter was to play genial host in the grand manner to hundreds of guests, among them a number of celebrities. Throngs came up the river by steamboat and countless others arrived by stage and horseback. The parlor was decorated with greenery and early flowers. A band played on the terrace. There was an elaborate supper with an abundance of champagne, and afterward there were speeches and toasts, and a large display of fireworks on the river. Indians danced and played their games for the entertainment of the guests. The festivities lasted until dawn.

The British author Sir Henry Vere Huntley chose the morning after the wedding to call on Sutter. He found him still "sitting at a table amongst bottles half and quite empty, wine-glasses and tumblers, showing what had once filled them, and stumps of half-used cigars, the floor covered with all the debris of a supper; the captain scracely recovered from his indulgences."

From this time on misfortunes crowded him. In 1853 there was a devastating flood, and in a despondent mood he considered selling the Hock Farm and moving to the Sandwich Islands. Then came Eliza's divorce after one stormy year of marriage, and Sutter's desertion by both his sons at a time when he most needed them. The moody, quarrelsome Emil set off to try his luck in the mines, while Alphons, who had military ambitions, joined William Walker's filibustering expedition to Nicaragua. In 1857 the Hock Farm was sold by the sheriff for a debt one of Sutter's fraudulent agents had contracted in his name and without his knowledge. He was fortunately able to redeem the property.

The following year the United States Supreme Court dealt Sutter a staggering blow when it reversed the decision of the lower court and refused to confirm the Sobrante grant, which constituted two-thirds of his lands. By this time there was virtually nothing left but the heavily mortgaged Hock Farm. But there were more sorrows in store. In 1863 the favorite Alphons died of a tropical disease contracted in Central America.

In the early morning hours of June 21, 1865, one of Sutter's final ties with California was severed when the house on the Hock Farm burned to the ground. "The fire was the work of an incendiary," the press reported. "There was no insurance." Sutter and his wife, now living alone, barely escaped with their lives, and the old pioneer stood helplessly by, watching the flames consume all his priceless records and papers of early days, his library, and the memoirs that he had commenced to write.

That December he and his wife arrived in Washington, D.C. Sutter had decided to seek redress for his losses by appealing to Congress. Early the next year his petition was presented. Although he had many friends in the capital who believed he was entitled to reimbursement for his aid to the emigrants, his services as one of the builders of California, and his injury through loss of the Sobrante grant, it was not until March 1870 that a "Bill for the Relief of John A. Sutter" was introduced.

But ten years, and then incredibly fifteen, were to pass without any constructive action being taken on the bill. He was by then, as he wrote, "sick in heart and body," tired of his vain appeals to Congress and the unfulfilled promises, and suffering from inflammatory rheumatism and kidney disease.

He and his wife were not in want, as has so often been stated. After the $15,000 tax refund due him on the Sobrante grant had been repaid by the state of California (it was doled out in $250 monthly installments), young John Sutter, by then the United States Consul at Acapulco, sent them money, or rather, sent it to his mother, for the old bitterness toward his father lingered. He had made a small fortune in his business, and in 1871 built his mother a comfortable brick house in the Moravian village of Lititz, Pennsylvania, where she and his father had been passing their summers during the years of fruitless waiting.

By the end of May 1880 Sutter was in better spirits. He wrote to a friend with some of his old optimism that in two weeks there would be a final settlement of his affair. He had received positive assurance that the bill awarding him $50,000 would be passed.

But 1880 was an election year, and Congressmen were eager to attend the political conventions. They adjourned abruptly on June 16. Among the stacks of unfinished business lay the bill for Sutter's relief.

This was the final blow. Two days later John Sutter was found dead in his little hotel room in Washington. The shock of disappointment had been too much for the heart already taxed by the years of anxious waiting. On the table lay an unfinished letter to his wife, telling her of this latest setback.

After a funeral service held at the hotel, his body, banked with California flowers from the capital's Botanic Garden, was taken to Lititz. Burial was in a quiet corner of the little Moravian cemetery there. General John C. Frémont, his feelings toward Sutter tempered by time and his own misfortunes, delivered one of the eulogies. He said, in part: "He died under the shadow of the Capitol of the people whom he had served so well . . . the uppermost feeling in my mind is one of surprise and regret that such a life—a life so filled with kindly acts, so valuable, so honorable, and so signalized by services to the country—should have met such cruel neglect and such harsh injustice."

22

The Iron Horse

THE FIRST steam passenger railroad west of the Rockies was built along the banks of the American River.

In answer to pressing demands for better and faster transportation to the northern mines, the Sacramento Valley Railroad was organized in 1854 to connect Sacramento City and Placerville. The engineer hired to plan and build it was Theodore D. Judah, a talented and resourceful young man from Connecticut who was an enthusiast almost to the point of eccentricity on the subject of the transcontinental railroad.

He reached Sacramento in mid-May of that same year, and two weeks later he handed in his report and preliminary survey to the directors. By the following February crews were already grading roadbed—and digging out gold. In March, Judah showed the editor of the *Sacramento Daily Union,* "a handsome ring" fashioned from "the first gold ever taken from earth in making [a] Railroad bank."

In mid-July, a fifteen-ton locomotive that had rounded Cape Horn was landed at Sacramento. Two weeks later a crowd of eager passengers, many of whom had never seen a railroad train before, squeezed themselves onto two flatcars for a fifteen-mile ride across the hot and dusty valley to the head of construction.

On Washington's Birthday, 1856, a gala excursion and grand ball celebrated completion of the line—not to Placerville as planned, but only the first twenty-two and a half miles. The cost of construction and equipment had totaled $1.1 million and promoters and investors had to be content for the time being with this first miniature railroad that made history—a line still in use today.

At the railhead, close to the junction of the North and South forks, the town of Folsom, laid out the year before on William Leidesdorff's old Rancho Rio de los Americanos, mushroomed into a bustling staging center. A traveler to the mines described the confusion.

At the depot

> stages backed up in a long row; prancing horses in front; swearing and sweating porters, baggage-masters, drivers, and passengers all about; John Chinamen . . . running distractedly through the crowd in search of their lost bundles; anxious ladies, prolific in crinoline and gorgeous in silks and satins (the California travelling costume), fretting and scolding over crushed bandboxes; and stern-looking men of an official cast of countenance shouting, fiercely, "This way, gents! 'Ere's the place for your baggage! Bring it along if you want it weighed; if you don't, it won't go—that's all!"

Thirty pounds of baggage was allowed; all extra baggage, twenty-five cents a pound. There was much wrangling over charges, and confusion over seats. Then at last they were off, "with fervent thanks . . . that we are clear of the smoke and trouble and turmoil of the railroad dépôt at Folsom."

Travel to the mines had been cut by a full day, and a new era in California transportation seemed about to open as Placerville and Auburn made plans to raise money for extensions of the railroad.

In 1859 Judah was hired to explore the mountains for a second wagon road across the Sierra to the new silver towns of Nevada. He returned from his summer's survey fired with enthusiasm for a route he considered practicable for a railroad as well. He envisioned it as the western link in the long-anticipated transcontinental line and talked of little else wherever he went; people were soon calling him "Pacific Railroad crazy."

Still, they listened with interest to what he said, for Californians were anxious to have a rail connection with the East; without it they feared the state would never grow as it should. It was almost impossible, however, for them to believe that trains could ever cross the steep and rugged Sierra.

But Judah had vision and determination, and he continued to explore the mountains for the best rail grade. In the fall of 1860, on his way back from one of his twenty-odd reconnoitering expeditions, he stopped at Dutch Flat to see Dr. Daniel W. Strong, a fellow railroad enthusiast. In the back room of Strong's drugstore, Judah wrote the articles of association for the Central Pacific Railroad of California, and he and the doctor made the first subscriptions.

On June 28, 1861, the company was incorporated. Earlier in the year Judah had talked a group of Sacramento merchants into backing him. Prominent among them were four men, later known as the Big Four: Mark Hopkins and Collis P. Huntington, who lent the room above their hardware store for the meeting at which the company was organized; Leland Stanford, a wholesale grocer who had started his career as a storekeeper in the mining camp of Michigan Bluff; and Charles Crocker, a dry-goods merchant.

Not everyone was convinced that Judah's route—which left the foothills at Auburn, followed the ridge above the American's North Fork to the heights, and crossed the summit south of Donner Pass—was the most practicable course over the Sierra. At the 7,239-foot summit the heaviest snowfalls in the United States had been recorded; the ascent was long, steep, and winding, and would call for many tunnels, while much of the roadbed would have to be hewn in solid granite. Many thought the rails should logically connect with the Sacramento Valley Line at Folsom, follow the natural passage of the South Fork's canyon, and cross the summit at Johnson Pass. And for a time it seemed as though the directors had decided on this route.

Certainly Alcander John Bayley thought they had when in the summer of 1861 he started to build a three-story brick hotel at Pilot Hill to replace a more modest wooden structure that had recently burned. He expected to cater not only to train passengers transferring to stages that would carry them on to Auburn and other gold towns along the North and Middle forks, but to the crowds of excursionists who came to see the Alabaster or Coral Cave, a limestone cavern of numerous rooms and passages filled with strange formations in rainbow colors. The cave, at the foot of Whiskey Bar Hill in Kidd's Ravine just a few miles down the road, had since its opening that April attracted more than three thousand visitors. It was such a popular sight, a special stage ran there from Folsom.

But when the hotel was nearly finished Bayley learned that the railroad would pass through Auburn, over the route surveyed by Judah. Negotiations with the toll road proprietors along the South Fork had been broken off because of their stubborn insistence that they be given a controlling interest in Central Pacific in return for their rights.

Known ever after as "Bayley's Folly," the stately red brick building with its double piazzas, observatory, broad carriage drive, and extensive plantings became the Bayley family home. It was for years the most palatial mansion in that part of California.

Alcander Bayley had come to the goldfields from Vermont in 1849, and after prospecting with little success in and around Coloma and Hangtown, he opened a "storage house" in the fast-growing city of Sacramento. The next year he was back in Coloma, managing Winters' Hotel at a salary of $500 a month. In this first flush of prosperity he married Miss Elizabeth Jones, theirs being the second wedding to take place in El Dorado County. For the wedding trip to Sacramento he hired the only horse and buggy in the county, paying two

ounces a day for its use. On their return ten days later, Uncle
Billy Rogers, owner of the rig, "magnanimously agreed to
deduct $20.00 from the bill, and settle for $300.00."

In November 1851, Bayley celebrated the opening of his
own hotel, the Oak Valley House, set on 640 acres at Pilot Hill,
with a grand ball that lasted two days. Ten years later this
wooden structure burned and he built his Folly.

He was destined to go on with more successful ventures as
owner of a prospering merchandise store at Pilot Hill, the
Grand Central Hotel at Lake Tahoe, and as a stock raiser, vine-
yardist, and winemaker at Oak Valley Ranch. The old house
still stands staunch beside the road to Coloma, slightly forlorn, only its second floor habitable. Its surrounding acres are
used as a horse farm.

Few who may wander along the quiet back road winding
down to Cooper's and Kidd's Ravine are even aware of passing the famed Alabaster Cave. Because it is now considered un-
safe, its entrance has been blocked with boulders and rubble,
and there is nothing left to suggest the "scene of wonder and
curiosity" that once drew throngs of tourists from all over California.

The insistent thump of pile drivers pounding bridge supports
into the bed of the American River formed a background to
the speeches and band music at the Central Pacific's ground-
breaking ceremonies held at Sacramento in January 1863. The
river had just overflowed and flooded the town, and layers of
straw were spread over the mud to give Leland Stanford, the
company's president and by then governor of California, footing to turn the first earth with a silver spade. The work of
building what was to become the western half of the transcontinental railroad had begun symbolically and in fact on the
bank of the American River.

That the Pacific Railroad had become a reality by an act
of Congress was owing largely to Theodore Judah's unflagging
efforts and enthusiasm. He could now look forward to devoting

all his energies to constructing the most difficult and challenging part of the entire transcontinental line. But ten months later he would be dead from yellow fever contracted while crossing the Isthmus on his way to New York. He was then thirty-seven.

The Pacific Railroad Act, signed as a military measure by President Lincoln on July 1, 1862, called for the construction of a railroad and telegraph line by two companies, the one to build eastward from the Pacific Ocean, and the other westward from Missouri. The Central Pacific, under contract to the government, would extend its rails just to California's eastern boundary, but in 1866 this was changed to read that point wherever the eastward and westward tracks should meet.

Many of the Central Pacific's first major problems were linked with the river. Bridges had to be built strong enough to withstand the fury of its floodwaters, extensive high fills constructed to elevate riverside track above the reach of torrents during storms and thaws, and towering trestles that became celebrated features of the road made to leap seemingly impassable chasms in the mountains. And the river nearly claimed the company's first locomotive, the *Governor Stanford.* As it was being hoisted from the deck of the riverboat *Artful Dodger,* cables slipped and it narrowly missed drowning.

Progress was agonizingly slow. Men who might have been recruited as laborers had either volunteered for service in the Civil War, or gone over the Sierra to the silver mines. It took eleven months to build eighteen miles of road that crossed the American and crept up into the foothills to Roseville—and the real challenge had not even begun. The first train, a work train, rolled over the rails in November 1863. By the next spring, when tracks had reached Newcastle, passenger service was started.

By the end of the following year the labor shortage was so acute the company petitioned the War Department for five thousand Confederate prisoners to be sent west as construction workers. Then the war ended, and that scheme was dropped.

Out of two thousand men hired and sent to the foothills, nine-teen hundred decamped for Washoe. Company agents combed gold camps and towns and sometimes ended up hiring twelve-year-olds and men of seventy—but even these were scarce.

It was then that Charles Crocker suggested hiring Chinese, a proposal that was dismissed lightly since the frail-looking Orientals were obviously unfit for backbreaking labor. Only when threatened with a strike did James Strowbridge, the construction superintendent, reluctantly agree to try a few Chinese. A crew of fifty was dispatched to him, and at the end of the first week came his plea: "Send up more coolies!" During those few days they had completed the longest and smoothest stretch of grading on the road.

Another fifty were promptly put into a freight car at Sacramento and sent to the end of the line. Concepts of their hardiness and endurance had been sharply revised: they were the first to get on the job in the morning and the last to quit. They were cheerful and willing, lived quietly in their own camps cooking rice, dried oysters, and cuttlefish, and drinking nothing stronger than tea.

The Chinatowns of California were scoured for these reliable workers, and every able-bodied man tempted with the promise of steady work at $40 a month. Within six months there were two thousand Chinese in blue cotton suits and basket hats pushing the work ahead at an incredible rate. The company looked forward to increasing its work force to fifteen thousand Chinese. Since no such number could be recruited locally, contracts were made to hire and import workers directly from Canton.

"Without them it would be impossible to complete the line in time," Leland Stanford explained to those who bitterly criticized the policy of hiring Chinese.

Tracklayers followed right behind the graders, and by the summer of 1865, trains were running as far as Clipper Gap, where stages took them on over the mountains to Virginia City.

In September the rails had reached Colfax, and the Central Pacific by then had a monopoly of all Nevada-bound freight and passenger traffic.

Colfax had been named to commemorate a visit from Schuyler Colfax, Speaker of the House and ardent partisan of the transcontinental railroad. President Lincoln had long been anxious to welcome California into the Union with a visit from some high-ranking member of the government. He had selected Colfax, and his dispatching him west constituted his last official act. On the night of April 14, 1865, the President received Colfax at the White House, gave him parting instructions, and bidding him Godspeed, left for Ford's Theatre—and the assassin's bullet.

On his way to California, Colfax and his party stopped on June 27 at the cemetery in Silver City, Nevada, to take part in a ceremony erecting a marble headstone over the grave of Hosea B. Grosh, whose body had been moved there from Gold Cañon at the request of his father, who had also ordered the monument.

Cape Horn, a sheer granite bluff fifteen hundred feet above the American River, proved the most formidable obstacle of the year. Its slippery face offered no foothold, but the resourceful Chinese cleverly solved that problem. With reeds and bamboo sent up from San Francisco, they wove large round baskets with waist-high sides. Into these baskets the pick and shovel workers and the crowbar and powdermen would step at the top of the cliff; they were then lowered over the edge with block and tackle, to dangle precariously above the river. A hand signal was used to alert the crew manning the ropes at the top. Sometimes these ropes snapped; sometimes after the fuses were lighted the signal was not obeyed promptly enough. No record was kept of the number of Chinese who lost their lives at Cape Horn, but from five hundred to a thousand met accidental death during the six years of construction.

Cape Horn became the railroad's favorite viewpoint. Passengers peering down into the chasm from car windows, or more dangerously from the platforms of open observation cars, saw little between themselves and eternity. For years trains made ten-minute scheduled stops there so travelers could walk to the sheer edge and marvel at the engineering feat that had made the cut, and peer down at the river where gold had first been found.

Occasionally a train pulled off before all the passengers were aboard, as once happened to the Emperor of Brazil. But neither His Majesty nor anyone else was ever stranded. The oversight was soon discovered and the train brought to a jerking halt.

A murder that fascinated Californians with its bizarre details was reported to have taken place in October 1870 at Cape Horn. Leonidas Parker, a young San Francisco attorney, and his companion Gregory Summerfield, a man in his seventies, had stepped onto the open observation car just before the train reached the sharpest curve on the Cape, to get a better view of the gorge. Suddenly there was a scream of terror, and the old man was seen tumbling over the cliff.

The train stopped, but as there was no hope of retrieving the body, it moved on after a few minutes. The cars buzzed with excited talk about the mysterious tragedy. Had the motion of the train pitched Summerfield over the edge, had it been suicide, or, as many seemed to believe, had his companion pushed him? Feeling against Parker ran so high, when the train pulled into the next station, he was arrested. What he had to tell the Grand Jury later was startling.

The dead man was a scientific wizard who had discovered the key that unlocked the constituent gases in water and caused it to burn fiercely. But unlike Agassiz and others who were concerned with decomposing water so as to fit it for use as a fuel, Summerfield saw in his discovery mastery of the world: at will he could ignite oceans and rivers and destroy life on the globe.

He had walked into Parker's office one day near the end of

September (he was an acquaintance of Parker's father), had sworn him to secrecy, and told him of his discovery. Showing him a small vial, he had demanded a million dollars for its contents; the money had to be raised in San Francisco within a month. He had then demonstrated with a bowl of water and a few drops from the bottle. "A sharp explosion took place, and in a second of time the water was blazing in a red, lurid column half way to the ceiling," Parker stated; when the flame died out the bowl was bone dry.

After a vain attempt to reason with Summerfield, Parker alerted a group of leading San Franciscans to the significance of the discovery and had the old scientist demonstrate it for them. A committee was hastily formed to collect the million dollars, but as the month drew to its close, pledges for only half the sum had been received. To apply to Wall Street for the rest seemed the only alternative, and Parker made speedy preparations for the trip, persuading Summerfield to go with him.

By this time everyone who had met the old man was convinced that no amount of money could buy his secret and that the world was not safe as long as he lived. The committee suggested to Parker that he somehow do away with him on the trip east.

The young lawyer was shocked at the suggestion, but once they had convinced him that millions of other lives could be saved by sacrificing this one, and they cited dozens of instances in history that were precedents, he agreed. He had traveled over the Central Pacific route more than once, was familiar with all its gorges and precipices, and chose Cape Horn as the one best suited to his purpose.

Once the facts became public, popular sentiment was on Parker's side, and the Placer County Grand Jury acquitted him.

Only after the passage of many months was it learned that the Summerfield case was pure fiction from the pen of a well-known San Francisco attorney and former judge, William Henry Rhodes, a North Carolinian who had come to the goldfields in 1850. Like so many hoaxes of its kind, the elements of the story were beyond credibility, but the clever use of realistic detail lent it trappings of authenticity.

In May 1866, the Central Pacific's rail crept safely past Cape Horn, and by summer it reached Dutch Flat where the company had its beginnings. Eight miles beyond town, graders struck rich tertiary gold-bearing gravel, and guards had to be posted along the right-of-way to keep out miners, for the earth was said to be worth eight dollars a cubic yard.

The Sierra crossing called for fifteen tunnels. Summit, the longest, was a quarter-mile bore through solid granite so stubborn it flattened the points of picks. Although five hundred Chinese worked at it in eight-hour shifts around the clock, six days a week, progress could be measured only in inches— seven or eight a day. Then winter came on, the worst on record, and work in the open had to be suspended at the summit. Thousands of shivering Chinese were sent back to Sacramento or on over the ridge to work at lower elevations on the eastern slope, while thousands more were kept at the chiseling and blasting inside the tunnels. Forty-four snowstorms buried bunkhouses and supply stations under forty-foot drifts. To get to and from work, men carved a maze of passages under the snow, some nearly two hundred feet long, with airshafts to the surface.

For almost four months, three thousand men, mainly Chinese, worked, ate, and slept in burrows beneath tons of snow, like so many moles. Then the blasting had to be stopped for it began to trigger avalanches that would roar down the mountainsides without warning and sweep away work crews and sometimes entire camps. The bodies were usually not recovered for months.

The task for those on the eastern slope was little easier. Men carving the roadbed out of granite had to work under the snow in igloos, their tools and equipment lowered to them through shafts.

With the coming of spring, crews were rushed back to the summit, but it took weeks of chipping through solid ice before the abandoned cuts and fills could be reached. The assault on the mountains was renewed with intensity as twelve thousand men attacked the tunnels above Donner Lake and began grading the roadbed down the eastern side. But with the thawing of tons of snow and ice, new problems arose: streams, waterfalls, and mud slides swept away bridges and trestles, and only forty miles of road were finished before winter closed in again —another heavy one, with all the experiences and problems of the last one repeated.

The closing of the summit for the second winter convinced engineers of the need for snowsheds. During the next two years thirty-seven miles of heavily timbered galleries were built to meet the requirements of unusual snow conditions; some were to cost $30,000 a mile. A dozen sawmills and 250 carpenters were kept busy during these months.

But the first travelers from the East did not appreciate the endless sheds. Having seen nothing but desert for days, they felt swindled when deprived of views of the most scenic part of the trip. Complaints were so many an attempt was made to solve the problem by putting alternate sections on track and rolling them aside after the snows were gone.

Robert Louis Stevenson, on his way to San Francisco, has left his impression of travel through the snowsheds and down the western slope:

> When I awoke next morning, I was puzzled for a while to know if it were day or night, for the illumination was unusual. I sat up at last, and found we were grading downward through a long snow-shed. And suddenly we shot into an open; and before we were swallowed into the next length of wooden tunnel, I had one glimpse of a huge pine-forested ravine upon my left, a foaming river, and a sky already coloured with the fires of dawn . . . I had come home again— home from the unsightly deserts, to the green and habitable

corners of the earth. Every spire of pine along the hill-top, every troutly pool along that mountain river, was more dear to me than a blood relation. Few people have praised God more happily than I did. And thenceforward, down by Blue Canyon, Alta, Dutch Flat, and all the old mining camps, through a sea of mountain forests, dropping thousands of feet toward the far sea-level as we went, not I only, but all the passengers on board, threw off their sense of dirt and heat and weariness, and bawled like schoolboys, and thronged with shining eyes upon the platform, and became new creatures within and without.

But as with all man's attempts to conquer the Sierra, the struggle nearly ended in defeat. Blizzards, snowslides, and massive drifts defied snowplows and sheds, derailing and wrecking trains, and burying them under tons of snow, while melting snow and earth slides washed out tracks, collapsed fills, and caved in banks. Sometimes it was mid-April before the road could be opened. As late as 1952, well into the age of diesel power, thought to be the final answer to the challenge of Sierran winters, a blizzard and monster snowslide at Yuba Gap trapped the company's streamliner *City of San Francisco* and kept its 226 passengers and crew prisoner for three days and nights. Heavy blizzards today may still close tracks and delay trains for hours.

On August 29, 1867, the headings in Summit Tunnel met, after one year of work, and by the end of November track was laid through this granite cavern. By the following spring the worst was over, and the Central Pacific's goal became "a mile of track every working day."

On May 10, 1869, the rails of the two lines met at Promontory, Utah. A picked team of the Union Pacific's "Irish terriers" marched out before the assembled spectators, reporters, and photographers to lay the last rails west and spike them down. Then a group of Chinese workers in fresh blue jackets stepped up to set the final rails east, and James Strowbridge and the UP's construction superintendent, Samuel Reed, placed a polished laurel tie under them. It was symbolically the last tie, and after the ceremony was replaced by one of durable redwood.

A $400 spike made from "pure Mother Lode gold" was slipped into a predrilled hole in the laurel tie, and Leland Stanford, holding a silver-plated sledgehammer, stood ready to drive in this symbolic last spike. A telegraph wire was coiled around the hammer to catch the sounds of the final blows and carry them to waiting millions all over the country.

At a signal from the telegrapher, Stanford applied the sledge gently to the precious spike; the impulse triggered the release of a magnetic ball attached to a pole on the Capitol dome in Washington and fired a fifteen-inch Parrott gun at San Francisco's Fort Point, setting off a hundred-gun salute.

Within three minutes messages began pouring into Promontory: "The bells are ringing, and the people rejoicing." There had been no comparable jubilation since Robert E. Lee's surrender.

Church and fire bells pealed; steamboat and locomotive whistles shrilled; cannons boomed, bands played "America," and bonfires and skyrockets lit up the night skies. There were parades, banquets, and speeches greeting the dawn of a new era.

The East and West were one now. The Pacific Railroad that had begun as a dream beside the American River was a reality.

IV

THE EBBING OF
THE TIDE

23

The Final Phase

WITHIN THREE YEARS after the discovery of gold at Coloma, over $60 million had been taken from surface placers alone, and so intense was the search and so numerous the seekers, pay dirt was soon exhausted and the rocker and long tom were unable to wash enough low-grade earth to return a profit. Then miners began prospecting higher in the mountains, where to their surprise they found gravel deposits similar in appearance to those in the river. Some were embedded in the canyon walls hundreds of feet above the present stream; others lay on the surface of benches and ridges. What they had stumbled on were the channels of ancient streams, rich in gold.

During the Upper Jurassic period, a time of widespread volcanic activity, there was an infiltration of gold and other mineral-bearing quartz veins into rocks fractured by faulting. After the passage of some forty million years, when the climate had become semitropical and humid, and rocks were subject to weathering and deep decay, the gold was released, removed, and concentrated in incredibly rich placer deposits. Because of its high specific gravity, the gold, separated from its matrix, was washed into the lower parts of crevices and into the beds of swift-running streams, where it was caught in the natural riffles of rock. Then after still more millions of years had gone by, during another period of intense volcanic activity the sand, gravel, and boulders from these streams were entrapped by heavy falls of ash which dammed them, formed lakes, and

271

diverted drainage. This period was accompanied by severe earthquakes and faulting and great movements of land.

It was during this era of turmoil and upheaval that the Sierra Nevada province was moved largely as a unit and tilted westward, causing the rivers to flow in torrents down its western face and cut their deep and rugged canyons. These newer rivers, born on the volcanic surface, commenced their canyon cutting through the bedrock of the dead river channels, washing out the ancient gravels and gold and depositing them in their own beds, where they lay hidden from the knowledge of all but a few until 1848.

Where these ancient channels still lay under the volcanic cover, miners began working them with shafts and adits, a laborious and costly process, until one day some now-forgotten gold seeker thought of a cheaper and easier method, to be called "ground sluicing." He conducted a stream of water by ditch and canvas hose to the top of a bank and allowed it to flow down the face. Then with a little help from a pick and shovel, the softened mass was directed into a waiting sluice box in the bottom of which were riffle bars, blocks of wood, and rounded stones, covered with quicksilver, to catch the gold.

A little later, a "French gentleman" named Antoine Chabot, a sailmaker by trade, who was mining at Buckeye Hill, came up with a better idea: use water under pressure to undermine the gravel bank. Then still another miner, Edward E. Mattison of Connecticut, working at nearby American Hill, having seen Chabot's method, improved on it by adding a sheet-iron nozzle to the end of the canvas hose. By this simple expedient, hydraulic mining was born.

The next year Colonel William McClure, one of Yankee Jim's more distinguished citizens, who was a pioneer apiarist and orchardist, a miner and large shareholder in the ditch company that supplied the diggings with water, heard reports about this new process and paid Mattison a visit. He found two men

shooting streams of water against the foot of a high gravel
bank, the water under pressure of a sixty-foot drop from a
ditch and penstock on the hill above. He watched as the under-
mined bank collapsed into a mushy mass, bringing with it large
trees and boulders; watched as the streams of water were then
directed on the tons of fallen earth, and saw how it melted
away into the sluices almost as quickly as a snowbank. Every
so often the sluices were "cleaned up," and the quicksilver
amalgamated with the gold set aside to be retorted.

To obtain pressure, a trough set up on a tall trestle—called
a "telegraph" because it resembled a line of telegraph poles—
carried the water from the ditch to the penstock, which was a
simple funnel-shaped box, made from an old barrel. To this
was attached the heavy canvas hose, some five inches wide,
with its rude nozzle, leading to the gravel bank.

No such laborsaving device had yet been devised in the
mines, and the colonel was impressed with its possibilities. He
hurried back to Yankee Jim's to try it out and became the
first to introduce "hydraulicking" to the American River country.

Miners all over were soon adopting the method, and demand
for canvas hose was so great, local supplies were exhausted.
It is of record that at least one enterprising person, known to
posterity simply as "Old Joe of Coon Hollow," took advantage
of the shortage to make himself a quick fortune. He set up
the Hydraulic Hose Factory and was shortly supplying miners
with double canvas and leather hose. Rubber hose later replaced canvas, except for shorter lengths, and that in turn
gave way to still more durable iron pipe; while from Mattison's crude nozzle were developed formidable iron and steel
nozzles patented under such awesome names as Monitor, Dic-
tator, and Little Giant. These hurled streams of water with
the force of a cannonade and could send a half-ton boulder
flying through the air.

Bank blasting began to be used in conjunction with water to

loosen the more stubborn gravels cemented together. A mining engineer's report leaves little doubt that this method was effective. A ninety-foot drift dug in a T-form, with sixty-foot wings, was run into a hill under an old river channel, he writes. The tunnel was then filled with the contents of five hundred and ten kegs of powder, the entrance closely tamped, and the charge fired: "A dull report broke upon the ear, and a mass of earth, one hundred and fifty feet deep, two hundred feet wide, and three hundred feet long, rose a short distance into the air, and fell back thoroughly disintegrated and in a fit condition for washing."

But hydraulic mining called for more than a length of hose and a ditch. Adequate water could not be had at all points by merely backing up streams or digging basins to catch the winter rains, so an elaborate and costly system of canals, feeder ditches, flumes, tunnels, dams, and reservoirs was constructed to carry water from the river and its tributaries, to perform the same work the streams had been doing naturally over the ages.

Hundreds of miles of canals and feeder ditches were built at a cost of nearly $16 million. Miles of canvas-lined flumes spanned ravines and canyons, and where ridges had to be crossed, tunnels were bored. Every sailor within reach (and anyone else who could use a sailmaker's palm) was recruited at half an ounce a day and set to stitching flume lining.

The first ditch in the entire mining region of California was built at Coloma in 1850 at a cost of $10,000 to carry river water to the dry diggings. Two years later the South Fork Canal Company was started ambitiously, but soon failed. One expenditure that drew heavily on its resources was construction of "a large and well-appointed hotel" on Reservoir Hill, the proposed terminus of the main trunk. It was hoped to make it a fashionable resort that would attract patronage from as far away as Sacramento. But the proprietors were ahead of their time; Argonauts and gold-town merchants were not yet ready for leisure.

In 1856 John Kirk of Placerville began surveys for the resurrection and enlargement of the by-then defunct South Fork Canal system. He announced his intention to claim and divert water from the American River, Silver Creek, Echo and Clear lakes, with storage at Silver Lake. In 1860 he began, largely with Chinese labor, the construction of reservoirs at Medley, Audrain, and Echo lakes. Six years later water was being carried as far as Sportsman's Hall, and by 1873 the "Sierra Ditch," as it was known, had reached Placerville. Today this pioneer system, with enlargements and refinements, is being used as a part of the El Dorado Hydroelectric Project.

Flumes, wood-lined ditches and canals, trestles, tunnels, and sluices called for millions of feet of lumber, especially since each winter and spring the river swept away miles of these works which had to be replaced the next season; thus, the lumber industry, which is an economic mainstay of the area today, was launched. Sawmills sprang up along all forks of the river. With no thought for the future, the slopes were stripped of their fine stands of conifers.

"As most of the land has no owner, everybody cuts and slashes as if he cared for nobody but himself, and no time but today," Horace Greeley observed during his tour of the gold country. As the foothills were denuded, the sawmills moved higher up the river canyons. Greeley also deplored the wasteful methods of timbering: "Noble pines are pitched this way and that, merely for a log or two from the butt." The rest was left in unsightly heaps to rot.

Around 1879 hydraulic elevators were introduced to clean up the riverbed, first at Hoosier Bar by Samuel Laird, and then on the Middle Fork's Mammoth Bar by Colonel Walter Scott Davis, who had seen Laird's works. Although the colonel set up costly and elaborate machinery (which the river twice swept away), much of the labor was still handwork. After the water was turned aside by a diversion dam, the riverbed was picked and scraped to six inches below the surface and the loosened material shoveled into hand buckets. Then the actual bedrock was scraped and brushed with small bamboo brushes into sugar scoops, and their contents emptied into the buckets and sluices. For the finest and final sweeping, camel-hair brushes and horn spoons were used by patient Chinese laborers.

The result of all the blasting, washing, sluicing, and lumbering was devastating: the entire face of the country was changed. What would have taken centuries to accomplish by natural processes was produced within a few years. Soil to the depth of a hundred and fifty feet was washed from thousands of acres, exposing the underlying bedrock. Slopes stripped of trees and chaparral were not only ugly but subject to severe erosion and disastrous landslides. In at least one case miners, washing an ancient river channel, set their town sliding down the mountainside. Michigan City, perched on a narrow shelf between the North and Middle forks, started to slip one day, and the whole community had to pack up and move off in a hurry to a site higher up the ridge—the present Michigan Bluff.

Many rivers and creeks were dammed when tons of earth and rock from slides tumbled into them, changing their courses entirely, or backing their waters into lakes that were often sixty feet deep. Those streambeds not blocked were filled with boulders, gravel, and yellow mud called "slickens." Riverbeds were raised so high by this debris from hydraulic operations, summer navigation was no longer possible except for light-draft vessels. Slowly but surely San Francisco Bay was filling.

With every storm came destructive mud flows that spread a heavy residue of gravel and clay over the rich argicultural lands of the foothills and valley; and there were floods that turned the lowlands into an inland sea, drowned horses and cattle, swept away crops, farmhouses, and barns, and did untold damage to towns.

The salmon with which the American River abounded began to disappear, not only because its waters had become mud-laden, but because they were diverted by ditches, flumes, and dams, leaving many parts of the river completely dry.

> Mining is a necessary art [wrote Horace Greeley], but it does not tend to beautify the face of nature. On the contrary, the earth is distorted into all manner of ungainly heaps and ridges, hills half torn out or washed away . . . water courses . . . gouged out, and rivers, once pure as crystal, now dense and opaque with pulverized rock. . . . Not a stream of any size is allowed to escape the pollution. . . . California, in giving her hoarded wealth, surrenders much of her beauty also.

A forty-niner, writing at the peak of hydraulicking, recalls the American in its pristine purity:

> The river cañons where the old bars were located, were romantic places previous to being disturbed and torn up by the gold-digger. The water was as clear as crystal [and] swarming with fish. Salmon . . . ran up all the streams as far as they could get, until some . . . barrier which they could not leap prevented further progress. . . . Trout . . . were also plentiful, and the writer has caught them with hook and line weighing as high as ten pounds in the North Fork above Kelley's Bar.
>
> Upon every little bend or plat of land bordering the streams grew the white ash, alder, maple, laurel, honeysuckle and rank ferns and mosses. . . . Tussocks of . . . bunchgrass covered the bottoms, and wild grapevine clambered over every convenient tree. The water ousel . . . flitted from place to place in search of food, and the vigilant kingfisher darted from his perch on overhanging limb into the clear water and rose again with some finny victim in his beak. Deer wandered unscared amid these beauteous scenes. . . .
>
> Such was the condition of California streams when the gold-seeker first approached them—things of rare beauty,

joyous to behold, inconceivable to those who know them as they are found today—treeless, mud-laden, turgid, filthy and fishless; with matchless beauty gone, and natural purity forever lost. . . .

When pioneer orchards and vineyards began to be buried under debris, growers demanded that something be done to control or even prohibit hydraulic mining. But gold production was California's economic mainstay; the farmers' cries went unheeded, and the desolating activities were allowed to continue unrestricted for more than a quarter of a century.

By the 1880s friction between the two factions had practically errupted into open warfare. Miners boycotted valley-grown produce; flumes and ditches began to be destroyed. Two dams had already been blown up and a wooden one burned when at five o'clock on the morning of June 13, 1883, the English Dam on the Yuba's Middle Fork broke, releasing a solid wall of water that swept away bridges, roads, houses, barns, livestock, levees, another dam, and drowned at least six men, on its way to the lowlands. The break had not been accidental; a distinct explosion had been heard by those who lived nearby: there was evidence that the dam had been dynamited.

On June 12, 1882, Judge Jackson Temple issued a perpetual injunction enjoining the Gold Run Ditch and Mining Company from discharging or dumping "coarse" debris into the North Fork American or its tributaries. If, however, some method could be devised to impound the debris, application could be made for a modification or suspension of the injunction.

There was general rejoicing among the farmers at this first victory, but the working miner saw it as a deathblow. Both factions soon realized their error: the miner found it possible to build easily and cheaply from logs and brush adequate restraining dams to impound debris and so qualify for modification of the injunction; hydraulicking was shortly flourishing again.

Farmers on their part took a dismal view of these dams, pre-
dicting that they would give way with the first big storm and
release even worse mud flows.

But as agricultural products began to contribute to the
state's economy, there was a change in attitude toward farmers'
rights. On January 7, 1884, Judge Lorenzo Sawyer of the United
States District Court, "perpetually enjoined and restrained"
the North Bloomfield Gravel and Mining Company from dumping "tailings, boulders, cobble stones, gravel, sand, clay, debris
or refuse matter" into the Yuba River or its tributaries. He
too included that stipulation regarding application for modification or suspension of the injunction in the event some means
should be devised "to obviate the harm complained of by the
plaintiffs." That June, hydraulic mines on the Bear River were
placed under this injunction, and those on the American soon
after.

Judge Sawyer's restrictions were far more comprehensive
and explicit than Judge Temple's had been, and in order to
qualify for modification or suspension, hydraulic miners would
have to build substantial impounding dams, settling basins,
and elevators. Only the larger operators could afford to comply,
and hydraulic mining in general was doomed. A traveler, passing through the gold towns along the American River that
year, reported "thousands of white miners out of employment,
homes neglected, and ruin the order of the day."

But small groups of miners working in remote canyons along
the river soon found that they could operate illegally with
little chance of detection. Any investigator going into the
mountains to ferret them out did so at the risk of being shot
or lynched. Word of his coming sped ahead; hotels refused
him lodgings, hostile eyes followed him everywhere, and going
down some wilderness trail he took the chance of suddenly
facing the defiant stare of a cocked shotgun.

Contentions between the factions were finally settled in
1893 with establishment of a federal Debris Commission that

imposed still more stringent controls on hydraulic mining and gave California a River Commission whose duty it was to reclaim the rivers and prevent floods. This was the nation's third: only the Mississippi and the Missouri had preceded it.

There had been several early attempts to dredge the American with crude scows and plain bailing buckets, which succeded in bringing up quantities of mud and gravel but no gold. After hydraulic mining waned, dredging was tried again on the South Fork, near Folsom, with improved equipment and better results: since operations began in 1899, over $95 million has been taken out.

Dredging was another highly destructive form of mining, although more limited in scope than hydraulicking. Still, countless acres of valuable orchard land were turned into desolate rocky wastes as dredgers crept over them like ravenous monsters, literally eating up the rich soil and sluicing the refuse aside. Mounds of cobblestones forty to fifty feet high are seen along the South Fork today, mute evidence of the devastation.

With the exhaustion of the open placers, the character of both mining and the miner changed. It was no longer possible for a man to wander from place to place and pick up a fortune where nature had concentrated it in a pocket or a few yards of river gravel. Large investments of capital were necessary to build restraining works for hydraulicking, to run shafts and tunnels and build stamp mills for quartz mining, and construct elevators to clean up the riverbed. Miners in general were no longer nomadic; they settled in the gold towns and went to work for those big companies that had been formed to carry on the new kind of mining.

Within a decade of the discovery, most of the American River diggings had been abandoned to the Chinese who diligently worked over the tailings. The grand adventure was over. Mining had become an industry, and the roaring camps along the river were already a part of history.

24

Women and the River

MOST GOLD CAMPS could be searched in vain for a woman, and men were known to travel miles just for a glimpse of one. A young miner keeping bachelor hall with his uncle in a remote canyon heard one day that a young woman had come to a camp over the ridge. After supper that night he addressed his relation:

"Uncle Hiram, can I borrow Jack for a day or two?" Jack was a mule and in case of need their only means of communication with the outside world.

"What do you want with him, my son?"

"Well—you see, there's a lady come to Deadwood, and I aim to ride the forty miles there and back to see her."

"A lady. Well, take him son, and pay the lady a visit. I'm just downright sorry Jack don't ride double!"

Sometimes this worship was by necessity vicarious. In a camp near Coloma a miner who had in his possession a woman's fashionable boot treasured it above all else, and in moments of generosity would exhibit it at a dollar a head to men who felt they were getting a bargain. One day as he held it up for the admiring crowd to see, he announced: "The chunk ain't found that can buy this boot! 'Taint for sale, *no-how!*"

When the first white woman came riding into the diggings at Canyon Creek, the miners to a man dropped their tools and raced up the hill to meet her. They crowded around in an admiring throng and, after feasting their eyes awhile on this novel and satisfying sight, lifted her up, mule and all, and cheering loudly carried her triumphantly down the mountainside.

One afternoon a company of miners at work on Hangtown Creek got word that an emigrant train was approaching and that its chief attraction was a pretty girl from Kentucky. The men ran to the road and lined up along the side. As the party neared they saw that a young girl was riding ahead, and that she was indeed pretty. One of the miners never forgot that she had on "a blue calico dress with . . . heavy flounces around the bottom," a wide-brimmed straw hat, "milk-maid style . . . and a broad, black velvet ribbon around her neck," finery she had put on a few miles back.

Her appearance caused a stir among the "crowd of unwashed, uncombed, unshaven miners" starved for the sight of a lovely girl, and each one, nearly, had some remark to make aloud, or to himself, as she came up. "Them eyes of her'n are jest like my Mary Jane's," said one. "Now, that nose and chin and her hair, too, is exactly like my Marthy's down in Kennebunk," observed another. "But ain't she lovely, though!" sighed a third, and so on down the line.

That night while she was frying slapjacks for supper, a young

miner came up and offered to buy one. "She said they were
not for sale, but that she would give him one with pleasure."
She dropped it hot into his hand, and he returned the compli-
ment by dropping into hers "a very pretty gold specimen, which
she refused to accept. Upon a little persuasion from the . . .
youth she changed her mind, and slipped it into her pocket."

Occasionally the attentions lavished on a pioneer woman
caused trouble. A man named Crockett, who kept a tavern on
the Coloma Road, near Salmon Falls, had a remarkably pretty
wife. Instead of making him happy, possession of this luxury
kept him in a perpetual fever of irritation, for he was jealous
because there were always a dozen or two hairy miners gazing
"in a bewildered manner" at the handsome hostess, or waiting
around to get a peep at her. He carried a large revolver at all
times, and had been known to use it on provocation.

A great number of miners had looked at Mrs. Crockett on
the morning of our arrival, and her husband had not quite
finished foaming at the mouth in consequence, when we entered the house. It was some time before he condescended
to be civil; but having at length informed us that he was "so
riled that his skin cracked," he added that he was a "devil-
ishly good fellow when he was 'right side up,'" and commanded us to drink with him. After this he procured us a most
excellent breakfast, and, on the strength of our respectable
appearance, allowed Mrs. Crockett to preside at this repast,
which she did in a nervous manner, as if momentarily under
the expectation of being shot.

Most gold seekers were single, but those who did have wives
expected like the rest to return home soon immensely rich.
They were no more anxious to expose their wives to the rigors
of the trip and frontier living than the women were to undergo
them. Some married men seized on this chance to escape the
restraints and burdens of homelife and would have refused to
take their wives even if they had begged to go.

Still, a few plucky and determined women did come to the

goldfields with their men as early as 1849. Although it has been maintained that these women were "inferior in education and manners to the men," it is of record that there were among them many women of learning and culture, like Louise Amelia Knapp Smith Clappe, the wife of a physician, Dr. Fayette Clappe, known best by her pen name, Dame Shirley. Her witty and perceptive letters, written to a sister in New England, give one of the finest pictures of life in the river gold camps. "Shirley" went on to become one of San Francisco's most distinguished teachers and, on her return to the States, a lecturer on art and literature.

And there was Sarah Eleanor Royce, who became the mother of philosopher Josiah Royce. Later she wrote a fascinating account of her trip across the plains with her husband and two-year-old daughter and of their life in the diggings along the American River and elsewhere.

Then there was the poetess Eulalie, who came to Auburn a few years later as the bride of John Shannon, Jr., the fiery editor of the *Placer Democrat,* who, in the best journalistic traditions of his day, was to meet death at the hands of a rival editor.

On reaching Auburn, Shannon and his wife took rooms at the Junction House, a bustling stage hotel on the North Fork Hill Road. Ignoring the noise and confusion around her, the handsome Kentucky woman, who had won some recognition in the States for her verses and was a member of that circle of young writers revolving around Horace Greeley, set to work, and within a few weeks had finished the first in a series of "Travel Scenes" that was printed in the *Cincinnati Daily Times.* These were followed by "Leaves from the Diary of a Californian," for the same newspaper, and publication of a book of poems, *Buds, Blossoms and Leaves.* There was also a prolific output of verse and short stories for the *Placer Democrat,* and lectures in Auburn and other gold towns—all extremely popular with the miners.

But then in December 1854 the promising career was cut short when Eulalie died in childbirth at the age of thirty.

Few people today have heard of her, and yet she deserves recognition for her contribution to the state's literary annals, for she was California's first woman poet and the first Californian to publish a book of verse, while her fiction is counted among the earliest of California storytelling.

Some women had come before the Gold Rush. Nancy A. Kelsey was one of these. She was the first white woman to cross the plains and come over the Sierra. She reached California in 1841, with her infant daughter, Ann, and her husband, Benjamin, as members of the Bidwell-Bartleson Party.

When told that it was foolhardy for a woman to attempt such a dangerous trip, she said, "Where my husband goes I can go. I can better endure the hardships of the journey than the anxiety of an absent husband." The courage and good humor of this slim Kentucky girl not yet eighteen was long remembered. One man in the party recalled that once while struggling along a steep trail, having all he could do to keep his horse from slipping off, he looked back and "saw Mrs. Kelsey a little way behind me, with her child in her arms, barefooted I think, and leading her horse—a sight I shall never forget." Others remembered her astuteness and her "cheerful nature and kind heart."

Nancy had her first sight of California from the summit of Sonora Pass in October 1841. "We had a difficult time to find a way down the mountains," she recalled. Several weeks later the party reached Dr. John Marsh's ranch at the foot of Mount Diablo. Here Nancy and her family stayed until December 10 when, with Captain Sutter as escort, they set off "in a leaky rowboat" for New Helvetia. "We were fifteen days making the trip. The boat was manned by Indians, and Sutter instructed them to swim to shore with me and the child if the boat should capsize."

Sutter offered Ben Kelsey a place to live and a job whipsawing lumber, and he accepted. But Ben was afflicted with incurable restlessness, and after a few months he quit to go trapping. In 1843 he and his family joined a party going to Oregon, but within a year they were back, Nancy carrying a newborn girl in her arms.

Then in the spring of 1848 Ben "went to the mines to see if there was any truth in the report of gold discovery. He was gone ten days and brought back $1,000. The next time he went to the mines he took a flock of sheep up for mutton and brought back $16,000." Then he found rich deposits on a plateau along the South Fork, and a camp called Kelsey's Diggings sprang up. By the next year it could boast "six hotels and hay-yards, a dozen stores, and twenty-four gambling saloons," catering not just to local miners, but to those in nearby Chicken Flat, Irish Creek, and Fleatown.

Nancy and the girls joined him, and this time he stayed in one place long enough to get rich. With Indian labor, he is said to have taken out nearly a million dollars in gold from the Diggings.

But in 1850 they were off again, joining the rush to the gold mines of Humboldt County, in Northern California. Next it was Mexico, then Texas, where they were attacked by Comanches.

"The men were out hunting turkeys, and a neighbor woman and her children and I and mine were there alone," Nancy remembered. "I discovered the Indians approaching our camp . . . I loaded the guns and suggested that all hide. . . ." Her two oldest girls ran off to take cover in a thicket while the others hid "in a small cave in the bank of the ravine. I could hear the Indians above, but they did not discover us. I had forgotten to hide our money . . . with which we intended to buy cattle to bring to California. After they had pillaged the camp and taken the money (about $10,000) they started off and discovered the two oldest girls. They succeeded in catching my girl because her dress got tangled in the brush. She was twelve years old. The other girl reported that she could hear the blows and her sister's screams as they struck her down." Nancy did not find her daughter until the next day, not dead, but scalped and "partially deranged."

After Texas it was New Mexico where there was a fight with the Apaches, and then a return to California, to flit from place to place.

What became of the rest of the wealth Nancy must have known but she did not say. "I have enjoyed riches and suffered the pangs of poverty" was all she told the newspaper reporter who interviewed her when she was seventy. Then a "sturdy, spirited cheery old lady," but obviously poor, she was living alone in a little cabin on a farm "high in a nook of the Cuyama mountains" of Southern California; Ben had been dead five years.

On August 9, 1896, Nancy Kelsey died in her house, "unattended by physician," the death certificate notes, and was buried in a little nearby plot between her daughter, Mrs. Nancy Clanton, and an unidentified infant.

Some of the women who came then and later were plainly camp followers, others clearly husband hunters, like the one who gained a kind of immortality when her name was entered in the logbook at Sutter's Fort on September 21, 1847. The entry reads: "Lucinda the Widdow arrived." No more needed to be said for the much-married Lucinda had by then achieved the status of a professional widow.

While crossing the plains the year before, Lucinda had been married to a fellow emigrant for exactly ten hours. During that time the young man found that he had made the worst bargain of his life, and had the marriage promptly dissolved. Before the journey's end she had tried (and failed) to interest a second member of the party in matrimony. On her arrival in the river camps she was overwhelmed with offers, and accepted the most promising one, only to have her husband die soon after. She then married a sailor who shortly shared the same fate.

What followed is something of a record, for Lucinda is said

to have been married three times in six weeks. Sutter's Fort was a likely place to find yet another spouse, which may have been why she came, although her story hints that by this time she had concluded that matrimony was not her lot, and had turned to an "itinerant living," as best suited to her temperament. But here the logbook is silent; only her coming was heralded.

The scarcity of American women in California in 1849 suggested to the author and women's rights champion Eliza Farnham that she recruit a company of "intelligent, virtuous and efficient women" to emigrate there with her. She saw the absence of woman "with all her kindly cares and powers" as one of "many privations and deteriorating influences" gold seekers had to endure.

To discourage immature girls or frivolous adventuresses, all applicants had to be twenty-five or over; each would be asked to furnish a testimonial from her clergyman or other responsible townsperson vouching for her education, character, and capability; and finally each would be expected to contribute $250 toward the cost of the trip and have enough money left to support herself in San Francisco until she could find a suitable husband or job.

The plan won immediate endorsement from such notables as Horace Greeley, William Cullen Bryant, Katherine M. Sedgwick, and Henry Ward Beecher. The ranks were soon filled, and the packet *Angelique* chartered for an April sailing. Then Mrs. Farnham took sick, and without her leadership the project fell apart. When she was ready to sail that summer the company had dwindled to three.

The proposal received wide news coverage, and California papers featured it. All up and down the river "joy sat upon many a bachelor's countenance that had been wreathed in sorrow at the thought that his days were to end in this country with no wife," wrote a local editor.

Excitement was intense in all the gold camps as the time neared for the supposed shipload of young women to arrive, and miners flocked to San Francisco to be on hand when the vessel tied up. What happened when only three materialized has been preserved by a contemporary chronicler: "I verily believe that there was more drunkenness, more gambling, more fighting, and more of everything that was bad that night, than had ever before occurred in San Francisco within any similar space of time."

Word of this shortage of women made its way to France, and several companies of girls of good character landed in San Francisco. Before they could ever get to the river camps they were hired by gamblers and saloonkeepers at the unheard-of wages of $250 a month to sit beside the croupier and rake in the winnings, or to dispense drinks at the bar. Their employers guarded them vigilantly, for their presence assured an establishment increased custom; nevertheless, within a week or two they all had husbands. News of their success sped back to France, and women of another sort began to come.

"Nine hundred of the French *demi-monde* are expected," a San Francisco newspaper reported in October 1850. Then they began to flock in from all parts of the world—the Marquesas, Peru, Australia—and they were the first women to go to the river camps in any number, and they prospered wherever they settled; one noted prostitute claimed to have earned $50,000 in a few months.

Since practically any semblance of a woman could count on a speedy marriage, families began dispatching maiden aunts and spinster daughters whose matrimonial hopes had long since been blighted. The pamphlets of California colonization agents urged women to come, appealing euphemistically to all types: "The young person who loves the world and its pleasures will find here partners ready to procure her every enjoyment; while she who is inclined to domestic comfort will meet quiet and steady men whose door will open to welcome her."

Gold or no gold, after a year or two in California most Argonauts had decided that it was the place to live. Opportunities were unlimited, and the climate ideal. By then they were heartily sick of their hard-won freedom and slapjacks and beans, and they longed for the snug comforts of homelife, with a woman as the presiding divinity of the kitchen. Many of those who had been most anxious to escape family ties and other restraints of civilization were the first to admit readiness to settle down, and some in their eagerness even advertised locally for wives. A number married Mexican and Spanish girls, and some took Indian wives, while others, recalling a neighborhood girl to whom distance lent enchantment, started a correspondence with a view to matrimony and, if all went well, sent her passage money. Yet others went home to marry sweethearts and bring them back, while those who had families called on them to come west.

Many a woman found on her arrival that things were not nearly so rosy as pictured, that riches were still around the corner. But their services were in demand everywhere for almost any kind of work they had a mind to undertake. It was the first time in this country's history that women of all classes were allowed so much freedom beyond the home sphere, and they took full advantage of it. Those who could sing or play instruments, and had no scruples about the profession, took jobs as entertainers in gambling saloons. A few even turned professional gambler and opened their own houses. Some clerked in stores, ran boardinghouses and hotels, managed restaurants, opened private schools, and taught music, dancing, and French. One Hangtown wife baked dried peach and mince pies for a living; she soon had miners lining up outside her cabin to get these delicacies hot from the oven. She charged a dollar for peach pies and a dollar and a half for mince, and on peak days baked a hundred.

As the hardships of the journey lessened, more and more women came to California, and miners in general became married men, and the face of things all over the river country changed. Neat white cottages "shaded with young cottonwoods, or em-

bowered with trellises of passion-flower and Australian pea,"
took the place of ramshackle cabins. Dooryards were planted to
roses, lilacs, syringa, and forsythia, and orchards set out. Many
of these women brought with them the seeds and cuttings of
favorite trees, shrubs, and flowers. Today in every gold town—
even those that are mere memories—some of these plantings
can be found flourishing, often in the heart of the wilderness,
after well over a century.

Streets were cleared of their rubbish: "old boots, hats and
shirts, old sardine-boxes, empty tins of preserved oysters, empty
bottles, worn-out pots and kettles, old ham-bones, broken picks
and shovels . . ." Miners were forbidden to prospect in the middle of thoroughfares; mudholes were filled, roadways smoothed,
and plantings of poplar and locust trees made along the sides.

Society became organized, and the individualism of the old
camps gave way as men tended to do things collectively. Towns
began boasting fire and police departments, mayors and coun-
cils, military guards, and community brass bands. At women's
insistence men founded dramatic and philharmonic societies,
lyceums and lending libraries. Booksellers, music and dancing
masters, and tutors in mathematics and Latin prospered.

Much of the old rowdiness vanished. There was less swearing, less hard drinking, heavy gambling, and fighting as the
usages of polite society were resurrected. The bizarre dress and
"picturesque rags" of other days became less common; hair
and beards were trimmed, and boots wore an occasional polish.

Still, the metamorphosis was not entire. Although women
were the inspiration for the founding of a benevolent society
dedicated to the relief and protection of miners' widows and
orphans, its spirit was typical of the roaring gold camps—boisterous, rebellious, irreverent, and charitable. The Ancient and
Honorable Order of E Clampsus Vitus they called this fraternity, which was organized in Hangtown on November 25, 1855.

In spite of its serious purpose it was an avowed burlesque of
all other secret societies. Its highest officer bore the title Noble

Grand Humbug, and its motto was *Credo Quia Absurdum*. The
Knights met regularly just before and after full moon, but for
special meetings they were summoned by raucous blasts on
the Hewgag, a great tin horn administered by the Royal Grand
Musician. Its balanced program of nonsense, horseplay, and
charity attracted the most prominent men in town, and chapters
were soon being opened in nearly every gold camp along the
river. The convivial Clampers ruled the diggings, and newspapers of the day were full of notices of their good works.

All of the women, so far, had come to the river from other
places, but after a time native daughters began to be born along
it, and some of them grew up to gain recognition. The best-
known was the poet Anna Catherine Murphy Markham, whose
father was a miner at Iowa Hill, a gold camp perched on a ridge
above the North Fork and famed for its weekly output of $100,-
000 from the rich Blue Lead Channel running under the town.

As a child she played beside the river, found yellow violets
and azalea in its glens, shooting stars and iris on its sunny
banks, poppies, creamcups, and lupine in its grassy dales. She
smelled the heady sweetness of ceanothus and tasted the tart
apples of the manzanita; she watched "the lizard's dartling
gleam" as he sped across granite slabs, listened to the coyote
bay and the screech owl call, saw sun- and moonrise behind
the "mountain crests that break the sky." And she grew up to
sing joyously and convincingly of the Sierran river country she
knew so well and loved.

In 1898 she received considerable notice when she married
the poet Edwin Markham, soon to gain his greatest fame and
popularity with publication of "The Man with the Hoe," inspired by Millet's painting. After being elected county superintendent of schools, he had moved from Coloma to Placerville,
where, in 1886, he first saw a reproduction of Millet's work.

"In my large notebook, I wrote the four opening lines of the
poem, substantially as they stand today," he recalled. It was
Anna Catherine who discovered those lines and urged him to
finish the poem.

A long-time resident of Iowa Hill, where she taught school after finishing college, she had lived among hirsute miners for so long that she made a vow never to marry a man with a beard. After her marriage to the bearded Markham she was called on to explain.

"But he wrote such wonderful poetry about love that I forgot my objections," was her reply.

Women who lived in the gold towns profited abundantly from the dissolution of old precedents and prejudices, and the general liberation of thought. They found themselves in possession of an unwonted freedom, with opportunities to accept challenges in fields they would not ordinarily have entered. Maude Hulbert was one of these. In 1891, at a precocious sixteen, her name appeared on the masthead of the *Georgetown Gazette*, a newspaper which her father, Horace W. Hulbert, had founded in 1880. The elder Hulbert, too absorbed with his mining interests to devote much time to the *Gazette*, had made her an editor. She proved so capable, he found himself turning over to her more and more details of the paper's management, until there came a day when she was running it. She remained the *Gazette*'s editor and publisher until the paper's sale in 1924.

Maude's main problem during those first years, her daughter, Judge Amy Drysdale recalls, was to find a reliable printer. Every one she hired either got drunk or tried to make love to her, and Maude—being all business—discharged them instantly. Her search for a dependable printer took her finally to San Francisco, where she interviewed a number and hired one, John Christian Horn, who was slender and pale and seemed to be in need of some bracing mountain air.

He proved to have all the qualities she was looking for—and more, for two years later she married him. "Perhaps this was just to keep him," suggests their daughter, with a smile.

But editing and publishing a newspaper were not enough to satisfy Maude, so she learned telegraphy, and was soon operating the local system. This was a position of great importance in a day when the telegraph was the only means of communication between the big mines in the area and the outside world. Every night she went to bed with the telegraph key right beside her, ready in case of some mining accident or disaster, to be up in an instant and summon help.

Not even three children slowed her down for long. Once they were in school she accepted an additional post as correspondent for the *Sacramento Bee*. After her husband's tragic death in a fire in 1921, she assumed still another responsibility by taking over the management of his insurance business, and the duties of a notary public.

One of the high points in Maude Hulbert Horn's long and full career came in 1928 when she shattered all precedents by becoming El Dorado County's first woman justice of the peace, initially by appointment, and two years later by election.

Although women in the gold country were entering many fields that had long been restricted to men, and were rapidly proving their capabilities, it was still rare to find a woman in the cattle business. Yet young Maria Silva not only raised Durham cattle, but rode the mountain trails alone each June to take the herd she and her father owned to Stumpy Meadows along the Rubicon River.

She was born in Cooper's Ravine, below Pilot Hill, the daughter of Manuel Silviera de Avilla (whose name impatient Americans soon shortened to Silva), a miner who raised a little stock. It was the cattle that interested her—"I was brought up with those heifers," she says—and by the time she was twenty she had helped build up the herd from eighteen to seventy.

For years she was too busy to think about marriage, but when she did consider it, it was to accept the proposal of a fellow stock raiser, Henry Bacchi. Of Swiss ancestry, he, too, was born in American River country, at Garden Valley on the Georgetown Divide, and had taken up a homestead where the booming gold camp of Michigan Flat once stood, just north of Coloma. Together they worked to increase their herds and pasture lands and make theirs one of the largest cattle ranches in El Dorado County.

In spite of soaring taxes and dwindling open range which have driven most stockmen in the area out of business, or to other states, the Bacchi Ranch still operates. Today, at ninety-six, Mrs. Mary Bacchi, now a widow, works closely with her two sons, Byron and Francis, in the management of the home ranch, to which she has devoted nearly a lifetime, and one in southern Oregon where each year their Herefords are trucked for summer grazing.

No matter how numerous women became, men in the gold towns continued to regard them with awe and treat them with all the ardor and gallantry they had lavished on the first ones. For years to come, stage and steamboat runners were able to draw extra custom by shouting: "Ladies aboard!" And men would crowd windows and doorways to gaze with a kind of reverence on some pretty stranger come to town.

Nowhere in the world, stated an early settler, were women treated "with more respectful attention or consideration than in California. Without them the course of the country never could have advanced in the path of progress or amounted to anything worth the name." And, observed a woman who came during the Gold Rush: "This is the only country in the world where women are properly appreciated."

25

Folsom Dam

Taming the River

ON THE NIGHT of January 9, 1850, the American River rose above its banks and flooded the infant city of Sacramento. Mrs. Sarah Royce and her small daughter, Mary, fled their tent and raced the rapidly rising waters to take refuge on the top floor of a nearby wooden house; by midnight fifty other persons were sharing it. In the morning when she looked out of the window she saw nothing "for miles north and south . . . but water." It stood in the rooms below her almost to the beams of the second floor.

Six days later the high water was still there, but rescue had come in the form of the old riverboat *McKim*. That morning she and Mary climbed through the window into a boat that took them down the middle of the main street to the waiting steamer.

In March 1851, the American flooded Sacramento again, and Hardin Bigelow, a local merchant, set out with a small party to put up a levee at a point where the river made a broad sweep to the south and invariably poured over into the streets. To everyone's surprise but his own it worked, and the citizens were so impressed by his astuteness they elected him chief magistrate.

The next winter was a heavier one, and the river found a way into town above and below the levee. Thoroughfares were like

so many canals crowded with boats and barges carrying on the customary traffic; watermen plied for hire in the streets instead of cabs, and independent gentlemen poled themselves about on rafts, or on extemporized boats made of empty boxes. In one part of town, where the water was not deep enough for general navigation, a very curious style of conveyance was in use. Pairs of horses were harnessed to large flat-bottomed boats, and numbers of these vehicles, carrying passengers or goods, were . . . cruising about, now dashing through a foot or two of mud which the horses made fly in all directions as they floundered through . . . now grounding and bumping over some very dry spot, and again sailing gracefully along the top of the water, so deep as nearly to cover the horses' backs.

To that observer the flood seemed to cause little interruption in the normal course of business and pleasure, except "in the substitution of boats for wheeled vehicles." As rats were the scourge of all river towns, one great source of consolation to Sacramentans, he said, was "in endeavouring to compute how many millions of rats would be drowned."

The town was under water again during the winter of 1853, and it was then that merchants moved their stores and warehouses to the new city of Hoboken, laid out on higher ground to the east of them. After the water receded, Bigelow's levee was heightened and extended.

Eight mild winters followed, the river was docile, and floods were for a time forgotten. Then, in January 1863, 34.14 inches of rain fell in nineteen days, melting the heavy snowpack of December. The American breached the levees and Sacramento, by then a city of eighteen thousand, stayed under water from three to nine feet deep until nearly the end of March.

Around nine o'clock on the night of January 12, a steamer brought San Franciscans news of Sacramento's devastation, and they set right to work. By morning tons of provisions were already prepared (eleven thousand pounds of ham alone had been boiled), and before night two steamers carrying over thirty tons of cooked and canned food, twenty-two tons of clothing, several thousand dollars in cash, and small boats with crews for rescue work were on their way to the stricken city.

A visitor to Sacramento reported on March 6 that by then the water had receded some, but boats were still the only means of getting around most parts of the city. Hiring one, he rowed through the streets for nearly two hours to survey the damage, and saw such "a desolate scene" as he never hoped to see again. Drowned animals lay everywhere, and houses had toppled over or been swept from their foundations and carried several blocks. Sodden sofas, mattresses, chairs, and tables floated in front yards. Looking into the windows of a schoolhouse he saw the benches and desks aswim. "The new Capitol is far out in the water—the Governor's house stands as in a lake." Everything was "forlorn and wretched," business was at a standstill, and he wondered how the city could ever rise again.

Then more storms came, the American overflowed again, and for two weeks there was neither overland mail nor telegraph.

This time Sacramentans acted promptly to prevent such future disasters, heightening, strengthening, and extending the levees and raising the street level to four feet above the highwater mark. Then they dug a new mouth about three-quarters of a mile north of the natural one, deepened an overflow channel, and shifted the river's course slightly to the north.

But nothing they could do kept the American under control, and it continued to flood Sacramento for nearly ninety years more. John Sutter had been right when he opposed building a city on the river's lowlands.

When Horatio Gates Livermore of Livermore, Maine, came to Georgetown in 1850, he looked around with the eye of the Yankee businessman that he was and saw his future not in the productive gold diggings there, but in the fine stands of virgin pine that covered the Georgetown Divide. He had learned that the demand for lumber was great and sawmills were few; he could use the river to transport the logs and power the mill. Then he thought about diverting it into canals to irrigate the fertile valley for farming and using its power to turn factory wheels. He envisioned transforming Folsom into a replica of a New England manufacturing town. To demonstrate his faith in the future of farming, he planted five hundred acres in the foothills to orchards and vineyards and built a winery and fruit-drying plant at Folsom.

The biggest step in realizing his plan was to dam the American and build two canals, one for irrigation and the other with an eighty-foot fall for waterpower; he would use the impounded water as a gathering pond for the logs floated down from the Georgetown Divide.

The logical place for a dam was at Stony Bar, where high granite banks formed a narrow gorge. Construction was started in 1867, but a multitude of problems, including shortage of money, delayed its completion for twenty-six years.

Meanwhile, the younger Horatio Livermore had begun developing the lumbering side of the project. He incorporated the $1.5 million American River Land & Lumber Company, bought nine thousand acres of timberland lying between the South and Middle forks, and laid out a forty-mile logging railroad. Then the river was cleared of its largest boulders, a boom-enclosed pond constructed at Folsom, and a sawmill put up near town.

But after the log drives started it was soon seen that the American was unlike any of the civilized New England rivers the Livermores knew; they realized that this sinuous mountain torrent, which pounded logs to splinters and wedged them irretrievably between midstream rock shelves, could never be cleared of all its obstructions. River transportation proved so hazardous and costly, the mill was moved to a site near logging operations.

By the time the granite and concrete dam was finished in 1893, the elder Horatio Livermore was dead, and the question became whether to use the power to turn waterwheels, as he had originally planned, or electric generators, for electricity was then in its infancy. Young Horatio had watched with interest its first application in the mines, had seen Auburn turn on its first incandescent lights on October 19, 1889, and had studied the reports of transmission experiments conducted in Europe. He decided to build a powerhouse.

High voltage electricity had never been carried more than five miles, but he hoped to find some way of transmitting it the twenty-two miles from Folsom to Sacramento, for he had plans to bring electric lighting to the capital city and build an electric streetcar system there.

Again there were countless problems, but the Folsom powerhouse was finally finished, and an 11,000-volt, three-phase transmission line set up by the General Electric Company to carry the current to Sacramento. On July 13, 1895, the river's power began generating electricity, and on September 9, the forty-fifth anniversary of California's admission into the Union, a "Grand Electric Carnival" was held to mark this latest milestone in the state's progress.

The celebration was climaxed with an after-dark illumination of the Capitol when some 3,200 incandescent lamps outlined the dome and roof and lighted up the interior, and 2,000 colored bulbs were strung in the foreground trees. The local press reported that it was "a scene surpassing in effect that of any single similar effort heretofore attempted." A night parade, with illuminated floats set up on the new electric trolleys, ended the day's festivities.

This was the first demonstration in any American city of long-distance, high voltage transmission, and engineers came from all over the country to study the system.

In 1949, Congress authorized construction of a new multipurpose Folsom Dam, reservoir, and power plant. This involved a re-regulating dam and powerhouse downstream (Nimbus) and a diversion dam in the foothills, at Sly Park, where members of the old Mormon Battalion had camped in 1848 on their way to Salt Lake. This project was finally to provide the necessary flood control for Sacramento, conserve water, and generate power. In its first fifteen years, by preventing major flooding, the dam saved the capital city from damages totaling $113 million.

Today the river plays another role in the lives of Sacramentans. It furnishes them with both drinking water and recreation. A filtration plant purifies it, and the American River Parkway, which extends in segments as far as Nimbus Dam and Lake Natoma, offers varied sport. In the park there are hiking and riding trails over the bluffs, picnic grounds under the oaks, and an eighteen-hole golf course; while the river itself provides good fishing and swimming, rafting, and kayaking. The run from Nimbus Dam to Discovery Park is a favorite with canoe clubs.

Many office buildings and fine homes line the American's banks, and California State University occupies a 225-acre campus on its west shore, so close as to almost defy it.

Although residents of the capital city have come to trust the river, their confidence may be misplaced, for during the excessive rains of January and February 1973, stretches of riverside park were under water, and other parts of the city threatened by flood. Folsom Dam had reached capacity, and had the storms continued another day and a half or been of greater intensity, it could not have controlled the runoff.

When full, Folsom Lake covers 11,450 acres and has a seventy-five-mile shoreline that provides camp and picnic areas, boat launching ramps, and swimming beaches that attract millions of visitors each year.

The lake extends fifteen miles up the North Fork and ten and a half along the South, covering many of the river's earliest and richest gold camps: Mormon Island (where an auxiliary earth-fill dam has been built); Rattlesnake, Drunkard's, Whiskey, and Deadman's bars; Salmon Falls; Growler's Flat; and Pinchem Tight.

Nearly every camp has some tale behind its name, and so with Pinchem Tight. A Mr. Ebbert who ran the store there had no scales of a size to weigh out gold dust for small purchases. So, he would pinch the dust between his thumb and finger— loosely, of course, to get as much as possible—a habit that prompted his customers to watch him with eagle eye and warn: "Pinch 'em tight, Ebbert! Pinch 'em tight!"

To replace the natural spawning grounds of the king salmon at Salmon Falls, blocked off by these dams, the Bureau of Reclamation built a fish hatchery just below Nimbus. In late October and November when the salmon run occurs, the fish climb by ladder into the hatchery where they are milked, then given afterward to any Indians who want them. For ages, Salmon Falls was the Maidu's traditional fishing ground.

The Auburn–Folsom South Unit of the American River Division of the Central Valley Project (CVP is one of the nation's major water conservation and diversion developments) calls for still another large dam, power plant, and reservoir, which is under construction now at Auburn. The dam, a concrete, thin-arch structure, will stand seven hundred feet above the riverbed and impound two and a quarter million acre-feet. Releases from the reservoir will operate the power plant and supply Folsom-South Canal, a sixty-nine-mile concrete-lined ditch that will carry American River water to Lone Tree Creek in San Joaquin County, and eventually, as part of the planned East Side Canal, as far south as Bakersfield. The lake, with its 140-mile shoreline and planned recreational facilities that will include eleven thousand additional acres for public use, is expected to attract three million visitors the first year and five million annually after that.

In addition, there is the Forest Hill Divide Development that will invade the wilderness of Shirttail Canyon to build Sugar Pine Dam and power plant on North Shirttail Creek and pipe its waters to the Divide, to be doled out for irrigation, municipal, and industrial use.

However, the entire project has been curbed by President Nixon's January 1973 cut in CVP's budget, which will slow down construction on Auburn Dam, push its completion date well into the 1980s, and call a virtual halt to extension of the Folsom-South Canal. His request that state and local governments reassess a project's desirability is expected to put an end to continuation of the canal, since there is grave concern expressed by local government and environmentalists that the Lower American will be deprived of its flow if more water is diverted from it. As there is strong opposition on environmental grounds to the Auburn Dam, it is hoped by many that, with the President's determination to cut CVP's funds still more in the future, the dam will never be built.

The benefits of large dams, once thought to be the solution to all water problems, are being reviewed critically. Even for flood control, many engineers now agree that levees and small upstream controls on key tributaries are the most effective method of preventing floods.

Although it is now too late to keep the entire American River wild and free flowing, the North Fork from its source to the Iowa Hill bridge has recently been included with the Lower

American, from Nimbus Dam to its meeting with the Sacramento, in the California Wild and Scenic Rivers System. A bill
calling for protective legislation for five California rivers was
introduced by State Senator Peter H. Behr and, after a two-year
battle, passed both houses and was signed into law by Governor Reagan on December 20, 1972.

The North Fork has also been proposed for designation
under the National Wild and Scenic Rivers Act. Here the prospect is bright, for its inclusion in the California law in effect
recommends that the Secretary of the Interior designate it
under the federal act. In this case, an intensive study will be
made of its scenic, historic, archaeological, scientific, and recreational features and of its access routes and land ownerships.
A hydrologic survey will be made of its drainage, and a study
undertaken of its mineral and other resources. It will also be
subject to analysis under the Environmental Protection Act.
From these various findings a plan will be formulated both to
protect the area and provide for public use and enjoyment.

If Auburn Dam is built, changes in the river itself and the
surrounding country will be many. The chemistry of its waters
will be altered with storage in volume behind the dam; the
salinity and fertility of downstream soil will be changed, and
all indigenous plant and animal life affected, for any alteration
in plant and water systems changes food supplies, which in
turn directly influence all wildlife dependent on them.

Already highways are being cut into the heart of the wilderness, since present roads leading to such historic gold camps as
Forest Hill, Yankee Jim's, and Michigan Bluff will presumably
be under water. Even the famed Mother Lode Highway 49
which crosses the river just below the junction of the North and
Middle forks well be rerouted, for the scenic Y where the rivers
meet and the wooded slopes up which the road now winds
past glens that are wild gardens in spring will lie under the
lake. Tons of water will drown the site of some fifty famous
riverbars and lock up forever the vast treasure of the Big
Crevice.

26

The Struggle for Survival

As PLACER GOLD grew harder to find, men started looking about for other minerals, and they discovered silver near Kelsey's Diggings, copper in Hastings Ravine, iron near Clipper Gap, galena at Cool, and asbestos on the Georgetown Divide. And they found deposits of coal and pottery clay, granite, and limestone which is an important product of the region today. And they discovered marble, said to be, equal to the finest Italian marble. "A beautifully variegated block . . . weighing 2,700 pounds," taken from a quarry near Ringgold Creek, was California's contribution to the Washington Monument.

All these other resources were worked and made to pay, but there was none of that zeal which had marked the mining for gold.

Some men turned to dairying, sheep and cattle raising, and general farming. But it was to be apple and pear orchards, olive and citrus groves, vineyards, wine, and olive oil that would bring the river country its greatest agricultural fame. And it was at Coloma, first in many things, that the earliest plantings of grapes and apple and pear trees were made, and wineries opened.

Thermal belts were found to extend along the river canyons from Auburn almost to Michigan Bluff. Here orange, lemon, and lime trees were planted, and the area came to rank third in the state for citrus production. And the olive groves set out in these warm ravines produced prize-winning fruit and oil.

Although the mountain orchardist could not compete with the valley grower in per-acre production, it was for flavor and shipping qualities that the former's fruit was noted, and until the coming of mechanical refrigeration and diesel locomotives, it was in demand for eastern markets. But just as soon as it was found that carloads of the huge valley crop, which had up to then been sold to local markets, canneries, and drying plants, could be rushed across the country before they spoiled, the choice fruit of the river foothills was no longer shipped east. Many orchardists went out of business, and those former gold towns that had become large fruit-packing and shipping centers suffered economically.

Today there is new life among the river's growers, as an increasing number of consumers are discovering the delights of flavorful, mountain-grown fruit. The orchardists, striving to encourage this trend, have formed themselves into an association whose aims are to gain still wider recognition for the quality of their products and to promote sales on the ranch. To offer variety and extend the season, many growers also market their own wine, honey, nuts, olives, berries, mushrooms, dried fruit, cider, jellies, and Christmas trees.

From the earliest days of settlement along the river there were those who believed that its warm slopes and sheltered ravines were ideally suited for growing mulberry trees, and editors and lecturers urged silk culture to supplement gold mining. To encourage the industry, the state passed an act in 1855 offering bounties to mulberry tree planters, the amount paid based on the number of trees. But when hundreds of men began calling for their money, the act had to be hastily repealed to keep the state from bankruptcy. Thousands of mulberry trees had been planted by men who had no intention of raising silkworms, but saw here an easy way to get money from the public treasury.

A few did go into the business legitimately, and they made profits as high as $1,500 on an acre of trees when, during the late 1860s, European silkworms were struck by disease. But once the price of silk dropped, they could not compete, and within a few years silk culture along the river died out.

In May 1869, the side-wheeler *China* sailed into San Francisco with the first party of Japanese immigrants. There were ten samurai and farmers, members of a group of colonists headed by John Henry Schnell who had come from Japan to establish a silk and tea plantation at Gold Hill, just up the ridge from Coloma. Two more parties followed, bringing 300,-000 three-year-old mulberry trees, 150,000 tea plants, and a hardy variety of silkworm, called *aman*, that would also feed on black oak leaves. The last group included six women to reel the silk, and Okei Ito, a girl of seventeen, who was the Schnell family seamstress.

The Wakamatsu Colony, as Schnell called it, had its beginnings in the Japanese revolt of 1868, and the defeat of the Tokugawa shogun's forces by the emperor. Schnell, said to have been a German consular representative in Japan, had through his marriage to the daughter of a samurai become confidential adviser to one of the shogun's chief supporters, Lord Matsudaira of Aizu Wakamatsu.

For the defeated there had always been the choice of falling on one's sword in the honorable *seppuku,* or fleeing the country, which was punishable by death. But with the shogun's overthrow, emigration became legal, and Schnell and others of his party looked toward a haven in America.

By 1870 he was ready to harvest his first tea crop, but problems were already multiple. Miners refused to respect his property rights, took up claims on his land, and, in tearing up the earth in their zealous search for gold, destroyed hundreds of his plantings. Promised funds for the colony's support failed to materialize, and lack of money and mounting debts weighed heavily. Toward the end of that year he told his people he was leaving for Japan to raise capital. He took with him his wife and two small daughters, Mary and Frances, who had been

born at Gold Hill; they were the first children of Japanese ancestry to be born in the United States.

What became of John Schnell will probably never be known.
He did not come back to Gold Hill, and his colonists never
heard from him again. One story holds that on his arrival in
Japan he was arrested and executed for his part in the revolt;
another insists that he never went to Japan, and that the report of his execution originated with him to throw his creditors
off the scent.

When it seemed certain he was not going to return, his
people began scattering over the countryside in search of work.
Californians were by this time violently anti-Chinese, but Japanese were still few enough to be regarded with favor. Editors
pointed out that none of those objections raised against the
Chinese were shared by the Japanese. They were commended
because they had brought their wives and children with them,
and because they introduced many "new industries among us."
The carpenters and farmers from the Wakamatsu Colony therefore found work readily. At last there were only two left at
Gold Hill: Matsunoke Sakurao, a samurai, and the girl Okei
Ito, who was dying of malarial fever.

Francis Veerkamp, who had been farming at Gold Hill since
1852, took over the Wakamatsu lands and gave work to Sakurao
and care to Okei. Knowing that she would not live, she asked to
be buried on a certain hilltop where she used to sit, after the
Schnells left, and look longingly toward her homeland. In April
1871, Okei, just nineteen, died and was buried on the crest of
that grassy slope.

She was the first of those first colonists to die in this far-off
land, and her grave, still tended by descendants of Francis
Veerkamp, is visited annually by numbers of Japanese pilgrims
for whom she has become a symbol.

With the decline in mining, fruit growing, sheep and cattle
raising, dairying, and, of late, railroading—which once con-
tributed to the support of the region with large diesel engine

repair and freight-car-building shops—the hold most gold towns have on life is tenuous. Auburn looks to its new dam for prosperity, expecting to cater to the millions of visitors who will come to the lake for recreation.

Lumbering has been the one constant industry to give continuing life to many a gold camp. With the bulk of the area's timberland under U.S. Forest Service management, and the industry's own program of scientific harvesting and reforestation, along with the growing demand for lumber and its by-products, this is one major economic support that should never suffer any decline.

In season, skiers, hunters, fishermen, and river runners come out in force, bringing their trade to local business; and every clear weekend during the dry season motorcycle and trail-bike riders flock in to accept the challenge of the river's steepest slopes. The American is becoming increasingly popular with kayak and raft enthusiasts who are finding that it offers some of the most demanding white water in the state and magnificent scenic runs through its wild and rugged canyons. Its less turbulent stretches appeal to canoeists.

All forks of the river and its tributary Sierran lakes and streams support good populations of rainbow, brown, lake, brook, and cutthroat trout, and Kokanee salmon. In the Lower American there are catfish, bass, perch, and runs of steelhead and shad.

Deer are the only large mammals to have adapted themselves to man's invasion of their territory and benefited from some of his activities. They have so increased under protective game laws, there are said to be more in California today than when the first settlers came. They are so numerous in certain areas they are overgrazing their range, and while many die from malnutrition or are subject to disease on this account, numbers are driven from their habitat to seek food in orchards, vineyards, truck and alfalfa farms, and even home gardens. Wildlife biologists maintain that properly regulated hunting has a stabilizing influence on animal populations. By removing part of the surplus, forage competition is reduced, and animals are less subject to epidemics.

Neither the Tule elk, which once grazed in large herds on the wild pastures of the river's lowlands, nor the grizzly bear, at one time so plentiful in the foothills and mountains and the marshlands near the river, benefited from settlement of its territory. Individual elk herds containing as many as two thousand were not unusual in 1846, but these were soon reduced by hunters and the animal's natural intolerance to disturbance of its environment. When threatened with extinction in 1873, a protective law was passed by the state, but it was already too late. Today there are about 3,700 elk of three species in the wild: Tule, Roosevelt, and Rocky Mountain. Most of them have been introduced and are protected and managed. None lives along the American River.

The grizzly became the victim of an uncompromising campaign of extermination waged by the settlers who considered him too dangerous a neighbor. Presumably the last of his kind in California was killed in 1921.

His cousin, the gentler black bear, was more fortunate; he has maintained his own and even flourished on parts of the grizzly's old range. Bear hunting in California has always been limited to a relatively few sportsmen, and the kill is often incidental to deer hunting.

Snowshoe Thompson held the first exhibition of downhill skiing in California on the slopes east of Hangtown in the winter of 1855, and his subsequent heroic exploits in carrying the mails over the Sierra so popularized skis, they came into general use as a means of getting from place to place across the deep snow, and for sport. Miners living all year in the mountains found ski racing a cure for the tedium of winter days. As one contemporary observed, it afforded "an innocent amusement and health-giving exercise, thereby keeping the muscles in tune for the labor of the summer."

"Snowshoe" clubs were organized in many camps, and down-hill races and jumping contests held nearly every week during the season. But then as gold mining waned and men began leaving the mountain diggings, interest in skiing lapsed, and it was not until after World War I, when numbers of Europeans settled in California and began exploring the Sierran slopes with their skis, that there was a revival.

In general people seem to have been unfamiliar with the sport. One German skier of the early 1920s recalls how often, when she took the train to the ridges above the North Fork, fellow passengers looked at her skis curiously and asked, "What are those things you are carrying? And what do you do with them?"

Once they discovered the delights of skiing they took it up with enthusiasm and, as the miners had done, formed ski clubs, held jumping competitions and races, and built their own lodges along the railroad, from Cisco Grove to Donner Summit, for in those days no attempt was made to keep the two main trans-Sierran highways open in winter.

But once the State Highway Commission decided to make both all-year roads (at present nearly $3 million is spent annually on this task), and convert the Donner Summit route into the transcontinental freeway, Interstate 80, skiing became everyman's sport, and there are many weekends at the season's peak when traffic on these highways is bumper to bumper. Furnishing skiers with food, lodgings, and supplies brings in a good winter harvest to many former gold towns and stagecoach inns along the old emigrant routes, recalling that time when Mother Weltie, Dirty Mike, Tom Audrain,, "Straw" Berry, Dick Yarnold, and Sol Perrin were flourishing, and the roads were jammed with mule trains and Concord coaches.

Tourism is one of the river country's most stable economic resources. Old camps and towns, aware of their significant past, are restoring historic homes and buildings, and in some of the larger settlements, whole blocks and districts are being reno-

vated to recapture the aura of Gold Rush days and attract a constantly increasing number of visitors. Antique shops and art
galleries abound, and inns of other times, tastefully renovated
and furnished with period pieces, offer rooms and meals once
more. Some towns, like Folsom and Auburn, feature weekend
and summer theaters that present plays popular with the
miners.

There are plans to rebuild Damascus (north of Michigan
Bluff) as an example of a typical mountain gold camp. Concession businesses, and in winter, the sale of Christmas trees,
will pay its way.

The State of California, recognizing the necessity for protecting the historically important sites and buildings in Coloma
and preserving its character, has taken them into its park system. Here in this one charming hamlet, where time has practically stood still, are more significant links to the past than can
be found in any other gold camp in the northern mines. Under
its oaks are Maidu grinding rocks; at the foot of the hill on
which James Marshall is buried are the remnants of Chinatown
and the site of a Joss House, shaded by ailanthus trees. On the
riverbank stands a replica of the most famous sawmill in the
world, and under the pines and buckeyes on the slope,
Marshall's cabin. On this same rise are two historic churches
and their old burying grounds banked in a sullen drift of briars,
the wood and marble headstones weathered and pocked, some
erect, some leaning, some fallen.

There is the discovery site with overhanging willows and
alders, and the white clapboard house, set amid fruit trees and
tangled roses, where Edwin Markham lived. There is the red
brick gunsmith shop, and the ruins of the general store, and a
cannon said to have come from Sutter's Fort; the crumbling,
mossy walls of the old stone jail, and the armory of the Coloma
Grays, one of the few California military companies to serve
in the field during the Civil War.

Along the fringe of pines and oaks there are gnarled apple

trees and grapevines, and hoary locusts, relics of the first settlers. And there are vestiges of old gardens gone wild, with
clumps of daffodils trooping up the ravines, and dells empurpled
with violets.

And there is the cooling river, silvery in the forsaken sweetness of early morning, or ruffled with a sunset breeze that carries
some half-heard lay of the star-filled night to come.

Beyond the bounds of the park are two old inns, restored;
and a number of shops and an art gallery vie for favor with
the throngs of tourists who overrun the village on weekends
and throughout the summer.

By 1889, all that remained of John Sutter's imposing fortress
was its crumbling, two-story main building. That year it was
threatened with demolition by the proposed extension of a
street, and only the determined efforts of a group of citizens
aware of its historical significance saved it. The restoration and
reconstruction that were started by the state in 1891 have
brought the old stronghold into existence again. Approximating
its original plan, the fort now houses a priceless collection of
pioneer artifacts, letters, and papers in its archives, museum,
and reconstructed workshops, stores, and living quarters contained in the two-story adobe, and lining the walls of the quad-
rangle.

There is every reason to believe that there is nearly as much
gold left as was ever taken out of American River country,
mining men say. Although they maintain that little remains in
the river itself, aside from the fathomless Big Crevice, amateur
gold hunters continue to pick up flakes and nuggets. One novice recently found an 8.5-ounce nugget, worth some $3,600
as a collector's item, in the shallows of the Middle Fork. But
the greatest riches lie in the vast untapped deposits of the
ancient river channels, and unfound lodes in old tunnel drift
mines.

Today there are one or two small hydraulic operations on
tributaries of the North Fork, a few individual miners doing a

little work on old leads, and ever-growing numbers of recreational prospectors who pan or dive for gold during their holidays and are often rewarded with a little color. But gold mining as an industry has been shut down by high production costs. However, there are many who look forward to another Gold Rush—provided the price of gold continues to rise. It would have to be close to $200 an ounce to make it pay on a large scale, most old-time miners agree. But if it could then be stabilized, they foresee all the rich old mines in the area opening up again, new discoveries being made, dredging resumed, and the river canyons echoing once again with the rush and roar of monitors.

Land developers in unlimited numbers bombard the public with invitations to experience the peace and seclusion of summer, weekend, and year-round living in the groves along the river, far from traffic, smog, noise, and other people.

Establishment of extensive housing in remote areas necessitates supply centers, and soon units of stores appear, and then large shopping centers which may grow unchecked into a town, with traffic, smog, noise, and numbers of people. Gone then is the peace and seclusion of the grove as man brings with him the very evils he is seeking to escape.

Invasion of the wilderness for housing with its attendant clearing, grading, impervious surfacing, and reduction of open pore space in soil can pose problems of unknown magnitude for man. These actions alter the normal patterns of surface runoff and percolation, precipitate rapid erosion, and cause the loss of nutrients, phosphorus, and carbon to soil, preventing proper exchange of water between land and atmosphere.

Land and water usage also determines the fate of wildlife. Many birds and animals are territorial, depending on a plant and animal community of limited size for availability of food and cover. These often find it impossible to adapt by moving to another community, or by changing their food preferences. Large mammals, furbearers, upland game birds, and waterfowl have the least tolerance to disturbance, while nearly all birds and animals react negatively to any noise exceeding seventy-five decibels at a hundred-foot distance, or any unusual movement near or within their living areas.

Nor is the picture quite so perfect as the land agents indicate. The results of a four-year study show that air pollution has already touched the gold country. Blown into the Sacramento Valley by sea breezes, it is drawn up into the foothills where it may linger, or boil up and over the Sierra. On some summer days it is impossible to see across Lake Tahoe, a region once famed for its pure air and clear skies. The Jeffrey and ponderosa pines are the first victims of this pollution. Many are afflicted with chlorotic mottling which causes needles to degenerate from a healthy dark green to a sickly yellow, and instead of being retained four years, they are dropped at two or less. The result is an undernourished tree, which is subject to disease and attacks from natural enemies. Many of these stately trees are visibly unhealthy, and a number already dead.

To preserve the balance of the ecosystem and maintain wildlife population and quality in spite of a large resident and transient human population calls for further research and study of wildlife habitats and activities. Also essential are orderly development planning and total cooperation between landowners, developers, and federal, state, and county agencies and departments.

With two disparate forces at work, the future of the American River country is uncertain. While the Forest Service is striving to protect the fragile wilderness from overuse and preserve the solitude and primitive character of such areas as Desolation Valley, that glacial granite basin where the Rubicon and the South Fork rise, there is heard that insistent cry, Improve the roads! And in answer, more lanes are being added to Interstate 80, while conversion of U.S. 50 to total freeway status is being considered.

The long-range predictions (hopefully inaccurate) foresee a

connected series of small cities extending from Sacramento
through the river country to the 3,000-foot level.

The need for wilderness reserves is evident and imperative,
and it is being urged by those who appreciate their value as
"fountains of life," where, in the words of John Muir, men may
wash off the "sins and cobweb cares" of daily life by "saunter-
ing in rosiny pinewoods or in gentian meadows, brushing
through chaparral, bending down and parting sweet, flowery
sprays; tracing rivers to their sources . . . jumping from rock
to rock, feeling the life of them, learning the songs of them,
panting in whole-souled exercise, and rejoicing in deep, long-
drawn breaths of pure wildness."

27

The River and Time

"In rivers, the water that you touch is the last of what has passed and the first of that which comes: so with time present," wrote Leonardo.

A man's story ends after a few score years, but the river's story, reckoned by ages, has no end, for it is renewable and therefore eternal; timeless although not without change, its restless energy is never spent.

Even if the land should be covered with an ice mantle again, as some believe it may, the American will continue to flow, as it did many hundred thousand years ago, singing its muted song in silvery channels deep beneath the glaciers. Only if the forces of inner earth should break out, and mountains sink and valleys rise and seas cover the land once more, would the river vanish. Born of chaos it would meet its end in chaos.

But until that unforeseeable time, in spite of man's efforts to enslave it, it will remain a vital force that will triumph finally over all his transient works. Invested with an invisible power, the river is ever enlarging itself, deepening its canyons, widening its valleys, shifting its course, wearing down the mountains that gave it birth, destroying or giving increase to things that are born of its life-giving moisture, carrying its burden of rock and sand and gold to build up new land, new bars and banks, and, more slowly, new mineral deposits.

Although it loses itself in the depths of the Pacific, it is soon reborn as clouds which replenish the fountains that nourish it.

317

Fulfilling its cosmic cycle, the river's life pattern is a magic circle, an endless chain of clouds, rain, snow, ice, and crystal springs seeping from alpine moraines and mossy banks.

Throughout the summer, thunderstorms in traveling showers refresh the river's fountains almost daily, and in October the first snow whitens peak and forest. Within a few hours on a clear autumn day the brooding clouds mass and noon is dark as dusk. Then tiny flakes or single glinting crystals flutter in spirals, and the first faint whisperings are heard as they alight on leafy bosks. Falling at a time when golden asters, penstemon, and scarlet mimulus are still in bloom, and southbound flocks of birds call hauntingly in the wastes of the sky, this snow is soon gone.

The great storms that clothe the mountains in lasting packs of snow and ice and bury alpine lakes and rivers, rarely break before November's end. Once begun, storm follows storm, with intervals of clear, crisp days when keen fitful gusts whip trees and bushes bare.

Snow piled on snow builds out from the banks in arching drifts that compact and freeze and, in some narrow places, reach out and touch. In a world buried beneath a hush of snow, the river's is almost the only voice to be heard in the solemn canyons, and its wild rush and flash nearly the only life seen in a dormant landscape.

In spring when the thaw begins, uncounted snow-fed brooks glance down the slopes or thread their way through meadows in a shimmering tracery of silver. Responding each morning to the sun's call, they break from their icy covers and hasten to join the river, increasing in flow as the day grows, and lessening toward dusk when frost encrusts each leaf and grass-blade in rime, and ice again glazes the water's surface. The river, responding to this change in flow, rises and ebbs as regularly as the tides, often doubling in volume during the day.

It is in spring, too, that after each passing rain, mists of purest whiteness rise out of the river and from between its trees with the suddenness of phantoms. Growing rapidly in number, they steal swiftly through the dark glades and somber wooded gorges, and in the wind's lap are swept in billowing masses to crown the ridgetops. Like a ghostly army they occupy the river canyons. Then another shower comes and they vanish into the thin, sweet air as quickly as they came.

In fall, when seedpod is blown, nest, aerie, den, and burrow empty, when the vine growing wild along the banks is hung heavy with sweet bloomy grapes, the river's mood is one of calm expectancy. It still flows swift and voluble, but its crystal swell is less, and it reveals many of its secrets. Stretches of cobbled shore are newly bared, and midstream islets and boulders loom. Even the sheeny pebbles and gold-flecked sands of its bed, seldom clearly seen, delight the eye with their color, shape, and glitter in the bottom of lapping shallows. Feeder streams have slowed to a stony murmur or shrunk to chains of murky pools. The river waits for the drifting cumuli to gather and darken and replenish the springs. With the coming of the first snow, its cycle for the year is complete, its life renewed.

In a harmonious round of uncounted seasons, redwings will build their basket nests in the tall rushes of the river's lowlands; ouzels will fashion their huts of moss under its mountain falls and pipe their fluty songs yearlong in its spray. Trout will flash in its pools, swallows skim its surface, orange and blue butterflies drift among the flowers on its banks, and bees, their panniers laden with pollen, probe manzanita bells for nectar. Deer will browse on its slopes and drink from its edges, water shrews walk on its ruffling surface, and turtledoves mourn in the groves.

And the river, in the fullness of flood or in slack, will through unmeasured time, fill its great canyons with wild song.

Notes on Sources

1. The River Is Introduced, pp. 3–10

Life zones: Muir, *The Mountains of California*; Tresidder, "Life Zones in the Sierra"; first-hand observation. Brewer, *Up and Down California in 1860-1864*, described the canyon of the Silver Fork American. Muir wrote of the Sierra woods in *The Mountains* . . . . Wildlife: Orr, *Mammals of Lake Tahoe*; Dasmann, *Big Game in California*; Angel, *History of Placer County*, observed the water shrew. Geological background: Miller, *California Through the Ages*; Matthes, "A Geologist's View"; Jenkins, "Geologic History of the Sierran Gold Belt" and "Sierra Nevada Province." Muir wrote of the rivers in flood and the water ouzel in *The Mountains* . . . . Botanical and bird notes: first-hand observation.

2. The Red Man and the River, pp. 11–21

Background: Stirton, *Time, Life, and Man*; Camp, *Earth Song*; Forbes, *Native Americans of California and Nevada*; Kroeber, *Handbook of the Indians of California*, "Elements of Culture in Native California" and "The Nature of Land-Holding Groups in Aboriginal California"; Gifford, "Californian Indian Physical Types"; Cook, "Conflict Between the Californian Indians and White Civilization." Hutchings, "Scenes Among the Indians of California," observed the sucking shamans at work. Bryant, *What I Saw in California*, and author's grandfather are sources for the *temescal*. Gifford and Bolk, *Californian Indian Nights' Enter-* tainment, for beliefs and mythology. Mrs. Lizzie Enos, Maidu storyteller, for "The Valley Quail." Hutchings, "Scenes Among the Indians . . . ," witnessed the death and burial of a Maidu. Kroeber, *Handbook of the Indians*, is the authority for dress, skills, customs, and methods of hunting and fishing. Mrs. Berenice Pate, Auburn, shared her knowledge of Maidu basketry as well as her large collection of this art form. She is also the authority for many of the plants relished by the Maidu, for the method of flavoring acorn soup, for a minute description of the foothill Maidu huts, and for a description of the sacred Bear Dance. Bidwell, "In

321

California Before the Gold Rush,"
tells about Frémont's men eating
the spicy grasshopper meal. Gerstaecker, *California Gold Mines*,
described the Maidu earth houses,
watched Maidu girls parch seeds,
and observed the method of eating
acorn gruel or soup. Balls, *Early*
Uses of California Plants, for more
Indian uses of plants. Pfeiffer, *A
Lady's Visit to California in 1853*,
is an excellent primary source on
Maidu. Densmore, *The Music of
the Maidu*, contains information on
songs and ceremonies obtained
from the Indians.

3. Hunting the Land of Gold and Griffins, pp. 22–30

Background: Clissold, *The Seven
Cities of Cíbola*; Bancroft, *Cali-
fornia Inter Pocula* and *History of
California*, Vols. I and II; Hittell,
History of California, Vol. I; Josiah
Royce, *California*; Hunt and Sán-
chez, *A Short History of California*.
Hale, "Queen of California," gives
origin of the name "California."
Moraga, *The Diary of Gabriel
Moraga's Expedition of Discovery
in the Sacramento Valley*, and Mc-
Gowan, *History of the Sacramento
Valley*, for Moraga's explorations
and his naming of the river.

4. Jedediah Smith Defies the Land Barriers, pp. 31–38

Background: Sullivan, *Jedediah
Smith, Trader and Trailblazer*;
Smith, *Men Against the Mountains*;
Morgan, *Jedediah Smith and the
Opening of the West*; Farquhar,
"Jedediah Smith and the First
Crossing of the Sierra Nevada."
Letter from Jedediah Smith to
General William Clark.

5. The River Is Settled and Named Again, pp. 39–51

Background: McGowan, *History
of the Sacramento Valley*; Zollinger, *Sutter, the Man and His Empire*; Sutter, "General Sutter's
Notes"; Sutter, in Gudde, *Sutter's
Own Story*; Davis, *Seventy-five
Years in California*; Lienhard, *A
Pioneer at Sutter's Fort*, gives insights into Sutter's character and his
personal life. Dr. Sandels quoted in
Sioli, *Historical Souvenir of El
Dorado County*. Bidwell, "In
California . . . "; as Sutter's clerk
and friend he was in a position to
report on Sutter's finances and observe his character. Bidwell super-
intended the transfer of goods from
Fort Ross and described the primitive agricultural methods. Bryant,
another reliable primary source.

6. The River Trail Is Opened, pp. 52–65

Background: Frémont, *Memoirs
of My Life; Report of the Exploring Expedition to the Rocky Mountains in the Year 1842, and to
Oregon and North California in the
Years 1843-44*; Carson, *Autobiography*; Gianella, "Where Frémont
Crossed the Sierra in 1844"; talks
with Dr. Gianella enlarged on his
article. Preuss, *Exploring with
Frémont*; these almost daily jottings
in his diary supply an excellent
account of the trip and offer numerous insights into Frémont's personality.

7. Wagons over the Sierra, pp. 66–80

Hopkins, *Life Among the Piutes: Their Wrongs and Claims.* Bancroft, *History of California,* Vol. IV; "Story of the Murphy Party," in Foote, ed., *Pen Pictures from the "Garden of the World" or Santa Clara County, California*; Stewart, *The Opening of the California Trail,* all give an account of the Stevens-Townsend-Murphy Party. Schallenberger's reminiscences in "The Story of the Murphy Party." Bryant recorded the struggle around Truckee Lake and up to the summit; he noted the flora and the view. Lienhard, *From St. Louis to Sutter's Fort*; and Todd, in a letter in *New York Tribune,* described the ascent. Philip Badman quoted in Geiger and Bryarly, *Trail to California,* for the descent. William E. Taylor in Morgan, ed.,

Overland in 1846, noted the state of the road. Bancroft, *History of California,* Vol. IV, records the loss of the Townsend-Schallenberger journal. Bidwell, "In California..."; Colton, *Three Years in California,* described the Mexican cart. Mc-Glashen, *History of the Donner Party*; Lienhard, *A Pioneer . . .,* for the Donners' story and a sympathetic picture of Keseberg. Miss Maggie Schallenberger told the story of her father's Christmas dinner. Bidwell, "In California ..."; Sutter, in Gudde, *Sutter's Own Story*; and Sutter, "General Sutter's Notes," furnished primary source accounts of the Micheltorena-Alvarado revolt; Zollinger is an excellent secondary source. Geiger and Bryarly gave details of lowering wagons at Emigrant Gap.

8. "Manifest Destiny," pp. 81–94

Background: Gudde, *Sutter's Own Story*; Sutter, "General Sutter's Notes"; Bidwell, "In California . . . ," and "Frémont in the Conquest of California"; Frémont, *Memoirs . . .* ; Marti, *Messenger of Destiny.* Lienhard, *A Pioneer . . .,* told about Jim Savage, while Bidwell, "In California . . . ," described "Stuttering" Merritt. Royce, *California,* for a scholarly account of Gillespie's mission, the Bear Flag Party, and further insight into Frémont's motives and character. Bidwell, "In California . . . ," told about Todd and the Bear Flag; enlargement in Emparan, *The Vallejos of California,* and Murphy, *The*

People of the Pueblo. Sherman, *The Memoirs of General William T. Sherman,* and Colton described Dr. Semple. Kemble, "March of the California Battalion," and Bryant, who both marched with Frémont, gave details of the men's dress and told about the bugler. Sherman; and Nevins, *Frémont, Pathmarker of the West,* supplied details of the quarrel with Kearny. Nevins is the authority for Frémont's being a civil governor rather than a military, as is so often stated. Sherman accompanied Frémont to headquarters and remembered what he wore.

9. In Pursuit of Happiness, pp. 95–104

Background: Colton; Davis; Bidwell, "In California . . . "; Dana, *Two Years Before the Mast*; Lien-

hard, *A Pioneer . . .* ; Buffum, *Six Months in the Gold Mines*; Briones, "A Carnival Ball at Monterey in

1824"; Sherman, *Memoirs*, for both
glimpses and detailed accounts of
early California life. Bidwell, "In
California . . . "; Gudde, *Sutter's
Own Story*; Sutter, *New Helvetia
Diary*, for the story of Ruelle; and
Cutter, "The Discovery of Gold in
California," for an account of Lo-
pez. Bigler's original diary, quoted
in Paul, *The California Gold
Discovery*, described the cabin and
millsite. Marshall, "The Discovery

of Gold in California." Soulé,
Gihon, and Nisbet, *Annals of San
Francisco*, for ordinance of Jan. 30,
1847, changing the name of Yerba
Buena to San Francisco. "Steam
Travel," in *Alta California*, for
description of the *Sitka*; also Mac-
Mullen, *Paddle-Wheel Days in
California*. Both William T. Sher-
man and Colton wrote about
Christmas customs.

10. Gold! pp. 107–17

Colton recorded the weather on
Jan. 1, 1848; Bigler noted the alder
and manzanita in bloom. Bidwell,
"In California . . . ," described the
sawmill. Primary sources for ac-
counts of the gold discovery and
the immediate results: Gillespie,
"Marshall's Own Account of the
Discovery"; Marshall; Sutter, "The
Discovery of Gold," "General Sut-

ter's Notes," and *New Helvetia
Diary*; Gudde, *Sutter's Own Story*;
Bidwell, "In California . . . "; Lien-
hard, *A Pioneer . . .* ; Sherman,
Memoirs; Bigler, "Diary of a
Mormon in California." Secondary
accounts: Zollinger; Bancroft, *His-
tory of California*, Vol. VI, and
California Inter Pocula; Gay, *James
W. Marshall*.

11. Exodus, pp. 118–31

Kemble, "The First Drops of the
Golden Shower." The *Californian*,
Mar. 15, 1848, for the first news-
paper account of the discovery.
Background for the discovery's im-
pact: Sutter, *New Helvetia Diary*,
"The Discovery of Gold"; Gudde,
Sutter's Own Story; Lienhard, *A
Pioneer . . .* ; Colton; Mason, *Re-
port*. Angel, *History of Placer
County*, and Bancroft, *History of
California*, Vol. VI, for Chana's
story. Versions of the discovery of
Mormon Island are found in Lien-
hard, *A Pioneer . . .* ; Bancroft,
History of California, Vol. VI; and
Bigler, "Diary of a Mormon . . .".
Brannan's history is given in Soulé,
et al.; Scherer, *The First Forty-
Niner and the Story of the Golden*

Tea-Caddy; and Kemble, "The
'Brooklyn Mormons' in California."
William T. Sherman overheard
Clark and Mason. Kemble, "Con-
firming the Gold Discovery," and
"The First Party to the Gold
Mines." Bigler, "Diary of a Mor-
man . . . ," told the story of his
friend Benjamin Hawkins who saw
Brannan display the bottle of gold
and was caught up in the frenzy.
Bancroft, *History of California*, Vol.
VI, gives Bee's story, and quotes
Peralta. Bonsal, *Edward Fitzgerald
Beale*. Gillespie to Abel Stearns,
Oct. 15, 1848, in Hawkins, *First
and Last Consul*. William T. Sher-
man accompanied Mason on the
official tour of the mines; he des-
cribed the bustle at Sutter's Fort

and the July Fourth banquet. Sutter, in Gudde, *Sutter's Own Story*, also a source for the celebration. Bancroft, *California Inter Pocula*, quoted another witness to the general confusion at the fort. Lienhard, *A Pioneer . . .*, recalled Sutter's stories of military adventure. William T. Sherman told about Loeser. Bancroft, *History of California*, Vol. VI, for the general impact of the gold discovery.

12. The Golden Road, pp. 135–48

Shaw, *Across the Plains in '49*; and Haskins, *The Argonauts of California*, recorded the exaggerated reports about the quantity of gold and the ease with which fortunes were made. Bancroft, *History of California*, Vol. VI, for reports of the discovery reaching Honolulu, Mexico, and Oregon, and the consequent excitement. Chu and Chu, *Passage to the Golden Gate*, is the source for the excitement in Canton. Howe, *Argonauts of '49*, and Haskins, for excellent accounts of forming and outfitting companies, and for a listing of articles made expressly for the Argonaut. Haskins described the various gold-washers and told about the excess baggage. Hittell, *History of California*, Vol. III, described "diving armor." Moorman, *The Journal of Madison Berryman Moorman, 1850-1851*; and Hagelstein, *My Trip to California*, tell about the relief stations and the high prices. Buffum saw the beaches piled with discarded baggage and gold-washers. The *Sacramento Transcript* and the *Sacramento Union* for accounts of "The Wheelbarrow Man." Sioli listed the way-stations along the emigrant routes, and described many of them. Angel, *A History of Placer County*, gave the river-bar production on the American, and an account of the Big Crevice. Talks with Mr. C. C. Roumage, Auburn, enlarged on the history of the Big Crevice. William T. Sherman and Davis remembered the arrival of the *California*. McCollum, *California As I Saw It*, enumerated the craft. Crosby, *Memoirs of Elisha Oscar Crosby*, recorded the lack of transportation and men building their own boats. Waite, "Pioneer Mining in California," gave a vivid description of the mosquitoes. Sutter in Gudde, *Sutter's Own Story*, for the founding of Sacramento City. Morse, "The First History of Sacramento City," gave its monthly progress. *Placer Times* for an account of opening night at the Eagle Theatre. Leman, *Memories of an Old Actor*; and Taylor, *Eldorado*, for descriptions of the theater and the flood. Buffum; Huntley, *California, Its Gold and Its Inhabitants*; and Marryat, *Mountains and Molehills*, wrote about the "paper" cities. McGowan, *The Sacramento Valley* and *History of the Sacramento Valley*, for Hoboken's story. Marryat; Kelly, *A Stroll Through the Diggings of California*, noted the number of grog shops and recorded the names. Porter, *Aerial Navigation*; Lipman, *Rufus Porter, Yankee Pioneer*. The *Missouri Republican* for announcements of express lines to the gold-fields. Hunt and Sánchez, and Bonsal, for accounts of the "Lightning Dromedary Express." Bancroft,

California Inter Pocula, described the ways of the Yankee merchants. Sarah Royce, *A Frontier Lady*; and Taylor, *Eldorado*, wrote of the fort's decline. Kelly took note of the river, the herds of elk, and the flocks of geese.

13. The Manner of Men They Were, pp. 149–63

Gerstaecker; and Kelly described the "dandy" digger. Taylor, *Eldorado*, and Holden, "Condemned Bar in 1849," reported the miner's hard life. Taylor, *Eldorado*, described the quick riches in other occupations. Bancroft, *History of California*, Vol. VI; Buffum; Angel, *History of Placer County*; Banks and Armstrong, *The Buckeye Rovers in the Gold Rush*, wrote about the restlessness and the subsequent rushes. Buffum told how rumor affected the gold seeker. Angel, *History of Placer County*, described the mushrooming camp. Borthwick, *Three Years in California*, noted the ruins. Theory of Mother Lode in Bancroft, *History of California*, Vol. VI; and Lee, Stone, Gale, Hoyt, *Guidebook of the Western United States: The Overland Route*. Bancroft, *History of California*, Vol. VI; Pierce, *Lost Mines and Buried Treasure*, for story of the Lost Cabin Mine. Buffum described the thrill of discovery, and the impossibility of keeping a rich find secret. Marryat recounted the miner's funeral. Gerstaecker; and Haskins, sources for omens and necromancy. Judge Amy Drysdale, Placerville, recalled the Cornish miners' stories of Tommyknockers. Borthwick; Gerstaecker; Waite; Harte, "Society in the Mining Camps," describe miners' dress. Taylor, *Eldorado*; Huntley; Farnham, *California In-Doors and Out*, observed boys drinking and smoking, and heard them swear. Gillespie, "A Miner's Sunday in Coloma," for the story of the child gambler. Marryat; Bancroft, *History of California*, Vol. VI, for toasts. Browne, in *Washoe Revisited*; Clappe (Dame Shirley), *The Shirley Letters*; Taylor, *Eldorado*, sources for prolific and imaginative swearing. Marryat named the drinks. Bancroft, *History of California*, Vol. VI; Sioli; Jackson, *Anybody's Gold*, for temperance societies. Taylor, *Eldorado*; Huntley, are authorities for mining being a leveler. Downie, *Hunting for Gold*, noted the gamblers' generosity. Haskins told Mrs. Stuart's story, and wrote about the miners' fondness for children, as did Sarah Royce. Shinn, *Mining Camps*, told the story of the miners and the boy. Sarah Royce; Carson, "Early Recollections of the Mines"; Haskins; Taylor, *Eldorado*; Josiah Royce; Angel, *History of Placer County*, for prevailing honesty among first miners and swift punishment of offenders. Lienhard, *A Pioneer . . .* ; Carson, "Early Recollections . . ."; Soulé, et al.; Taylor, *Eldorado*, told of influx of rogues and the need for men to arm. Angel, *History of Placer County*; and Josiah Royce, saw the winter of 1849 as a social agent. Sutter, "Notes," for the theft of his cattle. Angel, *History of Placer County*, a source for nicknames. Author's grandfather for the jingle.

14. Camp and Town, pp. 164–80

Background for miners' cabins, kitchen arrangements, furniture, diet, bread, and slapjacks: Angel, *History of Placer County*; Browne, *Mining Adventures*; Holden; Shaw; Buffum; Taylor, *Eldorado*; De Quille, *The Big Bonanza*. Angel, a forty-niner, gave the recipes. Borthwick, and Buffum wrote about the after-dinner amusements. Haskins heard the bugler, he also reported on the dearth of reading material. Haskins; Angel, *History of Placer County*; and Huntley wrote about the coming of the newspaper vendors. Marryat remembered the shipments of books. Huntley; and Buffum for winter pastimes. Haskins described the July Fourth celebrations, and Kelly, the Christmas dinner. Haskins wrote about the typical Sunday in camp. Borthwick recalled the dining-room rush, and the miners' balls. Marryat; Buffum; Kelly; Angel, *History of Placer County*; Taylor, *Eldorado*; Wierzbicki, *California as It Is and as It May Be*, are all sources for prevalent sickness among the miners, for the lack of good medical care, the high prices charged by "doctors," and home remedies. Buffum recounts his recovery from scurvy. Buffum witnessed the floggings and hangings. Sioli told about the hangings in Coloma. Wilde, "The Ballad of Reading Gaol."

15. "California for the Americans!" pp. 181–88

Kelly; Ayers, *Gold and Sunshine*; Clappe (Dame Shirley), all witnessed mistreatment of foreign miners and the ensuing troubles. Chu and Chu, for the exodus from China. Hunt and Sánchez; Mark Twain, *Roughing It*; Soulé, et al.; and Huntley are sources for the anti-Chinese feeling and mistreatment. Miss Annie Yue, Auburn, furnished information about Auburn's Chinatown and the fate of the Joss House, and recalled her own experiences in school. Buffum; and Browne, *The Indians of California*, are primary sources for the campaign of extermination waged against the Indians. Josiah Royce; Hunt and Sánchez; and Cook are secondary sources. Mrs. Marie Potts, tribal historian, estimated the present number of Maidu. Mrs. Berenice Pate, Auburn, told about the Maidu's pride and interest in their heritage, and described the Bear Dance, which she attends each year.

16. Thespians Along the River, pp. 189–203

Ayers, a miner-turned-actor, for the history of several amateur companies, their repertoires and tours. Leman, an actor in McKean Buchanan's company, gave details of their productions and tours. McMinn, *Theater of the Golden Era in California*; Soulé, et al.; Jackson, *Anybody's Gold*, listed troupes and their plays, and individual performers who toured the mines. Borthwick, and Brewer wrote about Chinese plays and music. Rourke, *Troupers of the Gold Coast or the Rise of Lotta Crabtree*, for Lotta's story, and Lola Montez's part in her life. Ayers described the "Spider Dance"; he knew Montez and Pat Hull, and recounted their marital troubles. McMinn; and Holdredge, *The Woman in Black*, are further sources for Montez. Recollections of Lotta Crabtree from author's grandfather.

17. Last Chance, pp. 204–12

Angel, *History of Placer County*, for the founding of Last Chance. Bucke, "Twenty-five Years Ago," recalled his trip with Allen Grosh, to Last Chance. Lord, *Comstock Mining and Miners*, for a history of the Grosh brothers. Angel, *History of Nevada*, gives the brothers' story as told by their father. Mrs. Laura Dettenrieder's recollections of the Grosh brothers in Angel, *History of Nevada*. Sir Joseph Hooker quoted in Muir, *Our National Parks*. The grove's discovery, size of the trees, plantings, and other data in May and Sindel, "The Northern Outpost of Giant Sequoia." Muir, *The Mountains of California*. First-hand observation.

18. "The Pirate of the Placers," pp. 213–23

Angel, *History of Placer County*, recounts the story of "Rattlesnake Dick" Barter in detail. Lardner and Brock, *History of Placer County*, for the letter of Harriet Barter to her brother; it is headed: "Sweet Home, March 14, 1859." Background: Jackson, *Bad Company*.

19. The Discoverer's Fate, pp. 224–29

Bancroft, *History of California*, Vol. VI; Hittell, *History of California*, Vol. III; Angel, *History of Placer County*; Gay; Markham, *California the Wonderful*. Mrs. Doris Foley, Nevada City, remembered Marshall's friend, Miss Margaret Kelley, quoting him on his wish to be buried on the Coloma hilltop so that he could watch the "boys." First-hand observation.

20. The Great River Road, pp. 230–47

Borthwick recalled the stage depot; he and Marryat traveled by stage to the mines and wrote about the perils and beauties of the trip. Sioli; and Angel, *History of Placer County*, for a history of the first roads and early stage companies. De Quille, "Snowshoe Thompson." Browne took part in the silver rush, described in *A Peep at Washoe*; since he walked, he was able to report graphically on the state of the road, and describe the numerous way-stations. Lord wrote about the congested traffic. Sioli, for an account of the arrival of the Pony Express in Placerville, and Hank Monk's reception there. When Browne returned to Washoe in 1863, he took the stage and talked with the driver, as reported in *Washoe Revisited*; he also noted improvement in the way-stations. Truman, "Knights of the Lash," knew most of the early stage-drivers, and told their stories. Drury, *An Editor on the Comstock Lode*, was also a friend of Hank Monk; he described his appearance and told about the harness rivets. Truman; Ryder, "Stage-Coach Days"; Twain; Banning and Banning, *Six Horses*, all tell the story of Greeley's famous ride. Twain's version is used. Greeley, *An Overland Journey from New York to San Francisco in the Summer of 1859*, for his account of the ride. Sioli wrote about the robbery at Bullion Bend. First-hand observation.

21. The Fall of Sutter's Empire, pp. 248–53

Sutter, "Notes"; Sutter in Gudde, *Sutter's Own Story*; Zollinger.

22. The Iron Horse, pp. 254–67

Background: Howard, *The Great Iron Trail*; Griswold, *A Work of Giants*; Wilson and Taylor, *Southern Pacific*; Lewis, *The Big Four*; Bancroft, *Chronicles of the Builders of the Commonwealth*, Vol. V. Sioli for a history of the Sacramento Valley Railroad and the Central Pacific, and a biographical sketch of Bayley. Browne described the Folsom depot in *Washoe Revisited*. Hutchings, "The Alabaster Cave of El Dorado Co., Cal'a"; first-hand observation. Mrs. Mary Bacchi, Lotus, with whom we visited the cave, enlarged on its history. Chu and Chu for the role of the Chinese in the construction of the Central Pacific. Lee, et al., for a description of Cape Horn. Rhodes, "The Case of Summerfield," in *Caxton's Book*. Stevenson, *Across the Plains*. Howard, and Griswold for the celebrations attending the meeting of the rails.

23. The Final Phase, pp. 271–80

Jenkins, "Geologic History . . ."; Angel, *History of Placer County*, for mining methods along the American, and accounts of Chabot, Mattison, and McClure. Brewer is also a source for mining methods. Keyes, "Mineral Resources of the State of California," described bank-blasting and other forms of mining. Gilbert, *Hydraulic-Mining Debris in the Sierra Nevada*; John Hittell, *Mining in the Pacific States*. Sioli told about "Old Joe," and gave the history of the "Sierra Ditch." *Report to the Federal Power Commission on the El Dorado Hydroelectric Project*, contains some history of the early water projects. Lardner and Brock, for the story of Colonel Davis's hydraulic elevator. Further information furnished by his grandson, Mr. C. C. Roumage, Auburn. Brewer described the country's changed face. Angel, *History of Placer County*, remembered the river in its purity. Kelley, *Gold vs. Grain*, for friction between miners and farmers. Foley and Morley, "The 1883 Flood on the Middle Yuba

River." Judge Sawyer's decision in *Woodruff* v. *North Bloomfield Gravel and Mining Co., et al.* Logan, "History of Mining and Milling Methods in California," for dredging. Background: Ekman and Parker, *Old Mines and Ghost Camps of California*; Yale, "California's Mining History."

24. Women and the River, pp. 281–95

John Sanborn wrote to his brother Moses Sanborn, May 9, 1851, about the scarcity of women in camp. Hittell, *History of California*, Vol. III, for the story of the forty-mile ride, and the first woman in Canyon Creek. Marryat told about the woman's boot. Haskins saw the pretty girl from Kentucky ride into camp. Marryat had breakfast at the Crocketts'. Dunlap, "Eulalie, California's First Woman Poet"; "The Auburn Poetess" in Lardner and Brock. "A Californian Heroine," an interview with Nancy Kelsey in *San Francisco Examiner*. Zollinger for Lucinda's story. Mrs. Farnham told her own story. Bancroft, *California Inter Pocula*, wrote about the French girls of good character as well as the *demi-monde*. Paden, *The Wake of the Prairie Schooner*, told about the Hangtown wife and her pies. Taylor, *New Pictures . . .* , noted woman's hand in the camps, and the plantings. Borthwick itemized the rubbish in the streets. Sioli listed the organizations formed and gave the history of E Clampsus Vitus, as it was first called. Dane and Dane, *Ghost Town*, for more about the "Clampers." Hunt, *California's Stately Hall of Fame*; and Lardner and Brock for Anna Catherine Markham's story. Filler, *The Unknown Markham*; Wisehart, "Edwin Markham's Three Glimpses of God." Judge Amy Drysdale, Placerville, told her mother's story, and Mrs. Mary Bacchi, Lotus, her own. Bancroft, *History of California*, Vol. VI; Hittell, *History of California*, Vol. III, for woman's status in California.

25. Taming the River, pp. 296–304

Mrs. Royce told her own story. McGowan, *History of the Sacramento Valley* and *The Sacramento Valley*; and Morse, for a history of the floods, the damage, and levee building. Borthwick saw the horseboats. Brewer was in San Francisco at the time of the Sacramento flood, and visited there on March 6. Coleman, *P.G. and E. of California* and "The Livermore Family," for the Livermores' story. General background: *Report to the Federal Power Commission; The Journal of Electricity*; U.S. Dept. of the Interior, Bureau of Reclamation, CVP, American River Division, bulletins, fact sheets, and pamphlets. Sioli listed the gold camps and gave their histories. Mrs. Berenice Pate, Auburn, told about the Indians getting salmon at the hatchery. Senate Bill No. 107, "California Wild and Scenic Rivers Act." Mr. C. C. Roumage, Auburn, listed all the river-bars to be drowned by the dam.

26. The Struggle for Survival, pp. 305–16

Sioli; Angel, *History of Placer County*; Brock and Lardner, are sources for the river-country's mineral deposits and its agriculture. Mr. Floyd Locher, Auburn, furnished a comprehensive picture of the area's economic resources past and present, and its future prospects. "California Marble Blocks," *Alta California*. Angel, *History of Placer County*; Sioli; Murakami, "Wakamatsu Colony Centennial," for Schnell's story and that of Okei Ito. Daniels, *The Politics of Prejudice*; Ichihashi, *Japanese Immigration, Its Status in California*, for attitude toward Japanese, and a history of their immigration. Harris, *Down the Wild Rivers*. Dasmann. Brower, "Winter Sports"; Power, *Pioneer Skiing in California*; talks with early-day skiers, Mrs. Elsie Heimann, Mill Valley, and Mr. Lewis Clark, Alameda. Mr. C. C. Roumage and Mr. Rhoads Grimshaw, Auburn, are sources for the future of gold mining along the American. Tahoe Regional Planning Agency and Forest Service, U.S. Department of Agriculture, "Wildlife of the Lake Tahoe Region," for civilization's threat to wildlife and the general ecosystem. Wood, "Desolation Wilderness," for overuse of primitive areas. Muir, *Our National Parks*.

27. The River and Time, pp. 317–19

Leonardo da Vinci, *Notebooks*. First-hand observation. John Audubon, in *Audubon's Western Journal*, noted the American's rise and fall.

Bibliography

Books

Angel, Myron, *History of Nevada*. Thompson & West, Oakland, Calif.: 1881.

———, *History of Placer County*. Thompson & West, Oakland, Calif.: 1882.

Audubon, John W., *Audubon's Western Journal: 1849-1850*. The Arthur H. Clark Co., Cleveland: 1906.

Averill, Charles V., "History of Placer Mining for Gold in California," in Olaf P. Jenkins, ed., *Geologic Guidebook Along Highway 49— Sierran Gold Belt: The Mother Lode Country*. California State Division of Mines, San Francisco: 1948.

Ayers, James J., *Gold and Sunshine*. The Gorham Press, Boston: 1927.

Balls, Edward K., *Early Uses of California Plants*. University of California Press, Berkeley and Los Angeles: 1962.

Bancroft, Hubert Howe, *California Inter Pocula*. H. H. Bancroft Co., San Francisco: 1888.

———, *Chronicles of the Builders of the Commonwealth*, Vol. V. The History Book Co., San Francisco: 1891.

———, *History of California*, Vols. I–VI. The History Book Co., San Francisco: 1882-1890.

Banks, John, and Armstrong, J. E., *The Buckeye Rovers in the Goldrush: An Edition of Two Diaries*, Howard L. Scamehorn, ed. University of Ohio Press, Athens, Ohio: 1965.

Banning, William, and Banning, George H., *Six Horses*. The Century Co., New York: 1930.

Bates, Mrs. D. B., *Incidents on Land and Water, or Four Years on the Pacific Coast*. E. O. Libby Co., Boston: 1858.

Bigler, Henry W., "Diary of a Mormon in California," in Bancroft, *California Inter Pocula*. H. H. Bancroft Co., San Francisco: 1888.

Boggs, Mae Helene Bacon, *My Playhouse Was a Concord Coach*. Howell-North, Oakland, Calif.: 1942.

Bonsal, Stephen, *Edward Fitzgerald Beale*. G. P. Putnam's Sons, New York: 1912.

Borthwick, J. D., *Three Years in California*. William Blackwood & Sons, Edinburgh and London: 1857.

333

Brewer, William H., *Up and Down California in 1860-1864*, Francis P. Farquhar, ed. Yale University Press, New Haven: 1930.

Brower, David R., "Winter Sports," in Roderick Peattie, ed., *The Sierra Nevada*. Vanguard Press, New York: 1947.

Browne, J. Ross, *The Indians of California*. Colt Press, San Francisco: 1944.

——, *Mining Adventures, California and Nevada, 1863-1865*. Paisano Press, Balboa Island, Calif.: 1961.

——, *A Peep at Washoe* and *Washoe Revisited*. Paisano Press, Balboa Island, Calif.: 1959.

Bryant, Edwin, *What I Saw in California: Being the Journal of a Tour in the Years 1846, 1847*. D. Appleton & Co., New York: 1848.

Buffum, E. Gould, *Six Months in the Gold Mines: From a Journal of Three Years' Residence in Upper and Lower California, 1847-8-9*. Lea & Blanchard, Philadelphia: 1850.

Burnett, Peter H., *Recollections and Opinions of an Old Pioneer*. D. Appleton & Co., New York: 1880.

Camp, Charles L., *Earth Song, A Prologue to History*. University of California Press, Berkeley and Los Angeles: 1952.

Camp, William Martin, *San Francisco: Port of Gold*. Doubleday & Co., New York: 1947.

Carson, Christopher, *Autobiography*, Milo M. Quaife, ed. The Lakeside Press, Chicago: 1935.

Carson, James H., "Early Recollections of the Mines." *San Joaquin Republican* print, Stockton, Calif.: 1852.

Caughey, John W., *Gold Is the Cornerstone*. University of California Press, Berkeley and Los Angeles: 1948.

Cervantes, Miguel de, *Don Quixote*. A. L. Burt Co., New York: 1909.

Chu, Daniel, and Chu, Samuel, *Passage to the Golden Gate*. Doubleday & Co., New York: 1967.

Clappe, Louise Amelia Knapp Smith (pseud. "Dame Shirley"), *The Shirley Letters from the California Mines*. Alfred A. Knopf, New York: 1961.

Clissold, Stephen, *The Seven Cities of Cíbola*. Clarkson N. Potter, New York: 1962.

Coleman, Charles M., *P.G. and E. of California*. McGraw-Hill, New York: 1952.

Colton, Walter, *Three Years in California*. Cleaver & Co., Boston: 1886.

Cook, S. F., "Conflict Between the Calfornian Indians and White Civilization," in R. F. Heizer and M. A. Whipple, eds., *The California Indians*. University of California Press, Berkeley and Los Angeles: 1970.

Coy, Owen C., *Gold Days*. Powell Publishing Co., San Francisco and Chicago: 1929.

Crosby, Elisha Oscar, *Memoirs of Elisha Oscar Crosby*, Charles A. Barker, ed. The Huntington Library, San Marino, Calif.: 1945.

Cutter, Donald C., "The Discovery of Gold in California," in Olaf P. Jenkins, ed., *Geologic Guidebook Along Highway 49—Sierran Gold Belt: The Mother Lode Country*. California State Division of Mines, San Francisco: 1948.

Dana, Richard Henry, *Two Years Before the Mast*. Doubleday & Co., New York: 1959.

Dane, G. Ezra, and Dane, Beatrice J., *Ghost Town*. Alfred A. Knopf, New York: 1941.

Daniels, Roger, *The Politics of Prejudice. The Anti-Japanese Movement in California and the Struggle for Japanese Exclusion*. Peter Smith, Gloucester, Mass.: 1966.

Dasmann, William P., *Big Game in California*. California Resources Agency, Sacramento, Calif.: 1968.

Davis, William Heath, *Seventy-five Years in California*. John Howell-Books, San Francisco: 1967.

Delano, Alonzo, *Life on the Plains and Among the Diggings*. Miller, Orton & Mulligan, Auburn and Buffalo: 1854.

Densmore, Frances, *The Music of the Maidu*. The Southwest Museum, Los Angeles: 1958.

De Quille, Dan, *The Big Bonanza*. The Webster Co., Hartford: 1876.

Dettenrieder, Laura M., interview in Angel, *History of Nevada*. Thompson & West, Oakland, Calif.: 1881.

Downie, William, *Hunting for Gold*. The California Publishing Co., San Francisco: 1893.

Drury, Wells, *An Editor on the Comstock Lode*. Pacific Books, Palo Alto, Calif.: 1948.

Drysdale, Walter, *The Tommy Knocker* (pamphlet). Howell-North, Berkeley, Calif.: 1971.

Ekman, A., Parker, T. H., Storms, W. H., Penniman, H. W., and Dittmar, M. E., *Old Mines and Ghost Camps of California (Statewide for 1899)*, Reprinted by Frontier Book Co., Fort Davis, Texas: 1968.

The Emgirant's Handbook. Although the title page is missing, internal evidence indicates it was published in 1843.

Emparan, Madie Brown, *The Vallejos of California*. The Gleeson Library Associates, University of San Francisco: 1968.

Farnham, Eliza W., *California, In-Doors and Out; or, How We Farm, Mine, and Live Generally in the Golden State*. Dix, Edwards & Co., New York: 1850.

Farquhar, Francis P., *History of the Sierra Nevada*. University of California Press, Berkeley and Los Angeles: 1965.

Filler, Louis, *The Unknown Markham*. Antioch Press, Yellow Springs, Ohio: 1966.

Foote, H. S., ed., *Pen Pictures from "The Garden of the World" or Santa Clara County, California*. Lewis Publishing Co., Chicago: 1888.

Forbes, Jack D., *Native Americans of California and Nevada*. Naturegraph Publishers, Healdsburg, Calif.: 1968.

Frémont, John Charles, *Memoirs of My Life*. Belford, Clarke & Co., Chicago and New York: 1887.

———, *Report of the Exploring Expedition to the Rocky Mountains in the Year 1842, and to Oregon and North California in the Years 1843-44*. 28th Cong. 2d Sess. Sen. Ex. Doc. 174. Printed by order of the Senate of the United States. Washington, D.C., 1845.

Gay, Theressa, *James W. Marshall*. The Talisman Press, Georgetown, Calif.: 1967.

Geiger, Vincent, and Bryarly, Wakeman, *Trail to California, The Overland Journal of Vincent Geiger and Wakeman Bryarly*, Davis Morris Potter, ed. Yale University Press, New Haven: 1945.

Gerstaecker, Friedrich, *California Gold Mines*. Biobooks, Oakland, Calif.: 1946.

Gifford, Edward W., "California Balanophagy," in R. F. Heizer and M. A. Whipple, eds., *The California Indians*. University of California Press, Berkeley and Los Angeles: 1970.

———, "Californian Indian Physical Types," in R. F. Heizer and M. A. Whipple, eds., *The California Indians*. University of California Press, Berkeley and Los Angeles: 1970.

———, and Bolk, Gwendoline Harris, *Californian Indian Nights' Entertainment*. The Arthur H. Clark Co., Glendale, Calif.: 1930.

Gilbert, Grove Karl, *Hydraulic-Mining in the Sierra Nevada*. Professional Paper 105. Gov't. Printing Office, Washington, D.C.: 1917.

Glasscock, Carl B., *A Golden Highway*. The Bobbs-Merrill Co., Indianapolis: 1934.

Greeley, Horace, *An Overland Journey from New York to San Francisco in the Summer of 1859*. C. M. Saxton, Barker & Co., New York: 1860.

Griswold, Wesley S., *A Work of Giants*. McGraw-Hill, New York: 1962.

Grosh, Aaron B., letter to Mrs. C. B. Winslow, July 8, 1879, in Angel, *History of Nevada*. Thompson & West, Oakland, Calif.: 1881.

Gudde, Erwin G., *Bigler's Chronicle of the West. The Conquest of California, Discovery of Gold, and Mormon Settlement as Reflected in Henry William Bigler's Diaries*. University of California Press, Berkeley and Los Angeles: 1962.

———, *Sutter's Own Story*. G. P. Putnam's Sons, New York: 1936.

Hagelstein, George Michael, *My Trip to California*, LeVern Cutler, trans. and ed. Bulletin 66 (typescript), Stanford University, Stanford, Calif.: 1938.

Harris, Thomas, *Down the Wild Rivers. A Guide to the Streams of California*. Chronicle Books, San Francisco: 1972.

Harte, Bret, "Society in the Mining Camps," *The Writings of Bret Harte*, Vol. II. Houghton Mifflin, Boston: 1896.

Harwell, Charles Albert, "Some Birds of the Sierra Nevada," in Roderick Peattie, ed., *The Sierra Nevada*. Vanguard Press, New York: 1947.

Haskins, C. W., *The Argonauts of California*. Fords, Howard & Hulbert, New York: 1890.

Hawgood, John A., *First and Last Consul*. The Huntington Library, San Marino, Calif.: 1962.

Heizer, Robert F., *Languages, Territories, and Names of California Indian Tribes*. University of California Press, Berkeley and Los Angeles: 1966.

Heizer, Robert F., and Whipple, M. A., eds. and compilers, *The California Indians*. University of California Press, Berkeley and Los Angeles: 1970.

Hill, Jasper S., *The Letters of a Young Miner, Covering the Adventures of Jasper S. Hill During the California Goldrush, 1849-1852*, Doyce B. Nunis, Jr., ed. John Howell-Books, San Francisco: 1964.

Hittell, John S., *Mining in the Pacific States*. H. H. Bancroft Co., San Francisco: 1861.

Hittell, Theodore H., *History of California*, Vols. I-III. N. J. Stone & Co., San Francisco: 1898.

Holdredge, Helen, *The Woman in Black: The Life of the Fabulous Lola Montez*. G. P. Putnam's Sons, New York: 1955.

Hopkins, Sarah Winnemucca, *Life Among the Piutes: Their Wrongs and Claims*, Mrs. Horace Mann, ed. Cupples, Upham & Co., Boston, 1883.

Howard, Robert West, *The Great Iron Trail*. G. P. Putnam's Sons, New York: 1962.

Howe, Octavius Thorndike, *Argonauts of '49*. Harvard University Press, Cambridge: 1923.

Hunt, Rockwell D., *California's Stately Hall of Fame*. College of the Pacific, Stockton, Calif.: 1950.

——, and Sánchez, Nellie Van De Grift, *A Short History of California*. Thomas Y. Crowell, New York: 1929.

Huntley, Sir Henry Vere, *California, Its Gold and Its Inhabitants*. 2 vols. Thomas Cautley Newby, London: 1856.

Ichihashi, Yamato, *Japanese Immigration, Its Status in California*. R. and E. Research Associates Reprint, San Francisco: 1970.

Ingles, Lloyd Glen, *Mammals of California and Its Coastal Waters*. Stanford University Press, Stanford, Calif.: 1961.

Jackson, Joseph Henry, *Anybody's Gold*. D. Appleton-Century Co., New York and London: 1941.

——, *Bad Company*. Harcourt, Brace Co., New York: 1949.

Jackson, W. Turrentine, "Wells Fargo Staging over the Sierra." Reprinted from *California Historical Society Quarterly*, June 1970.

Jenkins, Olaf P., "Geologic History of the Sierran Gold Belt," in Olaf P. Jenkins, ed., *Geologic Guidebook Along Highway 49—Sierran Gold Belt: The Mother Lode Country*. California State Division of Mines, San Francisco: 1948.

——, "Sierra Nevada Province," in Olaf P. Jenkins, ed., *Geologic*

338   Bibliography

Guidebook Along Highway 49—Sierran Gold Belt: The Mother Lode Country. California State Division of Mines, San Francisco: 1948.

Kelley, Robert L., *Gold vs. Grain.* The Arthur H. Clark Co., Glendale, Calif.: 1959.

Kelly, William, *A Stroll Through the Diggings of California.* Simms & M'Intyre, London: 1852.

Keyes, W. S., "Mineral Resources of the State of California," in *The Pacific Coast Business Directory for 1867.* Henry G. Langley, San Francisco: 1867.

Kroeber, Alfred L., "Elements of Culture in Native California," in R. F. Heizer and M. A. Whipple, eds., *The California Indians.* University of California Press, Berkeley and Los Angeles: 1970.

——, *Handbook of the Indians of California.* California Book Co., Berkeley: 1953.

——, "The Nature of the Land-Holding Groups in Aboriginal California," in *Aboriginal California, Three Studies in Culture History.* University of California Archeological Research Facility, Berkeley: 1963.

Lardner, W. B., and Brock, M. J., *History of Placer County.* The Historic Record Co., Los Angeles: 1924.

Lee, Willis T., Stone, Ralph W., Gale, Hoyt S., et al., *Guidebook of the Western United States. Part B. The Overland Route with a Side Trip to Yellowstone Park.* United States Geological Survey. 63d Cong. 3d Sess. H. R. Doc. 1694. Gov't. Printing Office, Washington, D.C.: 1915.

Leman, Walter M., *Memories of an Old Actor.* A. Roman Co., San Francisco: 1886.

Lewis, Oscar, *The Big Four.* Alfred A. Knopf, New York: 1939.

Lienhard, Heinrich, *From St. Louis to Sutter's Fort,* Erwin and Elizabeth K. Gudde, trans. and eds. University of Oklahoma Press, Norman, Okla.: 1961.

——, *A Pioneer at Sutter's Fort, 1846-1850,* Marguerite Eyer Wilbur, trans. and ed. The Califía Society, Los Angeles: 1941.

Lipman, Jean, *Rufus Porter, Yankee Pioneer.* Clarkson N. Potter, New York: 1968.

Loeb, Edwin M., *The Eastern Kuksu.* University of California Press, Berkeley: 1933.

Logan, C. A., "History of Mining and Milling Methods in California," in Olaf P. Jenkins, ed., *Geologic Guidebook Along Highway 49— Sierran Gold Belt: The Mother Lode Country.* California State Division of Mines, San Francisco: 1948.

Lord, Eliot, *Comstock Mining and Miners.* U.S. Gov't. Printing Office, Washington, D.C.: 1883.

McCollum, William, *California As I Saw It.* Dale L. Morgan, ed. The Talisman Press, Los Gatos, Calif.: 1960.

McGlashen, C. F., *History of the Donner Party.* Stanford University Press, Stanford, Calif.: 1947.

McGowan, Joseph A., *History of the Sacramento Valley*, 3 vols. Lewis Historical Publishing Co., New York and West Palm Beach: 1961.
———, *The Sacramento Valley: A Students' Guide to Localized History*. Columbia University Teachers College Press, New York: 1967.
McMinn, George R., *Theater of the Golden Era in California*. Caxton Press, Caldwell, Idaho: 1941.
MacMullen, Jerry, *Paddle-Wheel Days in California*. Stanford University Press, Stanford, Calif.: 1946.
Markham, Edwin, *California the Wonderful*. International Library Co., New York: 1914.
Marryat, Frank, *Mountains and Molehills, or Recollections of a Burnt Journal*. Harper & Bros., New York: 1855.
Marti, Werner H., *Messenger of Destiny. The California Adventures, 1846-1847, of Archibald H. Gillespie, U.S. Marine Corps*. John Howell-Books, San Francisco: 1960.
Mason, Colonel Richard B., *Report* to General Roger Jones, Aug. 17, 1848. 31st Cong. 1st Sess. H. R. Ex. Doc. 17.
Matthes, François E., "A Geologist's View," in Roderick Peattie, ed., *The Sierra Nevada*. Vanguard Press, New York: 1947.
Miller, William J., *California Through the Ages*. Westernlore Press, Los Angeles: 1957.
Moody, Ralph, *Old Trails West*. Thomas Y. Crowell, New York: 1963.
Moorman, Madison Berryman, *The Journal of Madison Berryman Moorman, 1850-1851*, Irene D. Paden, ed. California Historical Society, San Francisco: 1948.
Moraga, Gabriel, *The Diary of Ensign Gabriel Moraga's Expedition of Discovery in the Sacramento Valley*, Donald C. Cutter, trans. and ed. Dawson, Los Angeles: 1957.
Morgan, Dale L., *Jedediah Smith and the Opening of the West*. University of Nebraska Press, Lincoln, Neb.: 1953.
———, ed., *Overland in 1846. Diaries and Letters of the California-Oregon Trail*. 2 vols. The Talisman Press, Georgetown, Calif.: 1963.
Morse, Dr. John F., "The First History of Sacramento City," in *Sacramento Directory: 1853-54*. Sacramento [Calif.] Book Collectors Club, Sacramento: 1945.
Muir, John, *The Mountains of California*. The Century Co., New York: 1911.
———, *Our National Parks*. Houghton Mifflin, Boston: 1901.
Murakami, James F., "Wakamatsu Colony Centennial" (pamphlet). No publisher cited, 1969.
Murphy, Celeste, *The People of the Pueblo*. Binfords & Mort, Portland, Ore.: 1948.
Nevins, Allan, *Frémont, Pathmarker of the West*. D. Appleton-Century Co., New York and London: 1939.
Orr, Robert T., *Mammals of Lake Tahoe*. California Academy of Sciences, San Francisco: 1949.

Paden, Irene D., *The Wake of the Prairie Schooner*. Macmillan Co., New York: 1947.

Paul, Rodman W., *The California Gold Discovery*. The Talisman Press, Georgetown, Calif.: 1966.

Peattie, Roderick, ed., *The Sierra Nevada*. Vanguard Press, New York: 1947.

Pfeiffer, Ida, *A Lady's Visit to California in 1853*. Harper & Bros., New York: 1856.

Pierce, R. A., *Lost Mines and Buried Treasure* (pamphlet). R. A. Pierce, Berkeley: 1964.

Porter, Rufus, *Aerial Navigation. The Practicability of Traveling Pleasantly and Safely from New York to California in Three Days*. Lawton Kennedy, San Francisco: 1935.

Powell, Lawrence Clark, *Philosopher Pickett*. University of California Press, Berkeley: 1942.

Power, Robert H., *Pioneer Skiing in California*. The Nut Tree, Vacaville, Calif.: 1960.

Preuss, Charles, *Exploring with Frémont*, Erwin G. and Elizabeth K. Gudde, trans. and eds. University of Oklahoma Press, Norman, Okla.: 1958.

Quaife, Milo M., ed., *Pictures of Gold Rush California*. The Lakeside Press, Chicago: 1948.

Reed, George Willis, *A Pioneer of 1850*, George Willis Reed, ed. Little, Brown & Co., Boston: 1927.

Report to the Federal Power Commission on the El Dorado Hydroelectric Project. FPC Project No. 184. Pacific Gas and Electric Co., San Francisco: June 1968.

Rhodes, William Henry (pseud. "Caxton"), *Caxton's Book: A Collection of Essays, Poems, Tales, and Sketches*. A. L. Bancroft & Co., San Francisco: 1874.

Rourke, Constance, *Troupers of the Gold Coast or the Rise of Lotta Crabtree*. Harcourt, Brace & Co., New York: 1928.

Royce, Josiah, *California*. Houghton Mifflin, Boston: 1897.

Royce, Sarah, *A Frontier Lady. Recollections of the Gold Rush and Early California*. Yale University Press, New Haven: 1932.

Schaeffer, L. M., *Sketches of Travels in South America, Mexico, and California*. James Egbert, New York: 1860.

Schallenberger, Moses, "Reminiscences," in H. S. Foote, ed., *Pen Pictures from the "Garden of the World" or Santa Clara County, California*. Lewis Publishing Co., Chicago: 1888.

Scherer, James A. B., *The First Forty-Niner and the Story of the Golden Tea-Caddy*. Minton, Balch & Co., New York: 1925.

Senate Bill No. 107: "California Wild and Scenic Rivers Act."

Shaw, Reuben Cole, *Across the Plains in '49*, Milo M. Quaife, ed. Citadel Press, New York: 1966.

Sherman, William T., *The Memoirs of General William T. Sherman*, Vol. I. D. Appleton & Co., New York: 1875.

Shinn, Charles H., *Mining Camps: A Study in American Frontier Government*. Alfred A. Knopf, New York: 1947.

Sioli, Paolo, *Historical Souvenir of El Dorado County*. Paolo Sioli, Oakland, Calif.: 1883.

Smith, Alson J., *Men Against the Mountains. Jedediah Smith and the Great Southwest Expedition of 1826-29*. John Day Co., New York: 1965.

Soulé, Frank, Gihon, John H., and Nisbet, James, *Annals of San Francisco*. D. Appleton & Co., New York: 1854.

Stevenson, Robert Louis, *Across the Plains*. Davos Press, New York: 1906.

Stewart, George R., *Donner Pass and Those Who Crossed It*. California Historical Society, San Francisco: 1960.

———, *The Opening of the California Trail*. University of California Press, Berkeley and Los Angeles: 1953.

Stirton, R. A., *Time, Life, and Man*. John Wiley & Sons, New York: 1959.

Sullivan, Maurice S., *Jedediah Smith, Trader and Trailblazer*. Press of the Pioneers, New York: 1936.

Sutter, John A., "General Sutter's Notes," in W. B. Lardner and M. J. Brock, *History of Placer County*. Historic Record Co., Los Angeles: 1924.

———, *New Helvetia Diary: A Record of Events Kept by John A. Sutter and His Clerks at New Helvetia, California, from September 9, 1845 to May 25, 1848*. Grabhorn Press, San Francisco: 1939.

———, "Reminiscences," recorded by H. H. Bancroft in *California Inter Pocula*. H. H. Bancroft Co., San Francisco: 1888.

Tahoe Regional Planning Agency and Forest Service, U.S. Department of Agriculture, "Wildlife of the Lake Tahoe Region: A Guide for Planning." South Lake Tahoe, Calif.: May 1971.

Taylor, Bayard, *Eldorado, or Adventures in the Path of Empire*. Alfred A. Knopf, New York: 1949.

———, *New Pictures from California*. G. P. Putnam's Sons, New York: 1894.

Thompson, R. A., *The Russian Settlement in California: Fort Ross*. Biobooks, Oakland, Calif.: 1951.

Tresidder, Mary, "Life Zones in the Sierra," in Roderick Peattie, ed., *The Sierra Nevada*. Vanguard Press, New York: 1947.

Twain, Mark, *Roughing It*. Harper & Bros., New York: 1899.

United States Department of the Interior, Bureau of Reclamation, Central Valley Project, American River Division, bulletins, fact sheets, and pamphlets. Gov't. Printing Office, Washington, D.C.: 1968-1970.

da Vinci, Leonardo, *The Notebooks of Leonardo da Vinci*, Edward MacCurdy, trans. and ed. 2 vols. George Braziller, New York: 1958.

Webster, Paul, *The Mighty Sierra*. American West Publishing Co., Palo Alto, Calif.: 1972.

Wierzbicki, F. P., *California as It Is and as It May Be, or A Guide to the Gold Region*. Grabhorn Press, San Francisco: 1933.

Wilde, Oscar, "The Ballad of Reading Gaol," in Richard Le Gallienne, ed., *The Le Gallienne Book of English Verse*. Boni & Liveright, New York: 1922.

Wilson, Neill C., and Taylor, Frank J., *Southern Pacific*. McGraw-Hill, New York: 1951.

Winthur, M. K., *Express and Stagecoach Days in California*. Stanford University Press, Stanford, Calif.: 1936.

Yale, Charles G., "California's Mining History," in Zoeth Skinner Eldredge, ed., *History of California*. The Century History Co., New York: 1914.

Zollinger, James Peter, *Sutter, The Man and His Empire*. Oxford University Press, New York: 1939.

Magazines

Bidwell, John, "In California Before the Gold Rush." *The Century Illustrated Monthly Magazine*, Nov.–Dec. 1890, and Apr. 1891, Vol. XLI (New Series XIX).

———, "Frémont in the Conquest of California." *Ibid.*

Briones, Brigida Cañes, "A Carnival Ball at Monterey in 1824." *Ibid.*

Browne, J. Ross, "A Peep at Washoe, or Sketches of Adventures in Virginia City." *Harper's New Monthly Magazine*. Dec. 1861, Jan. and Feb. 1862, Vol. XXIV.

Bucke, Richard Maurice, "Twenty-five Years Ago." *Overland Monthly*, June 1883, Vol. I (Second Series).

De Quille, Dan, "Snowshoe Thompson." *Overland Monthly*, Oct. 1886, Vol. VIII.

Dunlap, Boutwell, "Eulalie, California's First Woman Poet." *Overland Monthly*, Dec. 1919, Vol. XLIV.

Farquhar, Francis P., "Frémont in the Sierra Nevada." *Sierra Club Bulletin*, June 1930, Vol. XV.

———, "Jedediah Smith and the First Crossing of the Sierra Nevada." *Sierra Club Bulletin*, June 1943, Vol. XXVIII.

Foley, Doris, and Morley, S. Griswold, "The 1883 Flood on the Middle Yuba River." *California Historical Society Quarterly*, Sept. 1949, Vol. XXVII.

Gianella, Vincent P., "Where Frémont Crossed the Sierra in 1844." *Sierra Club Bulletin*, Oct. 1959, Vol. XLIV.

Gillespie, Charles B., "Marshall's Own Account of the Gold Discovery." *The Century Illustrated Monthly Magazine*, Feb. 1891, Vol. XLI.

———, "A Miner's Sunday in Coloma; From the Writer's California Journal, 1849–50." *The Century Illustrated Monthly Magazine*, May–Oct. 1891, Vol. XX (New Series).

Hale, Edward Everett, "Queen of California." *Atlantic Monthly*, March 1864, Vol. XIII.

Holden, Erastus, "Condemned Bar in 1849." *California Historical Society Quarterly*, Dec. 1933, Vol. XXIII.

Hutchings, James M., "The Alabaster Cave, of El Dorado Co., Cal'a." *Hutchings' California Magazine*, Dec. 1860, Vol. V.

———, "Scenes Among the Indians of California." *Hutchings' California Magazine*, Apr. 1859, Vol. III.

The Journal of Electricity, "The Electric Carnival." Sept. 1895, Vol. I.

Kemble, Edward C., "Confirming the Gold Discovery." *The Century Illustrated Monthly Magazine*, Feb. 1891, Vol. XLI.

Marshall, James W., "The Discovery of Gold in California." *Hutchings' California Magazine*, Nov. 1857, Vol. II.

May, Richard H., and Sindel, Glen E., "The Northern Outpost of the Giant Sequoia." *Sierra Club Bulletin*, Oct. 1955, Vol. XL.

Ryder, David Warren, "Stage-Coach Days." *Sunset Magazine*, Sept. 1927, Vol. LIX.

Sherman, Edwin A., "Sherman Was There. The Recollections of Major Edwin A. Sherman." *California Historical Society Quarterly*, Sept. 1944, Vol. XXIII.

Sutter, John A., "The Discovery of Gold." *Hutchings' California Magazine*, Nov. 1857, Vol. II.

Truman, Benjamin C., "Knights of the Lash. Old Time Stage Drivers of the West Coast." *Overland Monthly*, Mar. and Apr. 1898, Vol. XXI.

Waite, P. G., "Pioneer Mining in California." *The Century Illustrated Monthly Magazine*, May–Oct. 1891, Vol. XX.

Wisehart, M. K., "Edwin Markham's Three Glimpses of God." *American Magazine*, Sept. 1928, Vol. CVI.

Wood, Robert S., "Desolation Wilderness." *Sierra Club Bulletin*, Mar. 1971, Vol. LVI.

Woodruff v. *North Bloomfield Gravel and Mining Co., et al.* Circuit Court D, California, January 7, 1884. *Federal Reporter*, Vol. XVIII, pp. 735–808.

Newspapers

Alta California. Jan. 10, 1852, "The Salt Lake Mail"; May 22, 1852, "The Emigrant Relief Expedition"; Dec. 3, 1852, "California Marble Blocks"; Jan. 5, 1859, "Steam Travel."

Californian. Mar. 15, 1848, "Gold Mine Found."

California Star. Mar. 18, 1848; Apr. 1, 1848; May 6, 1848; May 20, 1848; articles relative to the gold discovery.

Missouri Republican. Jan. 17, 1850, "California Mail Line"; Jan. 21, 1850, "The April Line for California"; Jan. 30, 1850, "Ho for California!"

New York Tribune. Aug. 20, 1846, reprint of a letter of William L. Todd, dated Apr. 17, 1846.

Placer Times. Oct. 20, 1849, "Eagle Theatre."

Sacramento Transcript. Aug. 6, 1850, "The Man with the Wheelbarrow"; Apr. 28, 1851, "The First Mail to Salt Lake."

Sacramento Union. Apr. 17, 1852, "The Wheelbarrow Man Turned Up
Again"; June 11, 1857, "Thompson's Carson Valley Express."
Articles by Edward C. Kemble: Sept. 11, 1866, "The 'Brooklyn
Mormons' in California"; Dec. 9, 1871, "March of the California
Battalion"; Mar. 8, 1873, "The Goodly Vine and Its Golden Fruit";
Mar. 22, 1873, "The First Drops of the Golden Shower"; Apr. 5,
1873, "The First Party to the Gold Mines."

San Francisco Examiner. Feb. 5, 1893, "A California Heroine, The First
White Woman Who Crossed the Plains and Sierra," Unsigned inter-
view with Mrs. Nancy Kelsey; Jan. 18, 1973, "Danger of Major
State Flood Told"; Apr. 2, 1973, "Big Dam Called 'Outdated,'" re:
Auburn Dam.

San Rafael Independent-Journal. Jan. 22, 1949, "The Livermore Family,"
by Charles M. Coleman; Dec. 21, 1972, "Reagan Signs Behr's 'Wild
Rivers' Bill."

Manuscripts

Larkin, Thomas O., letter to James Buchanan, June 1, 1848. National
Archives, Washington, D.C.
———, letter to James Buchanan, June 28, 1848. Copy in National
Archives, Washington, D.C.
———, letter to James Buchanan, July 20, 1848. Copy in National
Archives, Washington, D.C.
Sanborn, John Leavitt, letter to Moses L. Sanborn, May 9, 1851. Copy
in author's collection.
Smith, Jedediah, letter to General William Clark, July 12, 1827. Copy
in National Archives, Washington, D.C.

Index

345